J.L. Fellows
20·I·1971.

JOHN KEATS

A REASSESSMENT

EDITED BY

KENNETH MUIR

KING ALFRED PROFESSOR OF
ENGLISH LITERATURE
IN THE UNIVERSITY
OF LIVERPOOL

LIVERPOOL UNIVERSITY PRESS

1969

Published by
LIVERPOOL UNIVERSITY PRESS
123 Grove Street, Liverpool 7

First published 1958
Second edition (reset) 1969

Printed in Great Britain by
Richard Clay (The Chaucer Press) Ltd.
Bungay, Suffolk

To
L. C. MARTIN

Contents

Acknowledgements

CHAPTERS 5 and 7 appeared originally in *Essays in Criticism*, Chapter 9 in the *Proceedings of the Leeds Philosophical and Literary Society*, and parts of Chapter 10 in *Dictionary of Poetry and Poetics*, edited by Alex. Preminger, Frank Warnke, and O. B. Hardison, Jr.

Acknowledgements are due to the editors and to the Oxford University Press for permission to quote from Maurice Buxton Forman's edition of *The Letters of John Keats*.

NOTE TO THE SECOND EDITION

During the past ten years a number of excellent books have appeared, including the biographies by W. J. Bate, Robert Gittings, and Aileen Ward, and Rollins's great edition of the letters. We have not found it necessary or possible to make any major alterations in these essays, but we have corrected a few obvious misprints.

Introduction

THE ESSAYS IN THIS BOOK are self-explanatory and require no introduction; but, as the authors write from different points of view, a brief general statement on Keats's development, to which they would all more or less subscribe, may be acceptable.

The world of beauty seized or created by the imagination clashes with the tragic world of reality. Keats had too much integrity to turn away from the actual world, and nearly all his greatest poetry is an imaginative expression of this conflict. Even in his early poems we can observe the impact of the real world on his romantic day-dreams. While he was writing *Endymion* he had realized that the poet must bear 'the burthen of the mystery', and he knew he could not shut out the 'still, sad music of humanity'. In 'Isabella' and 'The Eve of St. Agnes' he luxuriated in the world of romance, but his imagination had been enriched and disciplined by his experience, and he was fully aware that these poems, describing events of far away and long ago, were only a temporary escape from the pressure of reality. It is probable that 'Hyperion', too, began like this—as an escape into a world of abstractions from the pain of watching his brother die—but as the poem developed, his imagination, under pressure of the conflict between the two worlds of romance and reality, turned it into a reflection, and even an attempted solution, of the conflict. In the 'Ode to a Nightingale' he tried once more to escape, but the fancy proved to be a 'deceiving elf'. In the 'Ode on a Grecian Urn' the world of art seems to be as real as the world of harsh fact, and a clue to its interpretation: if we could recognize the two worlds as one the meaningless woe would be transcended in tragedy. 'Lamia' and 'The Fall of Hyperion' were written during the same period. In one Keats decides that the world of the imagination, though beautiful, is an illusion: Lycius dies of despair. In the other poem Keats expresses more clearly what he had learnt while writing 'Hyperion'. He himself therefore takes the place of the Apollo of the earlier version, becoming a great poet by gazing into the eyes of Moneta, as Apollo had been deified by gazing into the eyes of Mnemosyne. The way to the reconciliation of beauty and truth lies through the Vale of Soulmaking, and it consists in an acceptance of the miseries of the world. After this Keats wrote only one supreme poem, 'To Autumn'.

His experience flowered naturally into poetry. Both his letters and poems were comments on the allegory of his life; and his whole life was a struggle to resolve the conflict between the ideal and the actual, between poetry and fact. It was his profound sense of kinship with suffering humanity, and the tension between it and his sensuous love of beauty, which made Keats into a great poet. Yet some critics have regretted that he was not contented with being the Dreamer of 'The Fall of Hyperion'. This regret appears in its most conscious form in Dr. Garrod's lively and original study. He complains of the way Keats, having 'achieved some characteristic perfection' in the 'world of pure imaginative forms', is assailed by 'the old hunger and thirst for "reality"'. His poetry is continually being spoilt by the intrusion of the real world in the shape of philosophy, politics, action, or character. Not content with writing beautiful poetry he hunted powers not his own—'the power to express character, action, the heroic element in things, or the power that can penetrate the mystery of human suffering'. But, Dr. Garrod argues, Keats only achieves his best and purest work when he falls back 'from these grandiose strivings'.

This view of Keats, which has the inevitable effect of degrading him into a minor poet, is implicitly denied in several essays in the present book. We can hardly regret that he was faithful to his own experience, and that, superbly endowed with the sensuous equipment of a poet, he continued to seek truth.

It will be seen that we frequently differ from previous writers on Keats—we should not otherwise have written this book—and we have occasionally expressed our disagreements with some sharpness; but we hope no reader will suppose that we do not admire Dr. Garrod's great edition of the poems because we sometimes try to convict him of error, or that we are unappreciative of the work of the great line of scholars and critics from Arnold and Bridges to Murry, Ridley, and Gittings.

I

Keats and the Elizabethans

JOAN GRUNDY

'WE TRACK HIM EVERYWHERE IN THEIR SNOW.' This is almost as true of Keats and the Elizabethans as it was of Ben Jonson and the ancients. Ever since Charles Cowden Clarke noticed in 1812 how he ramped through the scenes of *The Faerie Queene* 'like a young horse turned into a spring meadow', critics of Keats's work have been eager to observe and record its various debts to, echoes of, and affinities with the Elizabethan poets. The influence of the Elizabethans has been traced in the subject-matter of his poems, in their form and structure, their language, versification, and general style. The study of 'influences' has merged imperceptibly into the study of 'sources', and the study of sources has often diverted attention from the poems themselves to the mental processes that produced them. The process of absorption and assimilation by which Keats made what he read his own has been demonstrated by such critics as M. R. Ridley and Caroline Spurgeon, but is best described perhaps in his own words, in the original version of the sonnet on 'The Human Seasons':

> He hath his lusty spring when fancy clear
> > Takes in all beauty with an easy span:
> He hath his Summer, when luxuriously
> > He chews the honied cud of fair spring thoughts,
> > Till, in his Soul dissolv'd they come to be
> > > Part of himself.

Much of Keats's reading seems to have become, to a remarkable degree, 'part of himself'. As a result, the literary allusiveness of his poetry is often extremely complex: incidents, images, phrases, even cadences may simultaneously awaken echoes of many different writers. Detailed analysis by a number of critics, notably C. L. Finney and Professor Douglas Bush, has disentangled and sorted many of these. Others, for example E. de Selincourt in his introduction to his edition of Keats (1905), have stressed the general formative influence of the Elizabethans upon Keats's mind and art, particularly as regards his understanding and sensitive use of Greek myth. (His creditors here include not only the poets who used myths—as which Elizabethan did not?—but also the translators, Chapman and Sandys.) The 'firm and sure-set liking' which Keats shows for these writers has been assumed to rest upon a real sense of affinity with them; consequently, the notion that he was in some way an Elizabethan born out of his time has come to be accepted almost as a truism. In his *Mythology and the Romantic Tradition* Professor Douglas Bush mentions some of these affinities:

Keats is commonly linked with the Elizabethans by virtue of his sensuous richness, but there are less obvious and no less important links than that. For one thing, in Keats as in a number of Elizabethans, it is almost impossible to draw a line between sensuous and spiritual experience. For another, Keats was the only one among the romantic poets who could quite naturally accept and carry on the allegorical interpretation of myth as he found it in Spenser, Chapman, Sandys, and others; . . . Like Spenser, too, he loves beauty in its concrete and human forms, and sees in myth a treasury of the 'material sublime'.[1]

Mr. Middleton Murry, looking rather at the quality of his mind and the nature of its insights, sees him almost as the reincarnation of Shakespeare. On the whole, it is the more old-fashioned Elizabethan writers, those whom Mr. C. S. Lewis would describe as 'golden', with whom he has been linked: it is these, after all, whom he is known to have read. An attempt has been made, however, to bring him into the Metaphysical fold. Thus Mr. George Williamson, speaking of the disappearance of the 'unified sensibility' in poets after the seventeenth century, writes 'Keats was working toward it in his second *Hyperion*',[2] and Mr. Cleanth Brooks finds that his 'most mature poetry can be brought under the general principles of symbolist-metaphysical poetry'.[3] Of course, Mr. Williamson and Mr. Brooks are not thinking of

1 Douglas Bush, *Mythology and the Romantic Tradition* (1937), p. 85.
2 G. Williamson, *The Donne Tradition* (1930), p. 25.
3 Cleanth Brooks, *Modern Poetry and the Tradition* (1939), p. 237.

particular affinities or influences; they are thinking simply of a way (and for them perhaps the *only* way) of writing poetry. But their statements, if correct, would establish affinities between Keats and these Elizabethans of the new school also.

What we might call the *material* debt of Keats's poetry to the Elizabethans seems therefore to have been proved beyond question. His enthusiasm for them is indeed self-evident, both in his letters and his poetry; research has only confirmed and documented it. Whether in doing so it has also increased our understanding of the nature of Keats's poetry, as distinct from the stuff out of which it was made (though we cannot wholly separate the two) is, I think, doubtful. There is always a danger that the road to Xanadu may end in a bog. Thus most of the discoveries about Keats's *unconscious* borrowings seem to me, in themselves, to interest without enlightening. These borrowings are usually either visual or aural in character; some image, phrase, or cadence floats up out of the mists of memory and finds a place in his poem. The connection often seems quite accidental; the particular passage seems often to have been remembered quite apart from its context, so that nothing is to be gained in the understanding of Keats's poem by going back to the 'source'. Thus in 'La Belle Dame sans Merci' the line 'And no birds sing' echoes the line 'Let no bird sing', which occurs in an elegy in the second book (Song 1) of William Browne's *Britannia's Pastorals*. Browne's heroine, Marina, comes across the elegy engraved upon a rock as she is wandering alone on an apparently desert island. The transmutation of Marina into the knight-at-arms may be a simple one compared with, others that have been suggested;[1] nevertheless, so far as I know, no one has yet tried to prove that the situation and characters of 'La Belle Dame sans Merci' derived from, or have been in the slightest degree influenced by, Browne's poem. The echo *is* an echo, of words and cadence, and it is nothing more. And this is true of many, perhaps of most, of Keats's echoes: the Indian maid in *Endymion* 'Brimming the water-lily cups with tears'; the 'silver snarling trumpets' of 'The Eve of St. Agnes', recalling Spenser's 'silver sounding instruments' (here, however, Keats makes of

---

1 Thus C. L. Finney, in *The Evolution of Keats' Poetry* (Cambridge, U.S.A., 1936), finding the source of the poem in Spenser's episode of Cymochles and Phaedra (*Faerie Queene*, II. vi. 2 sq.) writes 'Keats retained the lake in the setting of the story, but he converted the gondelay into a pacing steed' (vol. ii, p. 596).

the phrase something new); the 'particular beauteous star' of 'Hyperion'; the 'fair Hesperian tree' of *Otho*, and so on. Even when the similarity in context shows that the connection was not merely fortuitous, as in the passage in *Endymion* where cupids rain violets upon the sleeping eyes of Adonis, thus recalling the picture of Venus and Adonis which hangs in Spenser's Castle Ioyeous, our understanding of Keats's purpose is not greatly increased. It is interesting to know that his Adonis is to be connected with Spenser's rather than with Shakespeare's, though we should never have dreamt of connecting him with the latter anyway. But the tapestry in Castle Ioyeous has a significance quite different from that of Keats's Adonis—it typifies the lasciviousness of its owner, Malecasta—so that to stress the resemblance too much would be to introduce irrelevancies.

Because of the often accidental and quite arbitrary nature of Keats's unconscious borrowings, they probably have less to tell us about the nature of a particular work than have his deliberate borrowings and imitations. These are often at least a guide to his intentions. The Elizabethanism of the early poems is partly the result of mere youthful enthusiasm; in many of the poems of 1817 Keats is the 'great lover', joyously recording all 'these I have loved'. (The comparison with Rupert Brooke is not inappropriate.) Yet his discipleship is at the same time a deliberate act of choice. Keats read the Elizabethans for pleasure, but also, as a practitioner of poetry, for guidance and instruction in his craft. The Elizabethans were to him at the beginning of his career what the Metaphysicals were to Mr. T. S. Eliot at an early stage of his, congenial writers from whom, because they were so congenial and suited to his talent, he might have much to learn. In many of the early poems—the three epistles, 'Sleep and Poetry', some of the sonnets—Keats is doing in verse what Mr. Eliot did in prose: exploring and discussing the work he admires, to see what it has to offer for himself. The analogy must obviously not be pushed too far: Keats in these poems shows little of the critical insight and discrimination of Mr. Eliot, neither is his examination so cool and detached. The Elizabethans to a large extent provided him with his inspiration as well as with a model. But the theories evolved, adumbrated, or enunciated in these early poems were put into practice in *Endymion*. From this poem, taken closely with the *Poems* of 1817 and the letters written while it was being composed

(April 1817 to March 1818) we can see what were the principles upon which Keats's imitation of the Elizabethans was based. The failure of *Endymion* led him to abandon or at any rate to distrust those principles, while at the same time his intensive study of Shakespeare and Wordsworth suggested new ones. As a result, there is after *Endymion* far less deliberate imitation of the Elizabethans in Keats's poetry, although the unconscious echoing of them continues. Both in his conscious critical theories and in his natural development as a poet, Keats has begun to 'grow away' from them in certain fundamental respects.

The study of Keats's affinities with the Elizabethans is therefore likely to prove more profitable today than a renewed emphasis upon his use of them as sources. Was he *really* an Elizabethan born out of his time? To some extent I think he was. His difficulty *is* partly that he has been suckled in a creed outworn: like the twentieth-century agnostic who is by temperament and emotion drawn to Christianity but whose intellect will not allow him to accept its tenets, he finds it increasingly difficult to reconcile his instinctive 'Elizabethan' faith with his 'Romantic' (or simply nineteenth-century) reason. But to say that he was 'born out of his time' is by implication to recognize that his Elizabethanism was incomplete. That is important, for it is unhelpful to notice only the points of resemblance between him and the Elizabethans without noticing the differences also. The study of sources and influences has itself tended to exaggerate the Elizabethan character of Keats's poetry, while leaving the nature of his affinity with them vague and imprecise. Yet if the admitted similarity between his poetry and theirs is to have any significance, its scope and character must be defined. My concern in this essay is therefore less with Keats's use of Elizabethan matter, than with his total attitude to the Elizabethans, his affinities with them, and the limitation of those affinities.

II

In this context the word 'Elizabethan' stands in little need of definition. I use it to mean, chiefly, those Elizabethans whom Keats is either known or may be presumed to have read: Spenser, Sidney, Marlowe, Browne, Drayton, Chapman, Fairfax, Sandys, Jonson, Beaumont and Fletcher, and of course Shakespeare. As

an Elizabethan in sympathy if not in date, and one appreciated by
Keats for qualities similar to theirs, the young Milton should be
added to the list.

These writers have at least one quality in common that everyone
will acknowledge: bulk. Whether we take them individually or
collectively, we find in them God's plenty—or at any rate plenty.
From the long bejewelled speeches that sprawl across the pages
of *Tamburlaine* to the leisureliness of Spenser or the massive
translations of Chapman, long in line as in body, everything attests
their creative exuberance and vitality. Copiousness is everywhere.
It accounts for many of their characteristic virtues and vices; for
their richness, but also for their carelessness. It provides also the
first affinity between them and Keats. Like them, he had a 'teeming
brain' and his poetry is, among other things, an expression of
energy. In the volume of 1817 this energy appears as an appetite
for, rather than a record of, experience. Throughout these poems
Keats stands tiptoe upon a little hill and surveys the world as if it
were some great feast spread out before him:

> There was wide wand'ring for the greediest eye,
> To peer about upon variety.

'What next?' he asks, as though moving from course to course.
At times the earth itself cannot satisfy his appetite, and he looks
up to the sky, strains to see 'white coursers paw and prance' there,
and yearns for some adventures in wonderland. *Endymion* is written
partly to fulfil that yearning. The appetite expressed in this poem,
however, is more than an appetite for experience, for the raw
material of poetry; it is an appetite for poetry itself. 'I find that
I cannot exist without poetry—without eternal poetry', he wrote
in April 1817, '—half the day will not do—the whole of it—I
began with a little, but habit has made me a Leviathan.' And a
little later in the same letter: 'I shall forthwith begin my Endymion.' The love of poetry has made a Leviathan of that too. The
poem's profusion—of incidents, images, and descriptions—is
notorious; the story is smothered in rambling roses. But though
the celebration of 'these joys'—the joys offered by the realm of
'Flora, and old Pan'—is genuine enough, one is left with the
impression that Keats at this time does not care very much what
he writes, so long as he writes poetry. All experience is, in the
last resort, simply so much grist to the mill. The riotous abun-

dance of 'the slip-shod *Endymion*' is in fact not due entirely to careless rapture. It is also, partly, a sweet disorder in the dress, deliberately adopted because the poet believes that thereby he will produce more and better poetry. And it was his study of the Elizabethans that led him to this belief.

Keats held decidedly transcendental notions of poetry at this time. The early poems express his eagerness to 'think divinely', to catch 'sphery strains' from the 'blue dome', to

> write down a line of glorious tone
> And full of many wonders of the spheres,

to find the fair 'visions of all places'. The Elizabethans seemed to him to have done all these things:

> Is there so small a range
> In the present strength of manhood, that the high
> Imagination cannot freely fly
> As she was wont of old? prepare her steeds,
> Paw up against the light, and do strange deeds
> Upon the clouds? Has she not shown us all?
> ('Sleep and Poetry', ll. 162–7)

he asks. Their capacity for vision, and their freedom of imagination, these are the qualities that have impressed him most, and he connects the vision directly with the freedom. 'Poetry must be free!' is his creed. 'It is of the air, not of the earth, and the higher it soars, the nearer it gets to its home.'[1] Granted this freedom, it could become almost a kind of automatic writing; in 'Sleep and Poetry' Keats wrote of his longing to achieve

> many a verse from so strange influence
> That we must ever wonder how, and whence
> It came.

Freedom of range and complete receptivity were the important things. Whether a poet's imagination led him to contemplate earthly things of beauty or sent him soaring into 'some wond'rous region' to find the source of beauty itself, he must follow, for

> he ne'er is crown'd
> With immortality, who fears to follow
> Where airy voices lead.

1 *The Champion*, Sunday 28 Dec, 1817. Quoted by C. D. Thorpe, *The Mind of John Keats* (1926), p. 185,

B   7

And only the 'magic hand of chance' could trace correctly the 'huge cloudy symbols' of the high romance he found written among the stars. That this is the theory that lies behind *Endymion*, and that the theory derived, in its essentials, from Keats's study of the Elizabethans is clear from certain passages in the letters he wrote at this time. From these we see that he found (or thought he found) a precedent for the length, copiousness, and looseness of structure of *Endymion* in the Elizabethans.

Writing to his brother George in the spring of 1817, he speaks in rather awed tones of having to 'make 4,000 lines of one bare circumstance, and fill them with Poetry'. 'Why endeavour after a long Poem?' he asks. And he answers:

> Do not the Lovers of Poetry like to have a little Region to wander in where they may pick and choose, and in which the images are so numerous that many are forgotten, and found new in a second Reading: which may be food for a Week's stroll in the Summer?

The image here has been suggested by a passage in *Britannia's Pastorals* (II. iii), in which Browne is endeavouring to excuse his habit of digression. This is instructive: it shows that Keats chose to write a long poem because he thought it would give him, as well as the reader, a chance to wander as he pleased. The resemblance in shape between *Endymion* and *Britannia's Pastorals* is certainly not accidental, and the shape of *Britannia's Pastorals* itself may be related to the work of Spenser, Drayton, Ariosto, and to Elizabethan narrative art in general. 'Did our great Poets ever write short Pieces? I mean in the shape of Tales?' asks Keats. And he does not stay for an answer.

In a later letter, written in February 1818, at a time, that is, when he was engaged in revising *Endymion*, Keats again mentions the Elizabethans. His purpose is mainly to provide a damaging contrast to the self-awareness and self-satisfaction of the poetry of Wordsworth and Hunt, yet the remarks have relevance to his own practice in *Endymion*. He writes:

> Modern poets differ from the Elizabethans in this. Each of the moderns like an Elector of Hanover governs his petty state, and knows how many straws are swept daily from the Causeways in all his dominions and has a continual itching that all the Housewives should have their coppers well scoured: the antients were Emperors of vast Provinces, they had only heard of the remote ones, and scarcely cared

8

to visit them.—I will cut all this—I will have no more of Wordsworth
or Hunt in particular—why should we be of the tribe of Manasseh,
when we can wander with Esau? Why should we kick against the
Pricks, when we can walk on Roses? Why should we be owls, when
we can be Eagles? . . . I don't mean to deny Wordsworth's grandeur
and Hunt's merit, but I mean to say we need not be teazed with
grandeur and merit when we can have the uncontaminated and
unobtrusive. Let us have the old Poets, and Robin Hood.[1]

The very vehemence of this suggests that Keats is actually a
little uneasy: he was, after all, by this time already beginning to
worry about the absence in his poetry of any serious criticism of
life. It does, however, re-define for us his attitude to the Elizabethans. The earlier part of the statement praises them for their
careless profusion. The reference to wandering with Esau suggests
that he admires their (as he sees it) adventurous, undisciplined
method of composition; the phrase about walking on roses expresses his delight in their sensuousness; the question 'Why should
we be owls, when we can be Eagles?' indicates that he believes
them to have had more visionary power than a would-be teacher
and moralist like Wordsworth. (As a reflection on Wordsworth,
this need not be taken too seriously; Keats is obviously writing in
a fit of the spleen.) This again confirms that in writing *Endymion* he
had taken Elizabethan narrative poetry as his model. The third
point even hints, perhaps, at what was his highest aspiration for
the poem. He too wanted to be an Eagle. As poetry of vision,
Endymion may seem to us to be stillborn. Yet when we condemn
it for being rambling in form and overlaid with decoration, we
should remember that this is partly due to Keats's artistic theories,
and not to self-indulgence alone.

III

The freedom Keats claimed and exercised in *Endymion* was both
artistic and imaginative: freedom of range and simple lack of
discipline. The failure of the poem led him to revise his theories.
As a result, largely, of his intensive study of Shakespeare and
Wordsworth, he now came to associate the unfettered imagination, not so much with the idea of free flight (which he now

1 *The Letters of John Keats*, ed. M. B. Forman (1935), pp. 96–7.

restricts, perhaps, to Fancy: 'Ever let the Fancy roam'), as with the idea of a self-obliterating penetration into the nature and experiences of others, in which the intensity of the experience is more important than its range or variety. The effect of this was to turn his ambitions and sympathies (at any rate conscious sympathies) in the direction of the drama, and away from romance, with its ideal forms and unreal worlds. This meant that, apart from the dramatists and especially Shakespeare, he turned away from the Elizabethans as models, for the Elizabethans were to him primarily 'noble Poets of Romance'. That, even more than the sensuous quality of their verse, was the source of their initial appeal to him, as the *Poems* of 1817, with their oblivious delight in the Elizabethans' imagined worlds—of chivalry, mythology, and 'faery'—convey very clearly. Creativeness in this fundamental sense—creation or re-creation, not just of a work of art, but of new forms, a new world over and above that of nature—was characteristic of the Elizabethans; it was one of the ways in which their superabundant energy showed itself. They saw nothing unnatural in it; on the contrary, the poet, says Sidney, 'goeth hand in hand with Nature' by 'making things either better than Nature bringeth forth, or quite anew, forms such as never were in Nature, as the Heroes, Demigods, Cyclops, Chimeras, Furies, and such like'. Keats too, at the beginning of his career, joyously aligned himself with them in this. He too felt the urge to be a creator, a myth-maker. But in his new mood, after *Endymion*, doubts arose. The writer of romance became for him, not as he had seemed to be at first a visionary, but a dreamer, vexing the world with his 'wonders'. It is here that the difference between him and the Elizabethans becomes apparent. Sharing their instinctive liking for ideal forms and 'abstractions', he did not share with them, in any completeness at any rate, the attitude of mind, the philosophy almost, which made them accept such creative activity as, properly considered, the most divine act of which man was capable. To Sidney it was a matter of pride that, while Nature gives us a leaden world, 'the poets only deliver a golden'. Bacon observes that poetry 'was ever thought to have some participation of divineness, because it doth raise and erect the mind, by submitting the shows of things to the desires of the mind, whereas reason doth buckle and bow the mind unto the nature of things'. He does not question this view either of its character or function, but finds in the 'more ample greatness, more exact goodness, and more absolute variety' that poetry presents, something agreeable to the spirit of man which 'serveth and conferreth to magnanimity, morality, and to delectation'. The Elizabethan poet could make the too much loved earth more lovely; he could go further, and create,

> transcending these,
> Far other worlds, and other seas.

In neither case need he feel himself to be an escapist, for he could claim that he was portraying that highest form of Beauty which is Truth. Keats, born into a different era, with a different ethos, found it increasingly hard to ease his conscience with this Platonic argument. In 1817 he could declare that what the imagination seizes as Beauty must be truth, whether it existed before or not. The thought is echoed nearly two years later, at the end of the 'Ode on a Grecian Urn', yet it seems there to be less a philosophical conviction than a proffered consolation. The truth Keats is seeking in these later years, as the Induction to 'The Fall of Hyperion' shows, is in fact not so much ideal, as moral truth; his search is for an aesthetic doctrine that is also a moral doctrine. Here the Elizabethans can help him little. 'We hate poetry that has a palpable design upon us', he had declared (February 1818). This was a prejudice which the Elizabethans did not share. They knew that poetry must—and does—both delight and teach, and, interpreting this duty 'without a rigid definition, in an easy and Platonic description', they found it an easy matter to reconcile Ovid's banquet of sense with an Ovid moralized. This would not do for Keats. He wanted to achieve a purer art than the moralizing romantic poets among the Elizabethans had achieved, one 'uncontaminated' by the teacher (for, had he looked closer, he would have had to admit that no poet ever had a more palpable design on us than had Spenser in *The Faerie Queene*); yet at the same time he wanted it to be a more significant, responsible art than theirs seemed in its *least* moralizing moments. The 'dulce' and the 'utile' were not merely to be mixed in his poetry: they were to be identical.

Keats's later work, therefore, though it owes much to Elizabethan example in matters of expression and technique, is much less Elizabethan in its fundamental sympathies than *Endymion* had been. Keats tackles his new problem in various ways: in the narrative poems, 'Isabella', 'The Eve of St. Agnes', and 'Lamia', largely by ignoring it; in 'Hyperion' and 'The Fall of Hyperion', by adapting the Elizabethan allegorical method to his own purposes; and in the Odes by giving personal expression to a personal experience. The three narrative poems, particularly 'The Eve of St. Agnes' and 'Lamia', written in disregard of his new critical tenets, have also no ties with the old. They are their own *raison d'être*: their beauty seeks to capture and express neither ideal nor moral truth. Feeling himself unable as yet to achieve the morally significant art that he desires, he will not, it seems, strive any longer, as he had done in *Endymion*, after an ideally significant one. There is therefore no *faith* behind the poems, as, however distantly, vaguely, or conventionally, there always is behind an Elizabethan poem. They are fine poems of their kind (and therefore need, ultimately, no justification), but they lack, so to speak, a centre of gravity. Thus 'The Eve of St. Agnes' superficially Spenserian in its sensuousness and dream-like atmosphere, has beneath the surface no links with the poetry of Spenser. The characters are those of *Romeo and Juliet* reduced to a shadow-play, not characters at all in the dramatic sense of the word, but, rather, parts of a sensuous pattern. To those who refuse to give Spenser's allegory a chance to bite them (and Keats, it would seem, was at one with Hazlitt on this) *The Faerie Queene* also probably appears to be merely or primarily a sensuous pattern. In fact, it is a complex poem of many levels, in which the sensuous, the spiritual, the moral, and the intellectual are inextricably intertwined. In Keats's poem there is a *sensuous* complexity, but there is no complexity of levels or meanings. 'The Eve of St. Agnes' is a thing of beauty and a joy for ever. But to make its sensuous richness a ground for identifying its purely decorative art with the grave moral art of Spenser, as is often done, is surely wrong. Similarly with 'Lamia', for which the obvious comparison in Elizabethan literature is Marlowe's *Hero and Leander*. Even this poem has behind it a point of reference, perhaps only a point of view, which gives it, even in its unfinished state, more direction, more significance, than 'Lamia'. Marlowe's purpose may be only the cynically witty elaboration of a sensuous experience, but we are made aware of this purpose, and it gives the poem another dimension besides the narrative one. 'Lamia' is a dazzlingly exotic narrative, but its beauty, like that of 'The Eve of

St. Agnes', lies upon the surface. In fact, despite its artistic flaws, it is 'Isabella' that seems to me to be the most Elizabethan of these three poems, in the sense that it is, potentially at any rate, the most complex in its mixture of levels. Along with the idyllic study of Lorenzo's and Isabella's love, and the pathos of the 'pot of basil', there is a hint of social reference in the comments on the brothers, the literally haunting treatment of the supernatural Lorenzo's words

> 'those sounds grow strange to me
> 'And thou art distant in Humanity'

are an attempt to express something new in poetry—and above all the concentrated, almost ballad-like intensity of the description of the murder, with its touch of *Arden of Feversham* realism, and later of Isabella's discovery of it. The poem's artistic perfection is below that of the others, but its *promise* of a complex, significant, original poetry seems to me to be greater.

'Hyperion' differs from these three poems in being, from the start, built round an idea. The poem is, however, a failure, in Keats's eyes if not in ours, since it fails to fulfil his intention. 'The Fall of Hyperion' was to correct this, and to make his intention plain. The Induction attempts to show how the Beauty of the visionary (as distinct from the dreamer) can still be Truth: the rest of the poem was to provide concrete proof of this. The poem is, in fact, Keats's most ambitious attempt to fuse artistic beauty with moral truth, without abandoning those abstractions which were his only life, or the 'wonder' which, in spite of his misgivings, counted for so much to him in poetry. The method he uses is partly allegorical and thus invites comparison with the Elizabethans. In the Induction he does come closer than at any other time to achieving a moral power comparable with that of Spenser, by a method akin to his. The method, in the conversation between the poet and Moneta, is that of explicit moral statement, like the comments Spenser often introduces at the beginning of cantos. The description of Moneta draws some of its power from allegory: it presents one of those forms 'which do not live like living men' and yet are not alien to them, an unreality in which reality itself is mirrored. The lack of any *felt* meaning in the story that follows, on the other hand, comes largely from the fact that the characters fall between two stools and have neither the dramatic human

13

quality of fully realized individuals, nor the symbolic strength of true personification. They are at once too remote from human nature and not remote enough. It is here that the difficulties of Keats's position, as compared with that of the Elizabethans, becomes apparent. Lacking both their faith in the assured value of their own creations and their hearty appetite for a poetry that has a palpable design upon us, he is naturally not so fitted as they for the writing of allegory. Yet the limitations of his emotional experience, its subjective character and concentration upon a few themes—love, death, and mutability—and the complete absence of any indication that he understood *temperament*, as distinct from emotions, make it unlikely that he was particularly fitted to write drama either. Both in its strength and its weakness his 'allegory' is different in kind from theirs. It avoids crudity and over-explicitness (his aim is to let the actions and descriptions speak for themselves), yet in doing so it fails to signify all that Keats wanted it to do. This allegory really does not bite. Of Keats's poem, far more than of Spenser's, is it true to say that it is primarily a gallery of pictures. And the significance of the pictures lies in their beauty, in the vividness with which we are made to see expressed in face or voice or gesture the nature of the character's emotion. But neither the character nor the emotion is completely human. Even the portrait of Moneta is an extension of experience, rather than an interpretation of it. This fact, however, is important for another reason: it suggests a fundamental difference in direction between Keats's poetry and that of the Elizabethans. Keats, it seems to me, is not here symbolizing human experience in terms of pagan myth; he is, rather, trying to look at it from a new point of view, namely, that of a god. He looks both *at* and *with* Moneta; he feels

> a power within me of enormous ken
> To see as a god sees.

The feat he is attempting, a comprehensive, instantaneous survey of all human suffering, and with that survey, an understanding of and reconciliation with it, is 'negative capability' carried to its limit—a superhuman one. Elizabethan poetry has nothing quite like it. An Elizabethan poet surveys human life from the centre rather than from the circumference; his gods, kings of infinite space though they may be, are invariably bounded in this nutshell, given the characters and the stature of men. For in spite of its Platonism, the Elizabethan view of life is essentially anthropocentric; and the comprehensiveness achieved by an Elizabethan poet, whether we take as its representative Spenser or Shakespeare, is achieved through analysis, analysis of life in all its multiplicity and myriad-sidedness, rather than through synthesis, through a mighty summing-up of experience such as Keats seems to be attempting. Even of their religious poetry this is true: the incarnation moves them perhaps more deeply than anything else. Keats's Moneta is daringly conceived, perhaps more daringly than he realized, for she invites comparison with the King of Sorrows. She invites it, however, through her divine, not her human attributes, through that 'immortal sickness' which, though it transcends human sorrows, yet testifies to her infinite capacity to bear 'the giant agony of the world'. Thus Keats is here attempting an objective expression of a moral and religious absolute: he is reaching out after a poetry in which beauty, the static, objective beauty which he most admires and which he is most fitted to create, will express moral truth with a force that is not didactic but visionary. To some extent, this is the kind of vision he had been seeking from the start. The 'skyey knight-errantry' of the Epistles, the narration of the story of Endymion in 'I stood tiptoe', already indicate his desire for a vantage-point which will enable him literally to *comprehend* the mystery of life. In 'Sleep and Poetry', in one of those passages in which he outlines the progress he plans for himself, he describes this ultimate objective in words applicable to 'The Fall of Hyperion':

> Then the events of this wide world I'd seize,
> Like a strong giant, and my spirit teaze,
> Till at its shoulders it should proudly see
> Wings to find out an immortality;

with this we may connect the lines later in the poem

> A drainless shower
> Of light is poesy; 'tis the supreme of power,
> 'Tis might half slumbering on its own right arm.

It is a poetry of power that he wishes to write; in a more ambitious sense than Matthew Arnold intended, he wants to make poetry, through its power of revelation, a substitute for religion. In this he has moved beyond the Elizabethans. Poetry for them may be an aid to religion, or at least to morality; the poet, in creating ideal forms, may even be doing something god-like; nevertheless, the two spheres can never be identical. Weighing upon Keats is not only Platonism, but the heavy burden of the mechanistic 'philosophy' which he censured in 'Lamia'; the interpenetration of sense and spirit is not so clear, not so possible even, to him as it was to them. That perhaps is why he so persistently goes *outside* human experience for a view of human experience. Since he cannot fully experience the ideal in the actual, he seeks to contemplate the actual from the point of view of the ideal.

This is what he is doing in the two odes, 'To a Nightingale' and 'On a Grecian Urn'. Thus the picture on the urn, in its arresting of life, is also partly a summary of it; that is why it doth

> tease us out of thought
> As doth eternity.

(It is significant—for his art—that he finds the *picturing* forth of this meaning so satisfying.) The nightingale, in not being born for death, has a similar advantage: with it, we can again look at life from a point outside it, without, however, as yet having the ability to 'envisage circumstance all calm' which Moneta possesses. For these odes differ from 'Hyperion' and the other narrative poems in being also personal meditations, closer, in their personal and meditative qualities, to the Holy Sonnets of Donne, than to the generality of Elizabethan lyric. The odes 'To Psyche' and 'To Autumn' stand apart by reason of their complete objectivity and detachment; here the worlds of the imagination and of the senses are celebrated without any questioning of their value or significance. They are thus a reminder of the essentially concrete character of Keats's art.

IV

At the beginning of this essay I quoted Professor Douglas Bush's statement that Keats is commonly linked with the Elizabethans by virtue of his sensuous richness. This is true, and we can see the reason for it: Elizabethan poetry and Keats's both leave the same impression, the impression, surely, of an embroidered cloth, a rich tapestry of colour and sound and feeling. Professor Rosemond Tuve's convincing Berkeleyan demonstrations have, however, led us to doubt the evidence of our senses, so far as Elizabethan poetry is concerned, and have emphasized both the lack of particularity in Elizabethan sensuous writing and its strict subordination to a dominating abstract idea. A comparison of Keats's poetry with theirs in this respect makes apparent the much greater particularity of his poetry. From the early Spenserian imitations onwards, Keats's aim seems always to have been to re-create in poetry the experience he was describing. The Elizabethans, on the other hand, sought not so much to re-create experience as to create something new from it, not to give the illusion of transmitting sensation directly, but to show it acted upon and re-shaped by the mind. A poem like 'When icicles hang by the wall', in which the experience of the *thing itself* is re-created by the accumulation of realistic details, is rare with them. Seldom in their poetry do we find that endeavour after exactitude, that search for the exact expressive word, that is evident even in this passage from Keats's 'Calidore':

> sequester'd leafy glades,
> That through the dimness of their twilight show
> Large dock leaves, spiral foxgloves, or the glow
> Of the wild cat's eyes, or the silvery stems
> Of delicate birch trees, or long grass which hems
> A little brook.[1]

A typical Elizabethan passage to set beside that would be this from Drayton's *Endimion and Phoebe*:

> Out of thys soyle sweet bubling fountains crept,
> As though for joy the sencelesse stones had wept;
> With often turnes, like to a curious maze:
> Which breaking forth, the tender grasse bedewed,
> Whose silver sand with orient pearle was strewed,
> Shadowed with roses and sweet eglantine,
> Dipping theyr sprayes into this christalline.[2]

Keats wants you to see his scene as it was; Drayton is exercising all his ingenuity to embellish and enhance his. Keats's treatment of the natural world differs from that of the Elizabethans in this, that he does not try to make the too much loved earth more lovely. The loveliness it possesses in its unspoilt state is sufficient

---

1 'Calidore', ll. 47–52.
2 Drayton, *Endimion and Phoebe*, ll. 45–52.

for him: he does not normally 'quarrel with the rose', but is content to leave the 'finer tone' to the hereafter while he records and re-creates, as accurately as he can, the tone that is given us. To the Elizabethans, of course, it was always a matter of delight when Nature improved on Art, or Art on Nature; they loved to describe a garden

> Whose various flow'rs deceiv'd the rasher eye
> In taking them for curious tapestry,

or a veil such as Hero's:

> Her veil was artificial flowers and leaves,
> Whose workmanship both man and beast deceives.

Keats did not share this cult of the artificial. In his devotion to both Art and Nature he kept them separate, 'uncontaminated', and sought no sophisticated enjoyment of them. Stylistically, the difference might be summed up by saying that Keats's style is not so conceited as that of the Elizabethans. But underneath the difference in style there is a difference in total attitude.

Keats's affinity with the Elizabethans on the sensuous side of his work seems therefore to lie more in technique than in outlook, in the enrichment of his vocabulary, and in actual debts in images, stanza-forms and so on. Keats early made it one of his axioms that poetry should surprise by a fine excess and not by singularity. Perhaps it was the Elizabethans who had taught him this, for only a few weeks before setting down this axiom, he had written in praise of Shakespeare's sonnets, which 'seem to be full of fine things said unintentionally, in the intensity of working out a conceit'. And, of course, we have to remember that, whether the Elizabethans use sensuous language and imagery simply for decoration or 'to push us through an abstract process', they do use it, and that is probably what struck the pre-Tuveian readers, Keats among them, most forcibly. Keats did find sensuous richness in the Elizabethans, and their example encouraged and aided him in the development in his poetry of a sensuousness different in kind from theirs.

No doubt we could enlarge the term 'Metaphysical' sufficiently to include within it all those whom we should like to see among the saved. Such an enlargement, however, reduces rather than increases its value as a critical term, and I would, therefore, hesitate to apply it to Keats. It is true that in his search for the expressive word or metaphor he often achieves a compression that seems to have about it a certain quality of Metaphysical wit, as in the 'beaded bubbles winking at the brim' or the 'embalmed darkness' of the 'Ode to a Nightingale'. But the very fact that he does achieve them in his search for the expressive word emphasizes the difference. The wit, the intellectual quality in these phrases is only incidental; what primarily matters is the impression they make upon the senses, the success they have in re-creating the exact sensation Keats had in mind. When Marvell calls glow-worms 'Country Comets', we admire his wit; when Keats writes of 'Vesper, amorous glow-worm of the sky', it is primarily our feelings and senses that are stirred.

In a sense, Keats's affinities with the Elizabethans are recognized simply by calling him a Romantic. The Romantic movement was, after all, fundamentally a return to the kind of poetry that had been written by the Elizabethans, a poetry in which the senses, feelings, and imagination had a prominent place. To Keats the Elizabethans were also Romantic writers in the more specialized sense that they wrote romances, stories, that is, in which the fancy indulged itself freely in the creation of 'wonders' and 'the marvellous'. This perhaps first gave him his feeling of kinship with them. Like theirs, his art is, on one side of it, non-naturalistic, in the sense that it goes beyond nature and creates either new things or beautiful things made new. He, however, as I have shown, in one sense seeks to go further beyond nature than they ever dreamed of going. He does not succeed in this attempt; except for the Induction to 'The Fall of Hyperion' he is remembered primarily for what Arnold so felicitously called his *natural* magic. But there are hints in him also of a new kind of poetry of power. He might, had he lived, have found a way of using his objectifying gifts in the service of those abstractions which, as he once said, were his only life.

2

'Endymion'

CLARICE GODFREY

BOTH THE MOON and the myth of Endymion and Phoebe exercised a powerful fascination over Keats's imagination before he began to write *Endymion*. In the three Epistles included in the 1817 volume of *Poems*, Keats dwells on the beauty of the moon and her power to inspire the poet. The same idea is expressed in fuller form in 'I stood tiptoe', where a description of the moon as,

> Maker of sweet poets, dear delight
> Of this fair world, and all its gentle livers;
> Spangler of clouds, halo of crystal rivers,
> Mingler with leaves, and dew and tumbling streams,
> Closer of lovely eyes to lovely dreams,   (116–20)

leads to an imaginative account of the genesis of certain myths, and especially that of Endymion and Phoebe. The repetition in varied forms of a favourite idea or image is typical of Keats, especially in his earlier verse, and it was a natural step for him from a tentative, to a full, treatment of the myth.

In a letter to his sister, Keats told the story in these words:

Many Years ago there was a young handsome Shepherd who fed his flocks on a Mountain's Side called Latmus—he was a very contemplative sort of a Person and lived solitary among the trees and Plains little thinking—that such a beautiful Creature as the Moon was growing mad in Love with him—However so it was; and when he was asleep on the Grass, she used to come down from heaven and admire him excessively for a long time; and at last could not refrain from carrying him away in her arms to the top of that high Mountain Latmus while he was a dreaming—but I dare say you have read this and all the other beautiful

Tales which have come down from the ancient times of that beautiful Greece.[1]

This account of the myth serves as well as any other to show that, in itself, it offers insufficient detail or variety of incident for treatment in a poem of four thousand lines; yet that was the kind of treatment Keats chose to give it. The myth furnishes no more than the groundwork of Book 1, in which Endymion describes his meetings with an unknown goddess, and the end of the poem, where Phoebe carries Endymion away to enjoy with her an 'immortality of passion'. In the rest of the poem Endymion goes on a strange journey and Keats provides him with new adventures, drawing the material partly from his reading and partly from his imagination.

There is no evidence that Keats's friends or his earliest critics saw more in the poem that it appears to be on the surface—a long poem held together by a slender main theme, to which a profusion of description and digressive narrative, much of it in itself very fine, is loosely attached. Almost sixty years after Keats's death, however, Frances Mary Owen published a study of the poem, which she described as an allegory with 'a distinct development and very few digressions from its regular sequence'.[2] Since then most critics have followed her lead and seen in the poem conscious allegory worked out to a fairly detailed, if not very clear, plan. Although they are, in the main, agreed to interpret Endymion's adventures as a symbol of the quest of Man, or the Poet, for some kind of Ideal, they differ considerably in the significance they attach to detail and in the extent to which they have committed themselves. Interpretations which are superficially similar contain significant differences and, since the poem considered as an allegory is vague and obscure, the critic often seems to reveal as much of himself, and of his modes of thought, as he does of Keats, in what he sees there.

There is not room here for a detailed study of the various allegorical interpretations of the poem, but a summary of some of the main ones may be useful.

Sir Sidney Colvin and Professor Ernest de Selincourt both identified Endymion with the Poet and saw his adventures as a symbol for some kind of quest, in which he is successful only after

1 *Letters*, Letter 19, 12 Sept. 1817, p. 38.
2 F. M. Owen, *John Keats* (London, 1880), p. 84.

his soul has been 'taken out of itself and purified by active sympathy with the lives and suffering of others'.[1] Colvin saw Phoebe as a symbol of 'essential Beauty', and the Indian Maid as a Symbol of the individual beauties of things and beings upon earth, a passion for which beauties 'is in its nature identical with the passion for that transcendental and essential Beauty', for Phoebe and the Indian Maid are one.[2] Professor de Selincourt, however, claimed that, in *Endymion*, Keats was striving

to treat . . . the problem continually before his mind, and to present in a story whose beauty had long haunted him an allegory of the development of the poet's soul towards a complete realisation of itself,[3]

that Phoebe represents the ideal, which finds its way into the poet's heart 'through his emotional worship of nature',[3] and that Endymion's passion for the Indian Maid, like his interest in Alpheus and Arethusa, Glaucus and Scylla, represents the growth of the poet's love for humanity.

Robert Bridges, while claiming that Keats was 'not making an allegory but using a legend'[4] found in the poem an even more complicated 'inner meaning'. According to his interpretation, Endymion is Man, and it is the Moon which

represents 'Poetry' or the Ideality of desired objects, 'the principle of Beauty in all things'; . . . the supersensuous quality which makes all desired objects ideal.[5]

Phoebe, he suggests, as the personification and supreme manifestation of this quality, represents 'the ideal beauty or love of woman', while the Indian Maid 'clearly represents real or sensuous passion'; and, since Phoebe is the Moon as well as the Indian Maid, 'it follows that the love of woman is in its essence the same with all love of beauty'.[5] In Endymion's meetings with other lovers, Bridges traces an attempt to show that the 'ideality' of man's passion needs to be 'humanised' by sympathy with the sorrow of others.[5] He differs from the two critics previously

---

1 S. Colvin, *John Keats* (London, 1917), p. 172.
2 Ibid.
3 Keats, *Poems*, ed. E. de Selincourt, p. xl.
4 Keats, *Poems*, ed. G. Thorn Drury, with introduction and notes by Robert Bridges (London, 1896), vol. I, p. xxiii.
5 Ibid., pp. xxi–xxii.

mentioned, in claiming that the poem was carefully planned and that the four books correspond with the four elements—earth, fire, water, and air—which

typify respectively: I. Natural beauty; II. The mysteries of earth; III. The secrets of death; IV. Spiritual freedom and satisfaction.[1]

More recent critics, too, have found in the poem elaborate allegory worked out according to a careful plan. Professor H. C. Notcutt, who finds few details too small to bear some kind of allegorical significance, attributes to the poem 'a narrower and a wider meaning', claiming that Endymion's adventures symbolize both 'the new birth of poetry which came about as soon as the power of the pseudo-classical school declined', and also 'the experience of an individual, picturing the rise and development of the poetic passion in his mind, his earnest pursuit and gradual realization of the ideal that is set before him'.[2] Professor C. L. Finney, on the other hand, interprets one of the most important passages in the poem (I. 777–815) as an explicit statement of 'the neo-Platonic philosophy of beauty', and claims that 'if we interpret *Endymion* in the light of this passage, as Keats intended us to do, we see that the theme of the poem is the neo-Platonic quest of immortality'.[3] Elsewhere he calls this quest, 'the quest of the soul of man for reunion with God, or Original Essence'.[4] He too divides the poem into four parts:

Keats outlined four stages or gradations through which Endymion must pass before he wins the happiness of 'fellowship with essence'—first, appreciation of the beauty of nature, 'the clear religion of heaven'; second, appreciation of the beauty of art; third, friendship; and fourth, love. He developed these four stages in the four books of *Endymion*, devoting a book to each stage.[5]

Finally,[6] Mr. Middleton Murry, who condemns the systematic allegorical interpretation of the poem as 'something alien to the poetic idiosyncrasy of Keats', traces in the poem a fairly sustained

1 Ibid., p. xxv.
2 H. C. Notcutt, *An Interpretation of Keats's Endymion* (Capetown, 1919), p. 7. See also Notcutt, *The Story of Glaucus in Keats's Endymion* (Capetown, 1921), and *Endymion: A Poetic Romance*, with introduction by H. C. Notcutt (Oxford, 1927).
3 C. L. Finney, *The Evolution of Keats's Poetry*, vol. i, p. 298.
4 Ibid., p. 295.   5 Ibid., pp. 298–9.
6 For other interesting studies of the meaning of the poem, see H. I'A. Fausset, *Keats* (London, 1922), and Leonard Brown, 'The Genesis, Growth and Meaning of Endymion', *Studies in Philology*, xxx (1933).

record of Keats's personal experience, and summarizes the 'argument' thus:

> To obey Love and to pursue essential Beauty in all its manifestations lead to the same end. They alone lead a man to true happiness, to perfect self-forgetfulness, and to communion with the One.[1]

One thing stands out, and that is that, in most of the allegorical interpretations of the poem, the weight of the allegory is made to rest on a single passage (I. 777–815), in which Endymion defends his love against Peona's criticism and describes happiness as 'a fellowship with essence'. It is only on the assumption that the words, 'a fellowship with essence', mean 'union with some kind of transcendental reality' that Endymion's love for Phoebe can be said, with any confidence, to symbolize the pursuit of an ideal. Nowhere else in the poem is there any clear indication that this love is symbolic, or that it is different from human passion, except in that Phoebe, being a goddess, can win immortality for her lover and so make possible 'an immortality of passion' (II. 808). Any attempt to reconsider the meaning of the poem must start from this passage.

There is no doubt that Keats attached great importance to Endymion's speech and was anxious that it should be understood. Writing to his publisher to suggest alterations to lines 777–80, he explained:

> You must indulge me by putting this in for setting aside the badness of the other, such a preface is necessary to the subject. The whole thing must I think have appeared to you, who are a consequitive Man, as a thing almost of mere words—but I assure you that when I wrote it it was a regular stepping of the Imagination towards a Truth. My having written that Argument will perhaps be of the greatest Service to me of anything I ever did. It set before me at once the gradations of Happiness even like a kind of Pleasure Thermometer. . . .[2]

These lines, which form a 'preface' to the rest of the speech—and not, I think, to the rest of the poem as a whole—are:

> Wherein lies happiness? In that which becks
> Our ready minds to fellowship divine,
> A fellowship with essence; till we shine,
> Full alchemiz'd, and free of space.

1 J. M. Murry, *Studies in Keats* (Oxford, 1930), p. 59.
2 *Letters*, Letter 42, To Taylor, 30 Jan. 1818, p. 91.

There is nothing to indicate that the words, 'a fellowship with essence', describe only the highest of the gradations of happiness, and the gist of the passage might equally well be that each kind of happiness is in itself a 'fellowship with essence', the finest being that which makes the richest change in man's nature.[1] The use of the word, 'essences', in other parts of the poem, does indeed suggest that Keats used the term to describe his response to varying and particular forms of beauty.

In the opening lines of the poem, Keats describes some of the things of beauty which have power to soothe and delight, the beauties of nature and fine creations of the imagination of man:

> Such the sun, the moon,
> Trees old, and young, sprouting a shady boon
> For simple sheep; and such are daffodils
> With the green world they live in; . . .
>
> And such too is the grandeur of the dooms
> We have imagined for the mighty dead;
> All lovely tales that we have heard or read:
> An endless fountain of immortal drink,
> Pouring unto us from the heaven's brink.
>
> (I. 13–24)

He goes on,

> Nor do we merely feel these *essences*
> For one short hour.

Later in the poem, Endymion says of Phoebe,

> Now I have tasted her sweet soul to the core
> All other depths are shallow: essences,
> Once spiritual, are like muddy lees,
> Meant but to fertilize my earthly root,
> And make my branches lift a golden fruit
> Into the bloom of heaven.   (II. 904–9)

In other words, other beauties have but served to nurture his mind and to prepare him for his love for Phoebe.

---

1 The original version of these lines is helpful:
> Wherein lies happiness? In that which becks
> Our ready minds to blending pleasureable:
> And that delight is the most treasureable
> That makes the richest Alchymy.

(Keats, *Poetical Works*, ed. H. W. Garrod, Oxford, 1939.)

The word, 'essences', is clearly something more than a mere synonym for 'things of beauty'. A rough explanation of the word might be that it denotes things of beauty to which the poet makes a particular kind of response. The nature of that response is not described in the poem, but support may be found, in certain of Keats's letters, for Mr. Newell F. Ford's suggestion that 'fellowship with essence' means 'empathic fusion with particular things of beauty'.[1]

In October 1818, Keats wrote in a letter to Richard Woodhouse,

A Poet is the most unpoetical of any thing in existence; because he has no Identity—he is continually [informing] and filling some other Body—The Sun, the Moon, the Sea and Men and Women who are creatures of impulse are poetical and have about them an unchangeable attribute—the poet has none; no identity—he is certainly the most unpoetical of all God's Creatures. . . . When I am in a room with People if I am ever free from speculating on creations of my own brain, then not myself goes home to myself: but the identity of every one in the room begins so to press upon me that I am in a very little time annihilated. . . . [2]

In an illuminating comment on this letter, Woodhouse explained that Keats 'affirmed that he can conceive of a billiard ball that it may have a sense of delight from its own roundness, smoothness and volubility and the rapidity of its motion'. Woodhouse also believed that Keats was able 'to throw his own soul into any object he sees or imagines, so as to see feel be sensible of and express all that the object itself would see feel be sensible of and express'.[3] Keats's own words confirm this. In November 1817 he wrote to Benjamin Bailey,

The setting Sun will always set me to rights—or if a Sparrow come before my Window I take part in its existence and pick about the Gravel,[4]

and there are many references in his letters to a sense, sometimes

1 Newell F. Ford, 'Endymion—A neo-Platonic Allegory?' *E.L.H.* xiv (Mar. 1947).
2 *Letters*, Letter 93, p. 228.
3 Quoted from Woodhouse's *Scrapbook*, now in the Pierpoint Morgan Library, by (among others) W. J. Bate in his *The Stylistic Development of Keats* (New York and London, 1945), p. 6 n. 15. This study of Keats's style contains interesting comments on empathy in Keats's verse. See also R. H. Fogle, 'Empathic Imagery in Keats and Shelley', *Publications of the Modern Language Association of America* (Mar. 1946).
4 *Letters*, Letter 31, p. 69.

pleasant, sometimes distressing, of the identity of other people. Woodhouse's comment suggests that what Keats meant by 'identity' was the feeling of existence and individuality which the poet seemed to sense intuitively in other people and things. It is in the poet's nature, according to Keats, to have no such 'unchangeable attribute', and to lose all sense of his own identity in his concentration on other people and things. It is interesting that even a picture or a work of literature had for Keats a special 'feeling' or existence, in which he could lose himself, and that he sometimes used the words, 'intensity' and 'intenseness', in this connection, just as, in the speech about 'fellowship with essence', he calls love 'the chief intensity'. In April 1818, he wrote to the painter, Haydon,

I know not your many havens of intenseness—nor ever can know them—but for this I hope nought you achieve is lost upon me: for when a Schoolboy the abstract Idea I had of an heroic painting—was what I cannot describe I saw it somewhat sideways large prominent round and colour'd with magnificence—somewhat like the feel I have of Anthony and Cleopatra.[1]

Keats uses the word, 'essence', in *Endymion* in such a way as to suggest that it meant to him the 'identity' of a thing of beauty, and that the phrase, 'a Fellowship with essence', denotes some kind of emphatic fusion with particular things of beauty. The 'chief intensity', that which is most 'self-destroying', is love, and the 'essence' of love is what Mr. Middleton Murry calls 'the enchanted otherness, the divine idiosyncrasy' of the beloved.[2]

To return to Endymion's description of the 'gradations of happiness'. In its simplest form 'a fellowship with essence' comes from the response of the senses to beauty, as when we feel the texture of a rose-leaf. Higher in the scale comes the fine working of the imagination, so fired by 'lovely tales that we have heard or read', that it creates beauty through the power of association:

> hist, when the airy stress
> Of music's kiss impregnates the free winds,
> And with a sympathetic touch unbinds
> Æolian magic from their lucid wombs:
> Then old songs waken from enclouded tombs;
> Old ditties sigh above their father's grave;

1 Ibid., Letter 59, p. 129.
2 *Studies in Keats*, p. 51.

Ghosts of melodious prophecyings rave
Round every spot where trod Apollo's foot;
Bronze clarions awake, and faintly bruit,
Where long ago a giant battle was;
And, from the turf, a lullaby doth pass
In every place where infant Orpheus slept.

(I. 783–94)

At the top of the scale are 'richer entanglements', which have greater power to destroy all sense of self; these are human relationships. The 'crown' of these is made of love and friendship, and it is love which is 'the chief intensity'. It is of love that Keats says,

Nor with aught else can our souls interknit
So wingedly.

The lines which follow leave little doubt that by 'love' Keats means 'human love'. Endymion answers Peona's charge, that he has sacrificed worldly ambition to a love which she considers 'nothing but a dream', with the words,

Aye, so delicious is the unsating food,
That men who might have tower'd in the van
Of all the congregated world, to fan
And winnow from the coming step of time
All chaff of custom, wipe away all slime
Left by men-slugs and human serpentry,
Have been content to let occasion die,
Whilst they did sleep in love's elysium.

(I. 816–23)

The temptation to believe that Keats wrote these lines with the story of Antony and Cleopatra at the back of his mind is irresistible. His reading of Shakespeare is reflected to a marked degree in Book I of *Endymion*, and we know, from a letter he wrote to Haydon,[1] that he had been reading *Antony and Cleopatra* shortly after he began to write the poem. Not only is the story of Antony an apt illustration of Endymion's argument, but some of the imagery—'tower'd in the van of all the congregated world'—has a Shakespearian ring. This might, too, explain the curious imagery of 'slime' and 'men-slugs and human serpentry', as unconscious

1 *Letters*, Letter 15, 10–11 May 1817, p. 31.

echoes of words which had impressed themselves on Keats's memory. In his copy of the play many passages are marked, among them the description of the aspic's trail of slime, Antony's conversation with Lepidus about the 'slime and ooze' of the Nile and the serpents which breed there, and the phrase, 'my serpent of old Nile'.[1]

However that may be, what Keats is expressing here, and in much of the rest of the poem, is his conviction that love, even if it be no more than 'the mere commingling of passionate breath' (i. 833), is man's highest good. If other men have sacrificed all for love, how much more should Endymion despise 'this poor endeavour after fame' (i. 847), when he may hope for an eternity of love.

The best starting point for a study of the composition of the poem is Keats's own statement of his purpose in writing it. When the first three books were completed, he wrote to Bailey:

[*Endymion*] will be a test, a trial of my Powers of Imagination and chiefly of my invention which is a rare thing indeed—by which I must make 4,000 lines of one bare circumstance and fill them with Poetry; and when I consider that this is a great task, and that when done it will take me but a dozen paces towards the Temple of Fame—it makes me say—God forbid that I should be without such a task! I have heard Hunt say and may be asked—why endeavour after a long Poem? To which I should answer—Do not the lovers of Poetry like to have a little Region to wander in where they may pick and choose, and in which the images are so numerous that many are forgotten and found new in a second Reading: which may be food for a Week's stroll in Summer? . . . Besides a long Poem is a test of Invention which I take to be the Polar Star of Poetry, as Fancy is the Sails, and Imagination the Rudder.[2]

The fact that Keats took the trouble to copy this from a letter, now lost, which he had written to his brother in the spring, gives added weight to his words and makes it clear that his purpose had not changed during the composition of the first three books. That purpose was to put his powers to the test by taking 'one bare circumstance' and extending it in a poem of four thousand lines. The stress is put on invention, imagination, and fancy, and, far from indicating that the poem is an allegory on a theme of some importance to the poet, the letter suggests even an indifference,

1 See Caroline Spurgeon, *Keats's Shakespeare* (Oxford, 1928), pp. 123, 129, 148.
2 *Letters*, Letter 25, 8 Oct. 1817, p. 52.

CLARICE GODFREY

on Keats's part, to the reader's willingness to trace a train of
thought and to give its due importance to each part of the poem.
The reader may, in fact, 'wander' and 'pick and choose' his
favourite passages. It is the length of the poem, not the content,
which is decided in advance.

To say that Keats felt his way as he wrote, and that he was
inspired rather by a general desire to write poetry than by determination to develop one main theme, does not mean that his
choice of material was completely random and meaningless. The
search for allegory obscures the real effect of some parts of the
poem and does Keats less than justice. There are many ways in
which the four thousand lines might have been filled and there
is much interest in the particular direction Keats's imagination
took.

The four books of the poem are strikingly different from each
other in many respects, and not least in the kind of 'invention'
with which Keats extends the original myth. In Book I, elaboration of the myth largely takes the form of description—description of the country of the shepherds, of the festival in honour of
Pan, and of Endymion's meetings with Phoebe. In Book II, where
Endymion begins his strange journey, there is still a very large
proportion of imaginative description, but Keats introduces
variety by drawing upon his reading and incorporating into the
poem the myths of Venus and Adonis, and Alpheus and Arethusa.
Nevertheless, Endymion is a passive observer and listener—one
of the stories is told to him and the other overheard by him—and
the main story of the poem is developed only in Endymion's
meeting with Phoebe, who hints at her reasons for concealment
and promises soon to carry him away to 'heaven ambrosial'. In
Book III, where Endymion plays a more active role in the adapted
story of Glaucus and Scylla, description, though lavish, gives way
far more to the narration of incident. In this book, however,
though the story of Glaucus has some bearing on the main theme
of the poem, it is told at the expense of the story of Endymion and
Phoebe which is pushed into the background. When this story is
picked up again in the last book of the poem, Keats frees himself
from dependence on his reading and extends the myth by the
invention of new incidents, in which Endymion and Phoebe are
involved. There is markedly less pure description in this book
than in any other part of the poem.

30

Much significance has been attached to Endymion's strange
journey, but it may have had its origin simply in the fact that
most of the material from the original myth had been used in
Book 1 and the problem of filling four thousand lines had become
acute. There was a need for the introduction of some kind of
variety into the poem and the device of sending Endymion on a
journey gave Keats scope for filling the poem with the kind of
poetry which particularly delighted him at this time, that is with
passages of varied and detailed description. The need for a greater
variety of incident asserted itself later, and then the changes of
setting made possible the introduction of new characters. The
source of much of the description may be found in Keats's reading;
the rest springs from a fertile imagination which delighted in
colourful detail and tales of wonder. Sir Sidney Colvin pointed
out that parts of *Endymion*, particularly in Books II and II, have
much in common with the *Arabian Nights' Entertainments*, which
Keats knew well.[1] These tales abound in descriptions of under-
ground caves and palaces, of rooms and gardens full of jewels, of
talismans and magic spells, not unlike that worked by Endymion
at Glaucus' request. The magic fountains described in Book II
have much in common with the one which,

as it fell, formed diamonds and pearls resembling a jet d'eau, which
springing from the middle of the fountain rose nearly to the top of
the cupola painted in Arabesque.[2]

The other stories which are incorporated in the poem represent
more than a random search for material, for they have a certain
suitability and effectiveness. They are all tales of lovers who were
once thwarted, and in their eventual happiness Endymion may see
hope for himself. Through them Keats stresses the main theme,
that of the power and importance of love, and so achieves some
thickening of the texture of the poem. The treatment of the main
theme in a series of otherwise disconnected episodes has obvious
faults, but the treatment of each individual episode shows skill
which is obscured by the search for allegory.

Keats's adaptation of the stories of Alpheus and Arethus, and
Glaucus and Scylla, both of which he drew from Sandys's translation of Ovid's *Metamorphoses*, is particularly interesting, for he

1 *John Keats*, pp. 175, 184, 190, 191, 195.
2 *Arabian Nights' Entertainments*, ed., with introduction, by Jonathan Scott
(London, 1813), p. 89.

made changes in them so as to link them more closely with the
story of Endymion. In Ovid's version of the story of Arethusa,
which is told in Book v of the *Metamorphoses*, the nymph flees with
horror and loathing from the advances of Alpheus; in Keats's
poem, she appears as a thwarted lover, afraid of breaking her vows
to Diana. This an effective touch of irony, for the goddess is herself the victim of her own attributes. Her happiness with Endymion is delayed, because she dreads the smiles of the gods at her
'lost brightness' and foresees even more serious consequences:

> no bosom shook
> With awe of purity—no Cupid pinion
> In reverence vailed—my crystalline dominion
> Half lost, and all old hymns made nullity!
> (II. 791–4)

The irony is pointed by Alpheus' certainty that Diana must feel
the same 'pangs' and by Arethusa's exclamation—

> 'O, Oread-Queen! would that thou hadst a pain
> Like this of mine, then would I fearless turn
> And be a criminal.' (II. 961–3)

Endymion, too, prays to the one goddess who can help the lovers:

> 'I urge
> Thee, gentle Goddess of my pilgrimage,
> By our eternal hopes, to soothe, to assuage,
> If thou art powerful, these lovers' pains;
> And make them happy in some happy plains.'
> (II. 1013–17)

As Endymion utters this prayer, he turns and finds a path
leading to the sea. It is by no means certain that Keats intended
this to be understood as a reward to Endymion for his sympathy
with the lovers, for he reaches the sea in the natural course of
his wanderings. Before he meets Alpheus and Arethusa, he enters
a cave,

> O'er studded with a thousand, thousand pearls,
> And crimson mouthed shells with stubborn curls,
> Of every shape and size, even to the bulk
> In which whales arbour close, to brood and sulk
> Against an endless storm. Moreover too,
> Fish-semblances, of green and azure hue,
> Ready to snort their streams. (II. 879–85)

A meeting with Alpheus and Arethusa is appropriate in this setting, for Keats must have read, in Sandys's Ovid, that Diana cleft the ground and allowed Arethusa to escape 'through blind caves', until she reached the sea, pursued by Alpheus, whose river 'is swallowed by the earth not far from the shore'.[1]

The story of Glaucus, too, is changed by Keats, so that it has something in common with that of Endymion. Glaucus, even in the original, is a mortal living in close contact with nature and devoted to the sea ('deditus aequoribus'). Keats stresses this element of the story and makes Glaucus as passionately devoted to the seas as Endymion is to the moon. Glaucus, too, torments himself with longing for something which seems beyond mortal grasp, and wins immortality by a bold leap into the sea. His confidence is rewarded, as Endymion's finally is.

The rest of the story of Glaucus and Scylla was much changed by Keats, probably in order to make room in it for Endymion. In the original story, Glaucus rejects the love of Circe, who takes her revenge by turning Scylla into a monster. In Keats's poem, Glaucus tells how he was disgusted by Circe's cruelty, not by her love, which he describes in glowing terms. Circe punishes him by condemning him to a thousand years of wretched old age, and he is doomed to die at last, unless a youth, guided by heavenly powers, comes to his rescue. It is Endymion who is destined to save Glaucus and to restore to life all lovers drowned in the sea, and this he does by methods familiar to readers of fairy tales. There is no indication that he is particularly moved to pity for Glaucus; his main emotions seem to be an understandable reluctance to die—as he must if he refuses to help Glaucus—and pleasure that he has been chosen for so important a role. The episode ends with the triumph of love over death, for the dead lovers are restored to life. Thus the story becomes another illustration of the main theme of the poem.

The punishment inflicted on Glaucus by Circe has figured largely in some of the allegorical interpretations of the poem,[2] and the problem of why Keats chose to change the story in this particular way is an interesting one. The truth may simply be, however, that, seeking to extend the story of Glaucus, Keats

1 Ovid, *Metamorphoses, Englished, Mythologised and Represented in Figures* by G. Sandys (Oxford, 1632), see Commentary on Book v.
2 See, for example, H. C. Notcutt, *The Story of Glaucus in Keats's Endymion*.

recalled, or re-read, some of the detail of the two stories which
follow it in Book XIV of the *Metamorphoses*. The first is the story
of the Cercopians, who so offend Jupiter that he

> Contracts their limmes, their noses from their browes
> He flats, their faces with old wrinkles plowes.[1]

The next, and more important, is the story of Sybilla, who spurns
the love of Phoebus and is condemned by him to a thousand years
of miserable life in increasing senility. Her life is ended, as Circe
intends Glaucus' life to end, in 'unknown burial' (III. 599).

At the end of his adventure under the sea, Endymion hears his
goddess's voice, saying,

> *Dearest Endymion! my entire love!*
> *How have I dwelt in fear of fate: 'tis done—*
> *Immortal bliss for me too hast thou won.*
> *Arise then! for the hen-dove shall not hatch*
> *Her ready eggs, before I'll kissing snatch*
> *Thee into endless heaven. Awake! awake!*
>
> (III. 1022–7)

By his patience and trust, if not by valour and self-sacrifice,
Endymion has won immortal bliss, which Phoebe will share.
There is no suggestion that anything remains to be done and
certainly no hint that Endymion is not yet fit for immortality.
Delay can be made credible now only by some striking and un-
expected complication. With a thousand lines of the poem still
to write, Keats invents a convincing reason for delay by providing
Phoebe with a rival.

The situation is well and convincingly developed, for the Indian
Maid at first seems a very effective rival to Phoebe and a real
danger to Endymion's happiness. His very devotion to beauty
makes him unable to resist her charms and, moreover, she expresses a belief in the power of love, which echoes his own creed:

> There is no lightning, no authentic dew
> But in the eye of love: there's not a sound,
> Melodious howsoever, can confound
> The heavens and earth in one to such a death

[1] *Metamorphoses*, Book XIV, p. 457. Cf.

> his snow-white brows
> Went arching up, and like two magic ploughs
> Furrow'd deep wrinkles in his forehead large.
> (*Endymion*, III. 221–3).

As doth the voice of love: there's not a breath
Will mingle kindly with the meadow air,
Till it has panted round, and stolen a share
Of passion from the heart!   (IV. 78–85)

She, too, has loved a 'shadowy lover from the clouds' (IV. 190),
and her story of betrayal seems calculated to shake Endymion's
trust in his goddess. Endymion's faith is not shaken but, be-
wildered and dismayed by his new love, he abandons all hope of
happiness.

It is at this point that Phoebe keeps her promise, for, as Sleep
journeys slumbering towards heaven's gate to attend Phoebe's
wedding, Endymion is borne past him on a winged horse. Even
now the Indian Maid accompanies him and, as Endymion, the
helpless victim of his two loves, hesitates between them, Phoebe
in apparent despair fades from his sight. On his return to earth,
he despairs of winning immortal happiness and repudiates his love
for Phoebe:

                              'I have clung
          To nothing, lov'd a nothing, nothing seen
          Or felt but a great dream! O I have been
          Presumptuous against love, against the sky,
          Against all elements, against the tie
          Of mortals each to each . . . '
                                    (IV. 636–41)

Now, however, the Indian Maid refuses him and it is only when
he has given up all hope of love and decided to devote his life to
the welfare of the shepherds, that Phoebe reveals herself to him.

Endymion's perplexing division of soul is explained, for his
two loves were one, and Phoebe's apparently cruel deception is
shown to have been the means of purifying Endymion from his
mortal state, through suffering, for she says,

          And then 'twas fit that from this mortal state
          Thou shouldst, my love, by some unlook'd for change
          Be spiritualiz'd.   (IV. 991–3)

Whether there is any other significance in the identification of
the Indian Maid with Phoebe is doubtful. It can hardly be said
that the Indian Maid represents sensual love and Phoebe, spiritual,

or ideal, love, for, if there is any distinction in Keats's treatment of the theme of love, emphasis is laid rather more on physical passion in the descriptions of Endymion's encounters with the goddess, in the earlier parts of the poem. Moreover, Endymion's happiness is not the result of his choice of the higher love, for he makes no effective choice at all.

There is little doubt, however, that in Book IV we see a change in Keats's attitude to the poem. The idea, that Endymion is unfit for immortality until he has been spiritualized by suffering, is at variance with both the tone and the sense of Phoebe's words,

> 'tis done—
> *Immortal bliss for me too hast thou won.*
> *Arise then! for the hen-dove shall not hatch*
> *Her ready eggs, before I'll kissing snatch*
> *Thee into endless heaven.*　　(III. 1023–7)

It is impossible to determine at what point this idea began to develop in Keats's mind, but there may be reason to suppose that he began Book IV with the intention of providing Phoebe with a genuine rival, and that he gradually saw new possibilities in the situation.[1] However that may be, this book is marked off from the rest of the poem by a deepening note of seriousness: Endymion is given a wider range of emotion, and in the 'message', that man's nature may be purified by suffering, we may perhaps see what Keats would have made of the poem had he rewritten it, as he half wished to do.[2] As it was, he longed only to finish the poem, which no longer satisfied him, and his impatience is reflected in Book IV, in which apparently important conceptions are introduced in a strangely unsatisfying, and sometimes almost casual, way.

The change in the tone of the poem may reflect changes which had taken place in Keats's own life. After his return to London

[1] It is interesting that, although Phoebe and the Indian Maid are at one point present together as separate beings (IV. 430–55), later, when the moon rises, that is, when the being of the goddess enters into the moon, the Indian Maid fades (IV. 507–10), and the two are never seen together again. This may argue a change of plan.
[2] Keats wrote to Haydon:
'I would write the subject thoroughly again but I am tired of it and think the time would be better spent in writing a new Romance, which I have in my eye for next summer.'
Letters, Letter 24, 28 Sept. 1817, p. 51.

from Oxford, where he had written Book III, he was involved in
worry and distress. He was ill himself and surrounded by illness,
which, as always, weighed on his spirits. Tom Keats was showing
alarming symptoms and it seemed possible that he would have to
be sent abroad. Made more vulnerable by worry and ill-health,
Keats was further pained by the quarrels of his friends and irri-
tated by Hunt's proprietary and patronizing interest in *Endymion*.[1]
He faced his problems with characteristic courage and good sense,
and his letters show the depth of his spiritual and mental resources. It is significant that he came to the conclusion that man
may be 'self-spiritualized into a kind of sublime misery'.[2]

This experience is reflected in the description of the Cave of
Quietude (IV. 512–48), which gives an accurate picture of Keats's
own state of mind. He tells in it how a man may pass through
a time of great misery, in which 'many a venom'd dart At random
flies', until he finds refuge in a state of calm almost like indifference. When he had five hundred lines of the poem still to write,
that is, about the time when he was writing the description of the
Cave of Quietude, he described the same experience in a letter to
Bailey:

> The first thing that strikes me on hearing a Misfortune having
> befallen another is this. 'Well it cannot be helped—he will have the
> pleasure of trying the resources of his spirit'—and I beg now my dear
> Bailey that hereafter should you observe any thing cold in me not to put
> it to heartlessness but abstraction—for I assure you I sometimes feel
> not the influence of a Passion or affection during a whole week—and
> so long this sometimes continues I begin to suspect myself and the
> genuineness of my feelings at other times—thinking them a few barren
> Tragedy-tears. [3]

Although the poem is not a sustained record of personal experience, Keats's own mood is often reflected in what he wrote.
During the early stages of the composition of the poem, he was
tormented by a feverish desire to write but found composition
difficult, either because of his own restlessness, or because of
other distractions which interrupted him.[4] This experience is

1 See *Letters*, Letters 25, 26, 31, pp. 51–70.
2 Ibid., Letter 26, To Bailey, Oct. 1817, pp. 55–6.
3 Ibid., Letter 31, 22 Nov. 1817, p. 69. Cf. Letters 26 and 76.
4 Ibid., Letters to Reynolds (17 Apr. 1817), to Hunt (10 May 1817), and to
Haydon (10–11 May 1817), pp. 19, 22, and 28.

recorded in the introductory lines to Book II of *Endymion*:

> But rest
> In chafing restlessness, is yet more drear
> Than to be crush'd, in striving to uprear
> Love's standard on the battlements of song.
> (II. 38–41)

His uncertainty can be felt even in the halting and uneven composition of Books I and II, in which some lines flow easily, while others are hesitant and give the impression that the poet was feeling his way and searching for inspiration. Book III, on the other hand, was composed at Oxford during a period of unusual calm, when Keats wrote steadily and fluently.[1] This book is less disjointed, and markedly calmer in tone, than the rest of the poem; Endymion, whose fortunes depend to some extent on Keats's own state of mind, no longer dwells on his misery and frustration; and, except in the beautiful invocation to the moon there is little in the verse which clearly expresses Keats's own emotions and experiences.

Human love is the theme of the poem, which has a strange dream-like quality.[2] The dream, a young man's dream of passion which will never end, is broken in places and other matter intrudes. Keats wrote the poem at a vital stage in his development as a poet, at a time when his mind was 'like a scattered pack of cards'.[3] The lack of detailed plan made it possible for him to use the poem as an outlet for the ideas, emotions and intuitions which were crowding into his mind, and, as he changed, so did the poem. He outgrew the poem before he had finished writing it, but the experience had been valuable to him. He cleared his mind and strengthened his thought, and in style *Endymion* shows a great advance on the loose and facile verse of much of the 1817 volume.

Keats's method of composition in *Endymion* is open to criticism and the poem as a whole is disjointed and confused. In spite of that, the poem offers more than material for a study of Keats's

---

1 *Letters*, p. 38 n. 1.

2 The poem abounds in images of sleep and dreams. The relaxation of conscious control over the imagination in sleep seems to symbolize the freeing of the imagination in the poetic 'trance'. See *Endymion*, I. 453–61 and II. 829–39, and the Epistle 'To George Keats'. Though the poem as a whole is not a conscious allegory, it contains much symbolism.

3 *Letters*, Letter 227, To Shelley, 16 Aug. 1820, p. 507.

development. If it is read as Keats seems to have intended it to be read, *Endymion* yields up much fine poetry, and images which 'are so numerous that many are forgotten and found new in a second reading'. The faults of construction and style in the early work of the poet are no more striking than the richness of imagination, the frequent maturity of thought, and the strength and beauty of much of the verse.

3

'Isabella' 'The Eve of St. Agnes' and 'Lamia'

MIRIAM ALLOTT

KEATS'S NARRATIVE POEMS still suffer with his other work from the effects of late-Victorian adulation. 'By 1895', as G. H. Ford tells us in his study of Keats's rise to fame in the nineteenth century,[1] 'to deplore Keats was literary heresy', and the stock responses established by such enthusiasm are sometimes strong enough to withstand the most stringent post-Richards critical techniques. Even today, 'appreciation' of Keats often amounts to little more than a nerveless picking-over of the poems for evidence of 'rich sensuousness', 'poetic effects', vivid picture-making, and a vaguely defined 'principle of Beauty', varied by a little source-hunting and talk of influences. On the other hand, contemporary types of analysis have sometimes been applied to Keats's odes but hardly at all to his narrative poems. So that the narratives continue to be read in a critical vacuum and judgement on them is bewilderingly diverse.

For example, 'Lamia'. 'Lamia', as we are told by one critic, has 'a swiftness and brightness' new in Keats's art, but does not show that 'in narrative poetry . . . Keats was ever likely to achieve a success worth having'; it is 'tolerable poetry' but 'overrated'.[2] In direct contradiction, a second critic maintains that 'Lamia' is Keats's 'most notable narrative poem', being 'well-organised', 'conducted with a quick, certain movement fresh to Keats's poetry', and altogether having[3]

1 G. H. Ford, *Keats and the Victorians* (1944), p. 170.
2 H. W. Garrod, *Keats* (1926), pp. 61–3.
3 B. Ifor Evans, *Keats* (1934), pp. 103–4.

40

a liveliness and a firmness in outline, which distinguish it from 'Isabella' and 'The Eve of St. Agnes'. . . .

'Lamia' shows a high degree of control, a third scholar writes, but it need not therefore be distinguished from the other narrative poems:[1]

. . . in *Isabella*, and *The Eve of St. Agnes* and *Lamia*, Keats is controlled, first of all by the fact that he has a story to tell, one that he is not just making up as he goes along, and, in the second place—far more than in *Endymion*—by his artistic conscience.

'Lamia', argues a fourth, in spite of being 'a much clearer and less sprawling kind of narrative' than *Endymion* and improving on that poem's use of the couplet, is marred by 'a rather unhappy attempt at man-of-the-world cynicism' and[2]

remains otherwise a rather purposeless poem . . . it looks rather like an exercise in verse narrative.

These passages are selected more or less at random and do not illustrate the aberrations of the King Charles's head school of Keatsian criticism—W. W. Beyer, for example, regards 'Lamia' and most other poems by Keats as fathered by Sotheby's translation of Wieland's *Oberon*, which Keats read apparently some time in 1815.[3]

Some of the opinions quoted may seem almost wilfully obtuse —in particular, Garrod's and Hough's dismissals of 'Lamia', Keats's most remarkable narrative poem, as 'overrated' and 'rather purposeless'—but then Keats's work has never been easy to judge fairly. In the first place, almost too much is known about him and criticism still tends to be drawn out of true by the memory of his brief and painful life. Again, more importantly, his readers are in contact with a mind and imagination which were still in the early stages of their development when he died, so that any attempt to understand the nature of his achievement must involve a more than usually scrupulous and sensitive examination of the relationship in which his poems stand to each other. Keats himself was profoundly aware that his writings 'prefigured'

1 James Sutherland, *The Medium of Poetry* (1934), p. 62.
2 Graham Hough, *The Romantic Poets* (1953), p. 167.
3 W. W. Beyer, *Keats and the Daemon King* (1947).

only fitfully the kind of poetry which he wanted to write:[1] his later poems are a series of brilliant but sketchy gestures in the direction of maturity, but they frequently carry with them a sense of frustrated intention. Criticism of the later poems calls for a tact which has not always been forthcoming.

All Keats's writing, prose as well as verse, illustrates in its struggle for expressiveness a persistent but self-critical immaturity —he has no ambition to be consistent in his 'speculations' and no desire 'to be in the right'. This kind of flexibility illustrates the ease with which he moves from the rejection of 'fact and reason' (December 1817) to the assertion of 'one way' lying through 'application, study and thought' (April 1818), and accounts for the wide range of experiments which he made in the verse of his best period. Of course, behind the 'variables' Keats's driving impulses remain the same. Whether he moves towards 'feathers' or 'iron', whether he proclaims the primacy of 'sensation' or 'thought', Keats is guided by his belief in poetry as the most important human activity, at any rate for himself. Moreover, his conception of the most valuable poetry never really alters—his theorizing is less devoted to the analysis of different types of poetry than to finding out how best to become a 'Shakespearian' poet whose greatness derives from a sense of human conflict rather than from any feeling for wonders.

So, in spite of his perpetual oscillation throughout 1818, and well into 1819, between the two poles of 'Negative Capability', which does not reach out irritably after 'fact and reason', and 'application, study and thought', Keats at a deeper level moves steadily towards a mature formulation of beliefs which he had expressed as early as 'Sleep and Poetry'. In place of the naïve description of a poet's progress from the 'realms of Flora and Old Pan' to the 'agonies and strife of human hearts', he evolves, in May 1818, the superb Chamber of Maiden Thought parable in which he identifies sorrow and wisdom. Sorrow is not a relaxed indulgence of melancholy—clearly Keats's theory is here ahead of his poetic practice—but involves an intimate knowledge of human suffering, the knowledge which Moneta later exacts from the

1 Mr. F. W. Bateson attributes the incompleteness of Keats's achievement to the age in which he lived rather than to his immaturity: 'It was not to be possible to write the kind of poetry the mature Keats wanted to write for a hundred years.' F. W. Bateson, *English Poetry* (1950), p. 222.

poet in the second 'Hyperion'. One must 'convince one's nerves that the world is full of Misery, Pain, sickness and oppression' (3 March 1818). Later in the same year Keats longs to have[1]

the yearning Passion I have for the beautiful connected and made one with the ambition of my intellect. (13–14 October 1818)

By the middle of 1819, Keats has come to realize that the two conflicting impulses can be related to two different kinds of poet —the Boiardos and the Shakespeares. 'The English have produced the finest writers in the world', he declares, in June, because they have 'ill-treated them during their lives and fostered them after their deaths'. Without this ill-treatment a writer may be 'a noble Poet of Romance' like the prosperous and lavish Boiardo secure in his Apennine castle but he will never be 'a miserable and mighty Poet of the Human Heart' aware of 'the festering of society' and with his 'middle age all clouded over . . .'[2] (9 June 1819). Towards the end of this year—the year of his greatest poetic activity—Keats's continued hesitation between the two opposing attractions begins to show his awareness that ambition and his gift for romantic expression are at loggerheads. He could not complain that he had been excluded from the painful experience necessary for the making of a great poet, but he could ask himself with dismay whether this experience might not bankrupt his own kind of creative energy. Was the price of 'knowledge of life' the feeling for 'wonders' which had provided so far his best poetic stimulus? In September 1819, he had written to George and Georgiana Keats.[3]

Some think I have lost that poetic ardour and fire 'tis said I once had—the fact is perhaps I have: but instead of that I hope I shall substitute a more thoughtful and quiet power.

But this hope seems to conceal a fear.

If we judge by the context in which most of his own comments about the narrative poems appear, Keats almost certainly connected them in his own mind with his Shakespearian aspirations. To be 'a miserable and mighty Poet of the human Heart' meant dealing with men and women. He seems, in effect, to have thought of his narratives as part of the limbering-up process by which he might prepare himself eventually for the supreme goal—'the writing of a few fine plays'. The earliest hint which the letters

1 *Letters*, p. 241.   2 Ibid., p. 346.   3 Ibid., p. 421.

give us of this connection is the information that the opening stanzas of 'Isabella' were written out in his Folio Shakespeare: he sent for the book in order to complete the poem while he was staying at Teignmouth with Tom in 1818 (27 April 1818). Shakespeare as his 'Presidor' appears, of course, as early as May 1817, when his landlady's gift to him of the Shakespeare portrait which he had admired in her house seemed to him 'ominous of good'[1] (10–11 May 1817). It was in front of this same portrait, now decorated with Georgiana Keats's silk tassels, that he was sitting when he wrote to George in February 1819,

> I never look at it but the silk tassels on it give me as much pleasure as the face of the Poet itself. . . .

He goes straight on from this remark—as though immediately reminded by 'the Poet' of his own endeavours—to mention the group of narrative poems that he will send on with his next letter:

> In my next packet as this is one by the way, I shall send you the Pot of Basil, St. Agnes eve, and if I should have finished it, a little thing call'd the 'eve of St. Mark'. . . .

By July, writing from the Isle of Wight, he is able to record the progress of yet another narrative poem in the intervals of his first attempt at a full-scale tragedy, *Otho the Great*:[2]

> I have finished the Act (i.e. Act 1 of *Otho*), and in the interval of beginning the 2nd have proceeded pretty well with Lamia, finishing the 1st part which consists of about 400 lines . . . I have great hopes of success, because I make use of my Judgment more deliberately than I have yet done; but in the case of failure with the world, I shall find my content. . . . (11 July 1819)

When, a month later, Keats next reviews the achievement of this prolific year, he concentrates, significantly, on his narratives and on the '4 Acts of a Tragedy', openly placing them side by side with his dramatic aspirations:[3]

> I have written two Tales, one from Boccaccio call'd the Pot of Basil, and another call'd St. Agnes' Eve on a popular superstition; and a third call'd Lamia—half finished—I have also been writing parts of my Hyperion and completed 4 Acts of a Tragedy. It was the opinion of most of my friends that I should never be able to write a scene. I will endeavour to wipe away the prejudice . . . One of my Ambitions is to

---

1 *Letters*, pp. 29, 300.   2 Ibid., p. 358.   3 Ibid., p. 368.

make as great a revolution in modern dramatic writing as Kean has done
in acting . . .   (14 August 1819)

At this stage, with the year advancing into autumn, we begin
to notice his restless dissatisfaction with work that seems too far
divorced from life. In a letter which refers again to his dramatic
experiment and to his narratives, he finds Ariosto 'as diffuse' as
Spenser. At the same time his criticism of his own work shows
that he is dissatisfied with it for similar reasons. It is in the same
month that he asks Reynolds[1] to

pick out some lines from Hyperion and put a mark X to the false beauty
proceeding from art, and one ‖ to the true voice of feeling. . . .
                                                (21 September 1819)

And in another letter of the same date he comes out with his
attack on 'Isabella' for its lack of vitality, saying that he will not
publish it because[2]

There is too much inexperience of life, and simplicity of knowledge
in it . . . Isabella is what I should call were I a reviewer 'A weak-sided
Poem'. . . .   (21 September 1819)

His irritation with his work for its lack of human and Shakespearian qualities extends to 'The Eve of St. Agnes', but he gives
a qualified approval to 'Lamia'—possibly because in attempting
to deal dramatically with an emotional situation it seems to him to
possess a 'sort of fire'. About six weeks later the climax of all this
creative irritation is expressed in the revealing letter of 17 November to John Taylor. Thoroughly dissatisfied with his achievement
so far—so utterly different from what he really wants to accom-
plish—Keats writes,[3]

I have come to a determination not to publish any thing I have now
already written . . .

and he goes on to analyse his situation with remarkable insight:

As the marvellous is the most enticing, and the surest guarantee of
harmonious numbers I have been endeavouring to persuade myself to
untether Fancy and let her manage for herself. I and myself cannot agree
about this at all. Wonders are no wonders to me. I am more at home
amongst Men and Women. I would rather read Chaucer than Ariosto.
The little dramatic skill I may as yet have however badly it might shew
in a Drama would I think be sufficient for a Poem. I wish to diffuse the

---

1 *Letters*, pp. 381, 384-5.   2 Ibid., p. 391.   3 Ibid., p. 439.

colouring of St. Agnes Eve throughout a Poem in which Character and Sentiment would be figures to such drapery. Two or three such Poems if God should spare me, written in the course of the next 6 years, wo^d be a famous Gradus ad Parnassum altissimum. I mean they would nerve me up to the writing of a few fine plays—my greatest ambition when I do feel ambitious. I am sorry to say that is very seldom.

The simple truth is that though Keats was 'more at home amongst Men and Women' and preferred a Chaucer to an Ariosto, his creative imagination was continually pulled in the opposite direction: as he says here, 'I and myself cannot agree'. He admits that 'wonders are no wonders' to him, and yet he is inclined to 'untether Fancy' and let her loose. In this, I believe, his instinct was sound. It is when his imagination was free to display 'wonders' without being tethered to his dramatic ambitions or the journey-work of plot-making that it fell into the creative patterns of his finest writing. 'The Eve of St. Agnes' shows few signs of the potential dramatist, but it is at least the complete expression of a certain mood and attitude. The 'colouring' is an integral part of the poem, conditioned by the emotions and the situation which are being explored. We can see what Keats means and sympathize with him when he desires to diffuse this colouring in a poem which is intended to be objectively dramatic in character and sentiment, but this aim shows how far he was from understanding the source of what is best in his narrative poems—namely the expression in various symbolic forms of the romantic dissatisfaction with the actual. Yet it is also true—and only fair to add—that these romantic patterns are handled with increasing subtlety and control as he moves from his earlier to his later works in the narrative kind.

II

Keats is most successful in his narrative poems when he is least tied by the exigencies of a given story (unless, as in 'Lamia', the story itself follows a congenial Romantic pattern). It is not *as* narratives that these poems have value. The passages of most distinct interest and of greatest intensity occur when Keats's imagination is free to wander and usually have little to do with the development of 'plot' or character. The quickening of feeling in such passages, often expressing itself through closely integrated imagery, is normally associated with a particular emotional situation, at once personal and typically Romantic—in fact with the tension that arises when the imagination of the Romantic poet seeks to come to terms with what is actual. From *Endymion* to the second 'Hyperion' Keats's constant theme is the opposition between romantic enchantment and colder actuality. Behind the violent imagery of certain episodes in *Endymion*, the nightmare awakening of Lycius in 'Lamia', the despairing vision of 'La Belle Dame sans Merci', and the awful aspect of Moneta in the second 'Hyperion' lies Keats's awareness of contradictory impulses: he wished to go on writing poetry and at the same time to acquire the mature and 'philosophic Mind', but how was he to keep his sense of poetic enchantment alive while adjusting himself to 'reality'? In his final narrative poem, 'Lamia', he contends with a tremendous despair at the enormity—the impossibility, after all—of his task.

However familiar a problem the relationship between the ideal and the actual may be in romantic literature, Keats's attitude to it works itself out in his narrative poems through a patterned sequence of images possessing a force and frequency peculiar to himself. The frequent recurrences of this pattern make us realize that Keats's verse, though unequal and fragmentary in effect, betrays the driving compulsion of the genuine artist. He may have set out in *Endymion*, as his first long poem, 'to make 4,000 lines out of one bare circumstance', but it is what he is impelled to make of some of these lines that really matters. For the greater part of the poem he is at liberty to follow the bent of his imagination, with the result that each of the first three books turns on a central episode which reveals his peculiar sequence of images and carries a resulting emotional authenticity. Thus the account of Endymion's first experience of Phoebe's love in Book I, the Venus and Adonis episode in Book II, and the Glaucus and Circe story in Book III, all follow the same emotional 'curve'—they describe a lover falling into an enchantment, enjoying every kind of sensuous delight while it lasts, and then awakening to unpleasant reality. Adonis is less unfortunate than Endymion or Glaucus, since he only experiences a 'chilly drizzle' on awakening, but the others are plunged into despair. This emotional sequence is repeated in the other narrative poems—'Isabella' is the only exception, and even so possesses certain elements in common with the pattern—and it is obviously connected to some extent with a characteristic romantic reaction to erotic experience: a reaction epitomizing, in effect, all the romantic's difficulties in reconciling the dream and reality. The *Endymion* episodes already mentioned, and the stories of 'La Belle Dame sans Merci' and 'Lamia', move from a climax of delight to an aftermath which may involve despair ('the cold hill side') or disgust:

> ... all around her shapes, wizard and brute
> Laughing and wailing, groveling, serpenting,
> Showing tooth, tusk, and venom-bag and sting!
> O such deformities!   (*Endymion*, III. 500–3)

Even when the experience of love is a happy one, as it is in 'The Eve of St. Agnes' or in the story of Venus and Adonis in *Endymion*, life after the dream is less satisfactory and may even be alarming. It is only Venus' 'comforting' that mitigates Adonis' 'miserable strife' on being aroused from sleep, and Madeline's awakening, though she finds the real Porphyro at hand, is not so delightful as her dream—she senses a 'painful change' and calls out in distress (stanzas XXXIV–XXXV). This whole sequence may have some relation to the nature of Keats's creative mood—it is worth remembering here that the 'Ode to a Nightingale', for example, follows the same emotional 'curve'.

The details of the pattern in the narrative poems are almost invariably the same. To begin with, the lover falls into some kind of 'swoon' or 'sleep' (compare also the poet's 'drowsiness' at the beginning of the Nightingale ode); from this state he 'awakens' into enchantment. This enchantment is connected with a 'lady', who may or may not be supernatural—if she is really an enchantress, like Circe or Lamia, the whole experience is intensified and the outcome is disastrous. While the tranced intoxication lasts every sense is indulged—Keats always introduces flowers, fruit, wine, music, and perfume, the warmth and colour of summer are always suggested,[1] and erotic experience is always the supreme sensuous culmination. At last, suddenly and without warning, the

---

1 Even in *Isabella* Lorenzo tells his 'lady',

'Love! Thou art leading me from wintry cold,
'Lady! Thou leadest me to summer clime,
'And I must taste the blossoms that unfold
'In its ripe warmth this gracious morning-time.'

trance is over and the lover awakens to a world not only deprived of beauty but transformed into something repellent and hostile.

Perhaps the emotional pattern appears in its purest form in 'La Belle Dame sans Merci'. The lover confronts us, pale but with the rose of former ardour still fading on his cheek; he has been lulled to sleep by his enchantress in the midst of summer warmth, fragrance, and melody; and he awakens after a hideous nightmare to find himself on the cold hill side. Such concentration is rare. In the other narrative poems Keats has had to introduce extraneous elements for the purposes of filling out and decorating his story. Nevertheless the sequence of images in all the central episodes remains the same. In 'The Eve of St. Agnes' the crux of the poem is formed by stanzas XXVI–XXXVII, from Madeline's falling asleep until her final awakening. In stanza XXVI, Madeline puts off the day-time world with her 'rich attire'. 'Half-hidden' in her clothes, she is still only on the verge of the dream—'Pensive awhile she dreams awake'—and her 'wakeful swoon' continues until, disrobed, she falls into the inevitable deep sleep. While she sleeps, Porphyro brings in his feast, and the stanzas which describe these fruits and sweets (XXX–XXXI) fulfil the same function as the fruit and flower passages in the Venus and Adonis episode of *Endymion* (II. 387–533). The effect of this persistent seduction of all the five senses is to produce in the waking companion (and in us) a vicarious experience of the sleeper's tranced and amorous visions. Finally Madeline's dream fades, and, even when her first alarm is over, she and Porphyro still have to face the real world of frost and storm outside.

In 'Lamia' the sequence is identical. Whether he was fully aware of it or not, Keats was almost certainly attracted by Burton's synopsis of the Philostratus story because it presented him with a situation which allowed him to dwell at length on this obsessional sequence of emotions with all its customary physical accompaniments. Burton's account in *The Anatomy of Melancholy* mentions love and 'great content' followed by an awakening in which those experiences become 'mere illusions'; the victim, Lycius, is young and susceptible to 'the passion of love'; the fatal woman is a 'phantasm' whose apparatus of enchantment includes singing, wine and feasting. Burton also gives Keats two important new elements—the figure of the reasoning Apollonius, and the fact of the suffering of the enchantress—which were to have a profound effect on his poem.[1] Here it is enough to say that in 'Lamia' plot and the usual emotion sequence are two sides of a single coin. Lycius on meeting Lamia falls into a swoon; he passes from it to a new world, for he accompanies her through Corinth to the enchanted surroundings of her magic palace; and, while their happiness lasts, their senses are indulged by music, fragrance, summer warmth, and erotic pleasure; when the spell is finally broken the 'myrtles sicken', the music dies, and the 'flush' of love is replaced by the pallor of death.

So firmly established is this pattern of elements in the narrative poems, from as early as *Endymion*, that one is tempted to believe that even if Keats had never read Spenser and the Elizabethans, or loved Fanny Brawne, or become somehow involved with the mysterious Mrs. Isabella Jones,[2] he would still have expressed his sense of the harsh contrast between the ideal and the real by means of this symbolism. Quite apart from its use in 'Lamia' the pattern has a structural value which ensures that Keats does not risk incoherence when he relies on local impulse. What happens when he forces himself to 'plot' may be seen in Book IV of *Endymion*. The tiredness and confusion of the ending, with its perfunctory revelations and its contrived solution, throw into relief the richness of the compulsive imagery in the Glaucus episode of Book III. There is a similar flatness in 'The Eve of St. Agnes' while Keats is trying to get the action under way—when he reaches the 'dream' sequence he has only to let himself go to be at his best.

Whatever its incidental disadvantages, then, a sketchy narrative framework—like the leaves and twigs on which the spider is at liberty to spin its own intricate web (see his letter of 19 February 1818)—enables Keats to devise for his pressing emotions some episode that will express and objectify them satisfactorily. Thus it is not quite enough to say that 'the web is the thing',[3] without adding that any web has a characteristic pattern. How much Keats's pattern matters is brought home when we realize that the distinctive quality of the writing always forces the pattern on our attention whatever range of extraneous material there may be in

1 See below, p. 58.
2 For a discussion of Mrs. Isabella Jones and her connection with Keats's recurrent pattern of images see (i) Robert Gittings, *The Living Year* (1954), pp. 172–4, (ii) my notes on 'The Feast and the Lady', *N.Q.* (Aug. and Nov. 1954), and replies by Mr. Gittings, *N.Q.* (Sept. and Nov. 1954).
3 J. R. Sutherland, *The Medium of Poetry* (1934), p. 36.

the poem. For example, in the first book of *Endymion*, the pressure
of disenchantement seeks release in suddenly intensified imagery.
When Endymion finds himself awake and alone, deprived of the
'warmer air' and the 'scent of violets and blossoming limes'
which have vanished with Phoebe, then:

> . . . all the pleasant hues
> Of heaven and earth had faded: deepest shades
> Were deepest dungeons; heaths and sunny glades
> Were full of pestilent light; our taintless rills
> Seem'd sooty, and o'er-spread with upturn'd gills
> Of dying fish; the vermeil rose had blown
> In frightful scarlet, and its thorns out-grown
> Like spiked aloe. If an innocent bird
> Before my heedless footsteps stirr'd, and stirr'd
> In little journeys, I beheld in it
> A disguis'd demon . . .   (I. 691–701)

The landscape assumes a sudden surrealist horror and the arresting
imagery is quite different in quality from that in Keats's more
relaxed and 'decorative' kind of description. This quality is again
apparent in the imagery of the Glaucus episode in Book III, and in
'Lamia', Part I, where Keats describes the beauty and horror of
the snake. When the tension between delight and pain is at its
height Keats's 'web' is most intricate, 'interwreathing', like
Lamia herself, 'lustres with the gloomier tapestries', showing
itself 'rainbow-sided, touched with miseries', and deriving its
peculiar tautness from the poet's inability to 'unperplex bliss from
its neighbour pain'.

III

It is a commonplace that the path of Keats's development as a poet
and thinker may be traced in detail and with some exactness
through his letters and non-narrative poems. I seek in this section
to show that the same development may be observed in the succession of his narrative poems, and this task is not as super-
erogatory as it may appear at first sight. N. F. Ford, for example,
in his discussion of the difference between 'thought' and
'sensation' in Keats's terminology writes[1]

1 N. F. Ford, *Keats's Pre-figurative Imagination* (1951), p. 103.

by 'a life of sensation' Keats seems frankly to have meant a comparatively unreflective, predominantly sensuous and feelingful kind of
aesthetic experience (our mind turns at once to such poems as *Endymion*,
'Lamia', 'The Eve of St. Agnes', and 'I stood tip-toe . . .', the last of
which he called, revealingly enough, a 'posy of luxuries'— ll. 27–28).
It is the 'infant or thoughtless chamber of life in which we remain as
long as we do not think'.

Here *Endymion*, 'Lamia', and 'The Eve of St. Agnes' are obviously
considered to represent one kind or level of poetry in which sensation is of primary importance, and the question of development is
completely disregarded. In contradiction, I attempt to establish
that development in the narratives, quite apart from matters of
metrical skill and verbal discretion, is real. It may be considered
under two separate headings—its increasing subtlety and the
increasing care which is taken to limit 'wonders' and 'luxuries'
and to penetrate 'sensation' by 'thought'. *Endymion* and 'Lamia'
are separated by Keats's development as distinctly as an early poem
like 'I stood tip-toe . . .' and any one of the great odes, and even
in 'Isabella' the qualification of sensation by thought has begun.

It is true that Keats's first attempts, in 'Isabella', to counteract
the effect of 'luxuries' meet with only varying success. The poem
marks in some respects an advance on *Endymion* but it is perhaps
putting the case too favourably to say, with Mr. F. W. Bateson,
that '*Endymion* (finished November 1817) is adolescent, 'Isabella'
(finished April 1818) is adult'.[1] At this stage of his development
Keats's effort to write a more 'social' kind of poetry throws into
relief his difficulty in reconciling discordant elements—a difficulty
he seems to acknowledge from time to time in the poem: after his
somewhat irrelevant polemic at the expense of Isabella's profiteer-
ing and tyrannical brothers, he apologizes to Boccaccio

> For venturing syllables that ill beseem
> The quiet glooms of such a piteous theme,

and gives as an excuse his wish

> To make old prose in modern rhyme more sweet.

He again communicates an uneasy sense of being too far off course
in stanza XLIX:

1 F. W. Bateson, *English Poetry* (1950), p. 222 n.

> Ah! wherefore all this wormy circumstance?
> Why linger at the yawning tomb so long?
> O for the gentleness of old Romance,
> The simple plaining of a minstrel's song!

His difficulties are increased because of the nature of his chosen story and because there is too much of it. Keats's first task is to 'stead' Boccaccio 'in English tongue', and even though he makes his own elaborations and suppressions,[1] the special impulses of his imagination are checked. Though the story tells of an unhappy outcome to romantic love, this unhappiness does not arise from a distressed recognition that the romantic dream contains the seeds of its own decay: this time the dream is suddenly ruptured by violence from outside. The emotional emphasis, therefore, shifts to the treachery of the violent act and the cruelty of its consequences—and Keats at this stage of his development is not yet equal to dramatizing such a situation, though it is a situation from which the poem derives some of its more mature feeling. Later on, in 'Lamia', Keats was to wrestle more ambitiously with a story which both emphasized the self-destroying nature of the 'dream' and also drew attention to the external forces which might hasten its end.

Nevertheless, Keats is trying to 'reflect' in 'Isabella', and, if at times he seems to pull himself along by his own bootlaces in an effort to advance out of the 'infant or thoughtless Chamber', on other occasions he moves freely and firmly. A tenuous thread of 'thought' runs through the poem, from such statements as 'Too many tears for lovers have been shed' and 'the little sweet doth kill much bitterness' to

> 'Thy beauty grows upon me, and I feel
> A greater love through all my essence steal'

—lines spoken by the ruined Lorenzo from the other side of the grave—and in its course this 'thought' prompts a more purposeful and significant use of Keats's gift for the vivid, concrete image. His bees are 'the little almsmen of spring bowers' because they bring delight—'richest juice'—from the heart of danger and pain —'poison-flowers'—and so momentarily seem to 'unperplex' bliss. Again, the description of the Arno at the ford crossed by

---

1 See M. R. Ridley, *Keats's Craftsmanship* (1933), chapter II.

'the two brothers and their murder'd man' is not natural description for its own sake: the river fanning itself 'with dancing bulrush' and the bream keeping 'head against the freshets' draw attention to the vitality and delightfulness of the physical world —a world to which Lorenzo, 'flush with love', still belongs. It is the murdering brothers who are 'sick and wan', principles of destruction for whom also

> . . . the Ceylon diver held his breath,
>   And went all naked to the hungry shark;
> For them his ears gush'd blood; for them in death
>   The seal on the cold ice with piteous bark
> Lay full of darts . . .   (xv)

The 'thought' underlying such passages is never fully worked out, and Keats is perhaps undecided rather than discreet in hinting at a possible symbolic 'meaning' for the basil plant that flourishes on grief and draws

> Nurture besides, and life, from human fears. . . .

Yet in the stanzas describing Isabella's dream Keats seems to be feeling his way towards some statement about the relationship between decay and growth, death and love. There appears to be a momentary absorption of his whole personality as he contemplates the realities of physical decay and describes a mortal creature weeping at dissolution:

> Lorenzo stood, and wept: the forest tomb
>   Had marr'd his glossy hair which once could shoot
> Lustre into the sun, and put cold doom
>   Upon his lips, and taken the soft lute
> From his lorn voice, and past his loamed ears
>   Had made a miry channel for his tears.   (xxx)

Profoundly moved by this image, he utters through Lorenzo lines expressing the kind of feeling which has little concern with 'luxuries' and which is altogether beyond the range of the 'infant or thoughtless chamber':

> 'I am a shadow now, alas! alas!
>   'Upon the skirts of human-nature dwelling
> 'Alone: I chant alone the holy mass,
>   'While little sounds of life are round me knelling,

'And glossy bees at noon do fieldward pass,
  'And many a chapel bell the hour is telling,
'Paining me through: those sounds grow strange to me,
'And thou art distant in Humanity . . .'   (XXXIX)

Such writing helps to redeem the 'mawkishness' of the kiss in
stanza VIII and the mention of Isabella's 'dainties' in stanza XLVII,
the confused syntax and imagery of the lovers' dialogue in the
earlier stages of the poem, and the bathos of Lorenzo's farewell
to Isabella in stanza XXVI. Keats, like Landor, always fails to
modulate successfully from 'narrative' to conversation,[1] and in
this poem, as elsewhere, his weaknesses are most apparent when
he tries to represent the 'social' behaviour and actions of his men
and women.

If Keats does not fuse the different elements in 'Isabella', at least
he holds them together—both by his usually adroit management
of the stanza form and by his struggle to lift the given theme on
to a more 'thoughtful' plane. In 'The Eve of St. Agnes', on the
other hand, Keats's further advance into the 'Chamber of Maiden
Thought' is marked by his achieving a different kind of harmony.
The 'advance' may be questioned, since Keats is celebrating
romantic love and obviously indulging 'luxuries' to his heart's
content. He is easily identified with the Porphyro who urges
Madeline,

'Open thine eyes, for meek St. Agnes' sake,
'Or I shall drowse beside thee, so my soul doth ache . . . '
                          (XXXI)

This is less a dramatization of what the young man in the story
might feel than the expression of the hypnotic effect on Keats
himself of the delights he has conjured up. Porphyro and Madeline
—and Keats too—are magically transfixed:

        'twas a midnight charm
    Impossible to melt as iced stream:
     .   .   .   .   .
    It seem'd he never, never could redeem
    From such stedfast spell his lady's eyes;
    So mus'd awhile, entoil'd in woofed phantasies.
                       (XXXII)

---

1 See Donald Davie, *Purity in English Diction* (1952), p. 187.

Yet this 'warm, unnerved' indulgence is shaped and controlled
by the enchantment pattern and the 'awakening to reality' even
receives an emphasis from a kind of repetition.[1] When Madeline
first stirs and opens her eyes she weeps at seeing Porphyro 'pallid,
chill and drear' and her tears are those of shock at discovering
the startling difference between the real and the imagined lover.
But at this point Porphyro regains his colour and something of
his 'enchanted' aspect,

> he arose,
> Ethereal, flush'd, and like a throbbing star
> (XXXVI)

and is able to 'melt into her dream'. It we take what follows to
be the sexual consummation which is a usual part of Keats's
recurrent pattern of enchantment and awakening to disappointment, we are brought up sharply by what follows the 'solution
sweet'—the frost-wind and sleet, and the setting of St. Agnes's
moon. This is the emotional anti-climax demanded by the recurrent pattern, but the tone is not one of simple Romantic
impatience with reality, but rather of a certain resignation to
disappointment at the existence of different levels of experience,
some more and some less intense, and to difficulty, danger, and
biting winds as a part of reality. 'Reality', says Mr. Ford, 'was
against the dream. Nevertheless the dream is destined to prevail.'[2]
It is doubtless true that the whole story is a fantasy of wish-
fulfilment and in this sense a dream, but our main interest ought,
I think, to be in the remarkable change of tone within the story
at the awakening from enchantment to reality.

It is fair, then, to say that 'The Eve of St. Agnes' represents
Keats's attempt to see whether some of the elements in the 'dream'
will survive a colder air. Porphyro, in stanza XXXVII, now wide
awake and listening to the sleet pattering on the window, recalls
Madeline to actuality:

> 'This is no dream, my bride, my Madeline!'

She finds adjustment difficult:

> 'No dream, alas! alas! and woe is mine!'

1 As in 'Lamia', where the final 'awakening' is the sequel to an earlier intrusion
of 'the noisy world'. See below, p. 59.
2 *Keats's Pre-figurative Imagination*, p, 207.

and is afraid that she will be left desolate and forsaken (as all the other 'dreamers' in the narrative poems are left). Porphyro's reassurances, however, are drawn from a familiar waking world— 'arise! the morning is at hand . . . o'er the southern moors I have a home for thee'—and their escape is not only 'beset with fears' but physically impeded by the dark stair, the bloodhound, and the door which groans on its hinges in a final protest. Even if we agree with Mr. Ford that 'The Eve of St. Agnes' fulfils a wish, it is still true that the demands of a daylight plausibility are to some extent recognized.

The confidence which enables Keats to approximate dream and reality also helps him to integrate in his poem various elements extraneous to the enchantment pattern. The opening and closing stanzas, which bring in the old beadsman and the palsied Angela, provide a framework of contrast for the central episode: they show Keats relating different aspects of life to each other and trying to accept them all as parts of a greater whole. This is at least an attempt at a 'human and moral truth' such as Sidney Colvin desired but failed to find in the poem. The same attempt accounts for Keats's insistence throughout the poem on such contrasts as cold and warmth, whiteness and colour, moonlight and storm, 'harsh penance' and 'argent revelry', and on the passage of time that 'ages long ago' reduced the young lovers to a cold as enduring as that of the dead Angela and the frozen beadsman.

In 'La Belle Dame sans Merci' and 'Lamia', the lustres of Keats's poetic web are 'touched with miseries' and the moderate 'wishful' optimism of 'The Eve of St. Agnes' is rejected for something much more uncompromising. The 'knight-at-arms' awakens on 'the cold hill side', and Lycius is destroyed. The lady encountered 'in the meads' and the 'maiden bright' whom Lycius finds 'a young bird's flutter from a wood' both turn out to be fatal enchantresses who spell disaster for their victims and are themselves somehow doomed. In spite of their magic powers neither in the end has the 'sciential brain to unperplex bliss from its neighbour pain'. This takes us some way from the mood of the story of Madeline and Porphyro and probably reflects a further phase in Keats's emotional experience. He has felt compelled to turn to his particular obsession again and to re-state it with a heightened feeling for the delight of the 'luxuries' and the pain of their loss.

The heightening of contrast provides for structural tension. This is, of course, more immediately noticeable in 'La Belle Dame sans Merci', not only because it is a shorter poem and deals exclusively with the enchantment pattern—unlike 'Lamia' it avoids the weaknesses which accompany Keats's 'realistic' representation of human behaviour—but because of its verse form. Keats has no room to luxuriate in the ballad stanza, and spareness of form enables him to employ compression and understatement in the interests of emotional effect. The imagery establishes with precision and economy the usual emotional sequence, but the 'winter' of the silent birds and the withered sedge is brought forward more vividly than the past 'summer' of honey and flowers.

'Lamia', naturally, does not make the same direct impact on the mind and feelings as 'La Belle Dame sans Merci', but it is Keats's most ambitious attempt to wrestle with the triple problem of his obsession with the 'dream', his concern with the relative merits of philosophic and poetic 'truth', and his fear that the choice of one mode of inquiry will destroy his capacity for the other—that, in fact, he may commit a Coleridgean kind of self-murder, the philosopher in him killing the poet. The last part of 'Lamia', containing Lycius' attack on Apollonius, is of September 1819, and belongs therefore to the same mode of feeling which produced the 'Lines to Fanny' of late 1819, lines in which Keats simplified the issue without diminishing its importance for himself:

> My muse had wings,
> And ever ready was to take her course
> Whither I bent her force,
> Unintellectual, yet divine to me;—
> Divine, I say!—What sea-bird o'er the sea
> Is a philosopher the while he goes
> Winging along where the great water throes?
> How shall I do
> To get anew
> Those moulted feathers, and so mount once more . . .

And yet the final effect of 'Lamia' does not suggest that 'reflection' has stultified imagination: reflection in fact has caused a violent emotional reaction producing the 'fire' which Keats rightly stressed as the principal quality of the poem. On the other hand, some of the poem's weaknesses come about because Keats will not allow himself to concentrate on his central situation—which is an admirable vehicle for his enchantment obsession—without intro-ducing explanatory or 'realistic' elements to dilute its effective-ness. Even so, the poem as a whole is organized more closely and 'dramatically' than it is usually given credit for, and consequently makes on its own imaginative terms a successful statement of the ideas which Keats tries to expound—superfluously perhaps—in conceptual language towards the end of his story ('Do not all charms fly at the mere touch of cold philosophy . . .' Part II, ll. 229–38).

'Lamia' does not quite represent, as N. F. Ford maintains, Keats's attempt to scourge himself of all remaining belief that the 'dream' will prevail.[1] Such a theory would imply that Keats was less uncertain than the evidence shows him to have been about the danger to his poetic life of subordinating wonder to ratio-cination—this is not at all, it should be pointed out, the same thing as the opposition between 'wonders' and 'Shakespearian' reality. Moreover, the nature of his compassion for Lamia herself[2] —a new development in his poetry—and his hostility towards Apollonius are both out of keeping with this view. What Keats's poem as a whole communicates to us with great emotional honesty is his angry exasperation with Apollonius, his pity for Lamia, whose magic powers can neither prevail against Apollonius nor save her from the pain that accompanies her assumed mortal nature, his self-identification up to a point with Lycius, and his distressed sense that the final catastrophe is inevitable. He has no 'answer' to all this: no answer is possible. He cannot banish the 'dream': in describing it he asserts its value. Nor can he escape into it, refusing to contemplate the full 'heart and nature of man': the enchantress herself is subject to 'the painful change' and suffers as he does. He cannot ignore the philosopher, an unbidden guest who insists on making his inconvenient presence felt. All that is left for him to do is to express his pain and to utter his

1 *Keats's Pre-figurative Imagination*, p. 144.

2 H. W. Garrod's view of Keats's attitude to 'Lamia'—'No sympathy is wasted on Lamia: willow and adder's tongue are her proper portion for ever' (*Keats* (1926), p. 62)—is partly accounted for by his misinterpretation of Part II, l. 224. Keats selects 'the leaves of willow and of adder's tongue' for Lamia's 'wreath' because of their soothing and healing properties (see, for example, John Gerarde, *The Herball, or Generall Historie of Plantes* (1633), pp. 404–5, 1392). The pitiful fate of the 'lamia' in Burton's account of the story must have appealed to Keats in the first place through its hint of emotional conflict and of the sufferings of 'Men and Women'.

bitter protest against Apollonius—that is, against the kind of approach to life which seems to him to endanger the poetic imagination.

That Keats is as concerned as he has been all along with the insecure nature of the dream, quite apart from the added threat to it represented by Apollonius, is established early in the second part of his poem. Even before the feast—in fact partly causing that feast to be held—the 'noisy world' has intruded into the tranced state of the lovers with a distracting 'thrill of trumpets' which leaves 'a thought' in Lycius' head:

> For the first time, since first he harbour'd in
> That purple-lined palace of sweet sin
> His spirit pass'd beyond its golden bourn
> Into the noisy world almost forsworn.
>
> (II. 30–3)

Lycius' consequent attempt to heighten their happiness—

> 'I am striving how to fill my heart
> 'With a deeper crimson, and a double smart?'
>
> (II. 50–1)

is itself a confession that the delight has already passed its highest point, and the feast itself is a final folly:

> O senseless Lycius! Madman! wherefore flout
> The silent-blessing fate, warm cloister'd hours,
> And show to common eyes these secret bowers?
>
> (II. 147–9)

It is difficult enough in any case, Keats is saying in 'Lamia', for the enchantment and its valuable 'sensations' to survive in the common light of day without having to contend with the probing eye of the philosopher,

> Keen, cruel, perceant, stinging . . .
>
> (II. 301)

whose 'thought' is more ruthlessly abstract than that of the 'noisy world', and whose attitude to the dream is simply a barren denial of its utility.

Seen in this way the poem is obviously not a despairing rejection of the poetic mode of apprehension, though despair is an element in the poem: it is, on the contrary, an impassioned plea for its validity and an attempt—a last-ditch stand if one likes—to defend the enchanted dream, with all its fragility and potentiality for pain, against the threat of total dissolution. In his final outburst Keats is ready to assert the 'truth' of the dream against the 'falsities' of the philosopher. With a kind of inspired illogicality, Lycius in his dying breath affirms that Apollonius (not Lamia, who once seemed 'Some demon's mistress, or the demon's self') is a 'demon' with 'juggling eyes', guilty of 'Unlawful magic, and enticing lies'; more dangerous now than the 'ghost of folly' haunting 'sweet dreams', he is the 'grey-beard wretch' who perpetrates 'impious proud-heart sophistries' and risks the 'righteous ban Of all the Gods'.[1] Here, if anywhere, one feels the strength with which Keats finally asserts the validity of the poetic imagination: what the imagination seizes as truth comes home even now with more force than the conceptual logic of the reasoner. Lycius and Lamia, as it were, die in its cause—not altogether a lost cause, for Keats's record of their defeat suggests that the triumph of an Apollonius is, after all, something of a pyrrhic victory.

Keats's task in developing his theme is partly to 'dress the misery in fit magnificence', and he carries it out with brilliance in individual passages—especially where the misery and the magnificence are closely interrelated, as they are in the descriptions of the snake[2] and of the banqueting-hall which Lamia prepares in 'pale contented sort of discontent'. But the shaping power in the poem extends beyond these passages. It finds, for example, two functions for the preliminary episode about Hermes and the nymph, which might at first appear to be simply an opportunity for 'luxury' and decoration: for the episode first explains how Lamia is enabled to resume her 'woman shape' and then supports the poem's central idea, emphasizing that human 'dreams' vanish, whereas those of the immortals are 'truth':

> Real are the dreams of Gods, and smoothly pass
> Their pleasures in a long immortal dream.
>
> (I. 127–8)

---

1 'Lamia', II. 277–90.
2 W. J. Courthope describes them as 'too loathly for quotation'! See *A History of English Poetry*, vol. vi, p. 342.

Its closing lines,

> Into the green-recessed woods they flew;
> Nor grew they pale, as mortal lovers do,
>
> (I. 144–5)

hint at Lamia's destiny: the pallor of Keats's disenchanted lovers has been noticed several times in this essay, and here again at the end of the poem:

> . . . all was blight;
> Lamia, no longer fair, there sat a deadly white.
>
> (II. 275–6)

The whole structure of the narrative is in fact disciplined by Keats's theme. At the end of Part I, echoing the end of the pro-logue, Lamia and Lycius as human lovers pass into the formidable city—not into 'green-recessed woods'—and Corinth's night-noises are deliberately ominous:

> . . . all her populous streets and temples lewd
> Mutter'd . . .   (I. 352–3)

The figure of 'sharp-eyed' Apollonius looming up out of the shuffling crowd heightens the sense that human 'bliss' is every-where threatened. Part II is organized to convey the ebb and flow of feeling in the lovers' dying enchantment; it moves from the trumpeting intrusion of actuality, through the uneasy lull of the wedding-preparations, to the bright blaze of the feats and the final disaster. Within this firm structure the noticeable failures occur at precisely the points where Keats seems to have exerted himself in the interests of psychological realism and the world of 'Men and Women'. Lamia's subjection to Lycius, for example, anticipates the sentiment of a bad Victorian novel: while Lycius frowns with fierce masculine passion, Lamia kneels placatingly before him enjoying every moment:

> She burnt, she lov'd the tyranny,
> And, all subdued, consented to the hour . . .
>
> (II. 81–2)

The same flaw in sensibility—what George Eliot would have described as one of Keats's 'spots of commonness'—is responsible for the notorious passage about 'a real woman' being a better 'treat' than 'Faeries, Peris, Goddesses', and for such descents into prettiness as the lines which conclude, and almost succeed in spoiling, the first description of the snake.

But these weaknesses are incidental. In the final analysis one begins to feel that with the figure of Lamia Keats discovered an extremely potent symbol. The very anomaly of her position—situated somewhere between the real world and the dream (we are never sure whether she was originally 'a real woman' or a 'phantasm')—is relevant to the central experience of the narrative poems. She is able to undergo the 'dream' by entering the mortal world, and yet by entering it she also forfeits happiness. As an enchantress and the presiding deity of luxuries and wonders, she is inevitably the agent of pain and disillusion, yet she is herself doomed and pitiable. She sets about preparing for her own destruction with a 'high-thoughted' detached passion but, having done so, her 'weak hand' feebly protests at the last against annihilation. At the same time, in Lycius (and his creator), she has someone to speak for her—and also to die for her. Keats, whatever the cost, does not reject the kind of palace she builds, as Tennyson, bemused with Victorian earnestness, was to reject the Palace of Art barely twenty years later. And if 'Lamia' leaves us ultimately in perplexity this is not because Keats has lost his poetic integrity to the moralist or to the philosopher, but because his insight, keener after all than Tennyson's even at its best, has laid bare a series of paradoxes which it is beyond his powers to resolve.

4

The Meaning of the Odes

KENNETH MUIR

A GREAT DEAL HAS BEEN WRITTEN about the odes, and some of it will be known to serious students of Keats's work—Robert Bridges's condensed judgements. Dr. H. W. Garrod's account of the evolution of the stanza-forms used in the different odes, the subtle studies by Mr. Middleton Murry and Professor Cleanth Brooks of the 'Ode on a Grecian Urn' and Professor William Empson's account of the 'Ode on Melancholy' may be mentioned—but there would seem to be room for a plain and elementary statement of what the odes are about. In this essay I shall deliberately avoid direct critical analysis. Such analysis will be found in the essays which follow.

Between the middle of February 1819, when he laid aside 'The Eve of St. Mark', and the end of April, when he copied out the first of the odes, Keats wrote very little verse; and it is apparent from several remarks in his letters that he did not fully realize that his indolence was a necessary pause before another period of creation. It was closely linked with the Negative Capability he felt to be a characteristic of the best poets, alternating moods of activity and indolence being, in fact, the rhythm of the mind necessary for the exercise of Negative Capability. It is arguable, indeed, that since during the act of creation the poet must organize, choose, and reject, he can exercise Negative Capability only during his moods of receptive indolence—what Wordsworth called 'a wise passiveness'.

We can see from a passage in the long letter to George and Georgina that, by overcoming the feverish desire for poetic fame and by ceasing to be obsessed with his love, Keats managed to see life more steadily:[1]

1 *Letters*, p. 315.

64

Neither Poetry, nor Ambition, nor Love have any alertness of countenance as they pass by me: they seem rather like figures on a Greek vase—A Man and two women whom no one but myself could distinguish in their disguisement.

This passage is clearly the germ of the 'Ode on Indolence', though the poem may not have been written until a month or two later. Keats was wise to exclude this ode from the 1820 volume, because it is less highly wrought than the others, because the satirical tone of certain lines is out of key with the remainder of the poem, and because he had used some of its imagery elsewhere. He told[1] Miss Jeffrey that the thing he had 'most enjoyed this year had been writing an ode to Indolence'. 'The throstle's lay' links this ode to his own lines 'What the thrush said' and to Wordsworth's declaration that the blithe throstle was 'no mean preacher'. But the ode, like the letter, combines the praise of indolence with a repudiation of Love, Ambition, and Poetry. Keats included in the same letter two sonnets in which he had attacked the desire for fame, and there were times when he seemed anxious to escape from the bondage of love—that is the apparent meaning of 'La Belle Dame sans Merci'. In the 'Ode on a Grecian Urn', earthly passion is said to leave a cloyed heart, 'a burning forehead and a parching tongue'. In the 'Ode on Indolence' Keats seems to repudiate love altogether. But he was able to reject love, ambition, and poetry only by satirizing them:

> For I would not be dieted with praise,
> A pet-lamb in a sentimental farce.

The uncertainty of tone is the result of his personal situation. He could acquire the means to marry only by earning fame as a poet. The praise of a wise passiveness is spoilt by the juxtaposition of the irritable attack on vulgarity. Keats should have written two separate poems.

In the same letter to George and Georgiana, Keats wrote his parable of the world as a vale of soul-making—an idea which was implicit in the third book of 'Hyperion'. Near the end of the same letter he copied out 'La Belle Dame sans Merci' and the sonnet on Paolo and Francesca, both based on the fifth canto of the *Inferno*, and both related, we may suppose, to his love for Fanny

Brawne. Another sonnet, 'Why did I laugh tonight', concludes with the thought that death is 'intenser' than life, that it is 'Life's high meed'—a thought which was to recur in the 'Ode to a Nightingale'.

In the weeks before the writing of the odes we find that Keats was gradually realizing the creative function of indolence, he was anxious to achieve a state of non-attachment, and he was filled with a desire to find a meaning in human suffering so that his own and that of others could in some way be justified. He was torn between his continuing passion for Fanny and a wish to escape from the toils of ambition and love.

For an understanding of the odes, however, it is necessary to go back a year, to the 'Epistle to Reynolds', written in March 1818. In the course of this poem Keats gives examples of the coherent and creative dreams—the waking dreams—enjoyed by the poet and the painter. One of these is the picture of the sacrifice, which was later to find a place on the Grecian Urn:

> Some Titian colours touch'd into real life,—
> The sacrifice goes on; the pontiff knife
> Gleams in the Sun, the milk-white heifer lows,
> The pipes go shrilly, the libation flows:
> A white sail shows above the green-head cliff,
> Moves round the point, and throws her anchor stiff;
> The mariners join hymn with those on land.

Another picture, based on Claude's 'Enchanted Castle', with 'windows as if latch'd by Fays and Elves' perhaps contributed to the 'magic casements' of the Nightingale ode. Keats goes on to express a wish that all our dreams might take their colours

> From something of material sublime,
> Rather than shadow our own soul's day-time
> In the dark void of night

that is, that they should mirror objective reality rather than the frustrations and inner conflicts of the dreamer. He confesses that he dare not yet philosophize, and doubts whether he will ever attain to the prize:

> High reason, and the love of good and ill.

Whether we read *love* or *lore* (words easily confused in Keats's

handwriting) Mr. Murry is probably right in thinking that the
poet meant not the knowledge of good and evil, but rather a
recognition that particular evil is universal good, an ability to
see 'the balance of good and evil'. But Keats could not then make
his experience of life fit a philosophical theory. Things—the
problems of life—'tease us out of thought', as the Urn, and
Eternity, were to do. When the poet turns from the imaginary
world of his creating to the actual world, his imagination is

> Lost in a sort of Purgatory blind.

He is dissatisfied with escapist poetry, and not strong enough to
cope with the problems of good and evil. He convinces[1] his

nerves that the world is full of Misery and Heartbreak, Pain, Sickness
and Oppression.

The 'Chamber of Maiden Thought becomes gradually darken'd'
and he feels the 'burden of the Mystery'. Such speculations inevitably interfere with the enjoyment of the present, so that in
the epistle Keats declares that

> It is a flaw
> In happiness, to see beyond our bourn,—
> It forces us in summer skies to mourn,
> It spoils the singing of the Nightingale.

At the end of the Nightingale ode the real world breaks in on the
ecstasy of the bird's song.

In the concluding section of the epistle we learn that the particular problem which was agitating Keats at this time was the
struggle for survival in the animal kingdom—'an eternal fierce
destruction' symbolized not merely by shark and hawk, but by the
robin, 'Ravening a worm'. When he came to write the odes a
year later the death of Tom had become for Keats the prime
example of nature's cruelty. But we can see in the careless and
disconnected thoughts of the Epistle that many of the themes
treated in the odes were already in his mind.

The first of the great odes, 'To Psyche'—the first poem with
which Keats had taken 'even moderate pains'—is, as Wordsworth
said of another poem, 'a pretty piece of paganism'. Keats was
apparently looking for a surrogate for religion. He speaks nostal-
gically of 'the fond believing lyre', and looks back to a pantheistic

1 *Letters*, p. 144.

world when air, water, and fire were holy. He is mainly concerned with the relationship between Psyche and Cupid. In becoming her priest he builds a fane where she can receive her lover—not as formerly in darkness, but with a bright torch. In other words Keats is proposing love as a substitute for religion; but, as Psyche is the soul, the poem may also be linked with his conception of the world as a vale of soul-making and with the deification of Apollo in 'Hyperion'. A detailed examination of this ode will be found in the next essay.

The 'Ode to a Nightingale' begins with a description of a man falling into a drugged sleep, so that it comes as something of a shock when we learn in the sixth line that the poet is 'too happy' in the happiness of the bird. This paradox is resolved in the sixth stanza in which Keats tells us that he has often 'been half in love with easeful death', and that in listening to the nightingale,

> Now more than ever seems it rich to die.

An easeful death was to Keats, who knew that Tom's fate might be his, 'a consummation devoutly to be wished'. In the third stanza his account of the miseries of life:

> Where youth grows pale, and spectre-thin, and dies

is also coloured by thoughts of Tom; and a link between Tom's illness and the nightingale is to be found in Keats's copy of Shakespeare. He read *King Lear* on 4 October 1818, a few weeks before Tom died, and he underlined the words 'poor Tom' in Edgar's sentence:

> The foul fiend haunts poor Tom in the voice of the Nightingale.

Now, seven months later, when he heard an actual nightingale, Keats was haunted by Tom's ghost.

Keats, then, too happy in the happiness of the bird, dreams of escaping from the miseries of the world, first by a 'draught of vintage', and then 'on the viewless wings of Poesy'. The drink is to act, like the bird's song, as an opiate, allowing him to 'leave the world unseen'; and even in the richly sensuous evocation of the surrounding darkness we are reminded again of death in the phrase 'embalmed darkness'—an echo of the sonnet to sleep, death's counterfeit, the 'soft embalmer of the still midnight'.

Now Keats toys with the idea of dying:

> To cease upon the midnight with no pain.

with the bird singing his requiem.

Bridges complained of the illogicality of stanza VII, since the nightingale, like man, is born for death. But the bird, unlike man, is not conscious of the hungry generations; and it is no more illogical for Keats to pretend that he is listening to the same bird as the one that sang to Ruth, than it was for Wordsworth to imagine he was listening to the same cuckoo he had heard in childhood, or for Rousseau to cry out when he saw the periwinkle. Hazlitt, indeed, referred in the peroration of one of his lectures to Wordsworth's lines to the Cuckoo, to Rousseau, and to Philomel;[1] Wordsworth's poem, like Keats's stanza, ends with a reference to faeryland; and it is significant that the reading of the draft 'perhaps the self-same voice' is nearer than that of the published text to Wordsworth's 'wandering voice. . . . A voice . . . The same'. Another of Wordsworth's poems, 'The Solitary Reaper', may, as Mr. Garrod has suggested,[2] 'by some obscure process of association', have contributed to the same stanza of Keats's ode. The 'solitary Highland Lass', reaping the corn and singing 'a melancholy strain', recalled Ruth standing 'in tears amid the alien corn'. Wordsworth mentions the nightingale and the cuckoo; like Keats he uses the epithet 'plaintive'; and in both poems the song fades away at the end.

But in any case the apparent illogicality of the stanza is transcended when the underlying symbolism is understood: the song of the bird is the song of the poet. Keats is contrasting the immortality of poetry with the mortality of the poet. He is saying with Horace, *Non omnis moriar*. This is the climax of the poem and the point where the different themes are harmonized—the beauty of the nightingale's song, the loveliness of the spring night, the miseries of the world, the desire to escape from those miseries by death, by wine, or by poetry. Whereas when Keats wrote the 'Epistle to Reynolds' the problems of life spoiled the singing of the nightingale, the song now acquired a greater poignancy from the miseries of the world.

The ode is not the expresssion of a single mood, but of a succession of moods. From being too happy in the happiness of the

1 See the discussion on p. 145.   2 *Keats* (1926), p. 111.

bird's song, Keats becomes aware of the contrast between the bird's apparent joy and the misery of the human condition, from the thought of which he can only momentarily escape by wine, by poetry, by the beauty of nature, or by the thought of death. In the seventh stanza the contrast is sharpened: the immortal bird, representing natural beauty as well as poetry, is set against the 'hungry generations' of mankind. The contrast is followed back into history and legend with Ruth in tears and the 'magic casements opening on the foam of perilous seas'—which, as in the 'Epistle to Reynolds', conceal a bitter struggle for survival. Even the faery lands are forlorn. Reality breaks in on the poetic dream and *tolls* the poet back to his self. Fancy, the muse of escape poetry, is a deceiving elf. Keats expresses with a maximum of intensity the desire to escape from reality, and yet he recognizes that no escape is possible.

One kind of mastery displayed by Keats in this ode is worth noting—the continuous shifting of viewpoint. We are transported from the poet in the garden to the bird in the trees; in the second stanza we have glimpses of Flora and Provence, followed by one of the poet drinking the wine; in the fourth stanza we are taken up into the starlit skies, and in the next we are back again in the flower-scented darkness. In the seventh stanza we range furthest in time and place, as we have seen; and in the last stanza we start again from the Hampstead garden, and then follow the nightingale as it disappears in the distance.

The 'Ode on a Grecian Urn' is dialectically opposed to the 'Ode to a Nightingale'. Keats in an earlier poem, 'Bards of Passion', had imagined that in heaven the nightingale sings

> divine melodious truth;
> Philosophic numbers smooth.

But in the ode, though the poet temporarily endows the nightingale's song with meaning, the bird is still 'a senseless, tranced thing'. We are left thinking that neither the beauty of nature nor the beauty of art can console us for the miseries of life. In the 'Ode on a Grecian Urn' Keats tries once more. The life of the figures on the urn possesses the beauty, the significance, and the eternality of art; and this, in the third stanza explicitly, and throughout the poem implicitly, is contrasted with the transitoriness, the meaninglessness, and the unpoetic nature of actual life. The unwearied melodist,

> For ever piping songs for ever new,

and the uncloying love of the imaginary world of the artist,

> All breathing human passion far above,

are contrasted with the inevitable imperfections of human existence. Yet the moral is not 'mortal beauty passes, but not that of art'. This interpretation ignores the development of the poem. In the last stanza Keats proclaims that the sorrows and the meaninglessness of life can be transcended if we learn the lesson of the Urn, that 'Beauty is Truth, Truth Beauty'. As early as November 1817 Keats had told Bailey[1] that he was

certain of nothing but of the holiness of the Heart's affections and the truth of Imagination—what the imagination seizes as Beauty must be Truth—whether it existed before or not . . . The Imagination may be compared to Adam's dream—He awoke and found it truth.

A month later he told his brothers:[2]

The excellence of every art is its intensity, capable of making all disagreeables evaporate, from their being in close relationship with Beauty and Truth.

Now in the ode, as a result of the development of his mind during the earlier part of the year, Keats seems to go a stage further. The Urn is proclaiming that there is not merely a close relationship but an actual identity between beauty and truth. Whether the final words of the poem are supposed to be spoken by the Urn or whether they are intended to be the poet's own comment does not greatly affect the meaning. The words—

> That is all
> Ye know on earth, and all ye need to know—

are dramatically appropriate. Momentarily, and in response to the beauty of the Urn, the poet can accept the proposition—a natural development of his own earlier aphorisms—that beauty is an image of truth, and that therefore, if we see life steadily and see it whole, the disagreeables will evaporate as they do in a great

---

1 *Letters*, p. 67.   2 Ibid., p. 71.

work of art. Keats seems to protect himself from the criticism of common sense by leaving it doubtful whether his own views are to be identified with those of the Urn. Art claims that life could be as meaningful as art. When we are experiencing a work of art we are prepared to give our assent, though at other times we may be sceptical.

Keats was aware, as Yeats was aware, when he sailed to Byzantium, of the limitations of art. Even when he is congratulating the lover on the permanence of his unsatisfied love, he hankers after 'breathing human passion'; and when he is describing the scene of sacrifice which will remain for ever beautiful, he thinks of the desolate town, emptied for ever of its inhabitants. Art is invaded by human suffering. The cold pastoral, although perfect, is lacking in the warmth of reality. It is this undertone which prevents us from branding the message of the Urn as irresponsible, or 'uneducated', or 'intrusively didactic'.

The 'Ode on Melancholy' has links with several of the other odes. Keats had proposed to honour Psyche by making 'a moan upon the midnight hours', and his fane would have 'thoughts, new grown with pleasant pain'. The song of the nightingale had made him too happy, his heart aching, and his senses pained by a drowsy numbness. There is a strain of melancholy, as we have seen, in the fourth stanza of the 'Ode on a Grecian Urn'. Keats, moreover, had written some verses on the juxtaposition of joy and sorrow in the previous year:[1]

> Welcome joy, and welcome sorrow,
> Lethe's weed and Hermes' feather . . .
> Infant playing with a skull . . .
> Nightshade with the woodbine kissing . . .
> Oh! the sweetness of the pain!
>   . . . let me slake
> All my thirst for sweet heart-ache!
> Let my bower be of yew,
> Interwreath'd with myrtles new.

Now in the first stanza of the 'Ode on Melancholy' Keats introduces *Lethe*, *nightshade*, and *yew*, but he rejects them as being unnecessary means of arousing melancholy. He likewise rejects the stock properties—the skull, the gibbet, and the phantom-

1 *Poems*, ed. de Selincourt, p. 256.

ship—mentioned in a deleted stanza which had been partly derived from Burton's *Anatomy of Melancholy*:[1]

> This terrour is most usually caused, as *Plutarch* will have, *from some imminent danger, when a terrible object is at hand* . . . *by the sudden sight of some spectrum or devill* . . . the sight of a monster, a *carcase* . . . where a *coarse* hath been . . . with a *dead man.* . . . At *Basil* . . . where a malefactor hung in *gibbets.*

Horrors of this kind, and even the beetle, the death-moth, and the owl, are not only unnecessary as a means of arousing melancholy, they are to be shunned since they 'drown the wakeful anguish of the soul' and prevent us from experiencing to the full the subtler melancholy of which Keats is writing. Melancholy is to be sought in beauty and joy—in a rose, a rainbow, or the anger of a mistress. Because beauty is transient, because love and joy fade, enjoyment must be accompanied with melancholy. Beauty is lovely because it dies and impermanence is the essence of joy; so that only those who are exquisitely sensuous and able to relish the finest joys can behold the 'Veil'd Melancholy':

> She dwells with Beauty—Beauty that must die;
> And Joy, whose hand is ever at his lips
> Bidding adieu; and aching Pleasure nigh . . .
> Ay, in the very temple of delight
> Veil'd Melancholy has her sovran shrine,
> Though seen of none save him whose strenuous tongue
> Can burst Joy's grape against his palate fine,
> His soul shall taste the sadness of her might,
> And be among her cloudy trophies hung.

Keats is really writing about the poetical character. The fine sensitivity necessary for the writing of poetry makes the poet vulnerable both to joy and sorrow. The realization that love and beauty are subject to time intensifies his joy in them, as we can see from Keats's own poems or Shakespeare's *Sonnets*.

This ode is not quite perfect. The last three lines of the second stanza exhibit both the awkwardness that is apt to beset Keats when he is writing of women and also the lapses he is led into by the need to find a rhyme. It is difficult otherwise to explain 'let her rave'. The beautiful image at the beginning of the same stanza has been criticized for its irrelevance. The 'weeping cloud' and the 'April shroud' are admirable; but the information that

[1] Part I. See 2, mem. 4, subs 3.

the rain 'fosters the droop-headed flowers all' suggests, what Keats presumably did not intend, that the melancholy fit is creative.

'To Autumn', the last of the odes, requires little commentary. Keats's own account of the writing of the poem gives us a good idea of its theme:[1]

How beautiful the season is now—How fine the air. A temperate sharpness about it. Really, without joking, chaste weather—Dian skies —I never lik'd stubble-fields so much as now—Aye better than the chilly green of the Spring. Somehow a stubble-plain looks warm— This struck me so much in my Sunday's walk that I composed upon it.

Keats describes Nature as she is. He was in this like Peter Bell:

> A primrose by a river's brim
> A yellow primrose was to him,
> And it was nothing more.

'To Autumn' expresses the essence of the season, but it draws no lesson, no overt comparison with human life.[2] Keats was being neither allegorical, nor Wordsworthian. Goethe once remarked[3] that

for most men the vision of the pure phenomenon is not enough, they insist on going further, like children who peep in a mirror and then turn it round to see what is on the other side.

Keats in this poem is almost content with the pure phenomenon.

1 *Letters*, p. 384.
2 But see the essay on p. 96.
3 The passage was quoted by J. M. Murry.

5

The 'Ode to Psyche'

KENNETH ALLOTT

'TO PSYCHE' is the Cinderella of Keats's great odes, but it is hard to see why it should be so neglected, and at least two poets imply that the conventional treatment of the poem is shabby and undeserved. In his introduction to Keats (1895) Robert Bridges wrote of the 'extreme beauty' of the ode's last stanza and ranked the whole poem above 'On a Grecian Urn' (though not above 'On Melancholy'),[1] and Mr. T. S. Eliot in an unregarded parenthesis in *The Use of Poetry and the Use of Criticism* (1933) has commented more boldly, 'The Odes—especially perhaps the *Ode to Psyche*—are enough for his [Keats's] reputation.' I sympathize with these views. 'To Psyche' is neither unflawed nor the best of odes, but to me it illustrates better than any other Keats's possession of poetic power in conjunction with what was for him an unusual artistic detachment—besides being a remarkable poem in its own right. This may be another way of saying that it is the most architectural of the odes, as it is certainly the one that culminates most dramatically. Some of Keats's remarks about it are relevant here.

The following Poem—the last I have written is the first and the only one with which I have taken even moderate pains. I have for the most part dash'd off my lines in a hurry. This I have done leisurely—I think it reads the more richly for it and will I hope encourage me to write other things in even a more peaceable and healthy spirit.[2]

Keats almost certainly wrote this before he wrote 'To a Nightingale', 'On a Grecian Urn', and 'On Melancholy', and it is possible that he felt later that these remaining Spring odes were

1 *Collected Essays and Papers*, vol. i.　　2 *Letters*, p. 339.

written in a peaceable and healthy spirit. On balance this seems unlikely: 'To Autumn' is the only other ode one would expect him to characterize in these terms. The 'peaceable and healthy spirit' of 'To Psyche' can be explained by saying that Keats is more engaged as an artist and less directly engaged as a man in this poem (in spite of its superficial blemishes) than in 'To a Nightingale', and the unexpected degree of aesthetic distance is probably connected with his 'pains'. Those which can be sub-sumed under 'metrical preoccupation' have been fully discussed by Dr. Garrod and later by Mr. M. R. Ridley, but I suspect that Keats found a main difficulty in keeping his opulence from appearing obtrusive in what was for him a strain of unusually pre-meditated art. Apart from one or two lapses (mostly in the first stanza) I think he was successful—judged, that is to say, by the standards of success appropriate to the odes, which involve a somewhat different kind of expectation, as Matthew Arnold knew, from that with which one would read *King Lear* or the *Agamemnon*.[1] What I feel very strongly is that 'To a Nightingale' should not be quoted to exemplify Keats's control of his poetic gift unless we are ready to disregard the difference between swimming powerfully but hypnotically with the tide of feeling and being able when necessary to make use of its force to come ashore roughly where one has planned. To change the metaphor, 'To a Nightingale' and 'On a Grecian Urn' have in common a pattern suggesting mounting sexual excitement and its relief— the point being that at an early stage in these poems the poet ceases to choose where he is going. This is not true of 'To Psyche', for which, as I have already said, an architectural metaphor seems best.

> Yes, I will be thy priest, and build a fane
> In some untrodden region of my mind . . .

The poem itself is a Corinthian detail in the 'fane' promised to the goddess. Possibly such considerations were in Mr. Eliot's mind when he spoke of the ode: he may have felt, as I do, that Keats's artistry was more in evidence away from the emphatic somnambulisms of the Urn and the Nightingale. Responsible critics of Keats such as Mr. Middleton Murry and Sir Herbert

---

[1] See the conclusion to Arnold's essay on Keats in *Essays in Criticism*, 2nd series (1888).

Read might well dissent from this position and find the 'true voice of feeling' more distinctly in 'To a Nightingale' than in 'To Psyche'. Yet both these critics would probably agree that there is more detachment in the less familiar ode, and it gives the poem a peculiar interest. Of course why 'To Psyche' should 'hit so hard'[1] is left unexplained by these remarks, and to understand how our feelings have been engaged we need to go much further into it. I say 'our feelings' because many readers seem to rise from the poem in the perplexed frame of mind honestly expressed by Mr. Graham Hough in some sentences from his useful handbook, *The Romantic Poets* (1953).

> The *Ode to Psyche* seems . . . the most purely fanciful of the Odes. It would be easy to take it as a piece of lovely decorative mythology: but it is probably something more.[2]

Other readers must also have pondered the adequacy of Wordsworth's phrase for the invocation of Pan in *Endymion* ('A pretty piece of paganism') as a description of 'To Psyche', and felt with Mr. Hough that it would not quite do. When Mr. Hough tries to tell us what this 'something more' may be, he is less happy.

> . . . the last stanza . . . is not merely a piece of devotion to an obsolete myth; but a recognition by Keats that his own exploration is to be of the interior landscape, that his ultimate devotion is to be neither to the objective world, nor to any power outside himself.

I find the last stanza less confusing than this explanation of it, and I do not think its meaning can be stated so compendiously.

Before turning to my own analysis of 'To Psyche' I need to support the charge that the poem has suffered from being discussed in the course of scrutiny of the odes as a group of poems whose interest is assumed to lie in one or other of two directions —either in the individual quality of the poems commonly regarded as the most important, or in the unique nature of some group-character which the critic is bent on discovering. In such contexts even the consideration of metrical form can be slanted unfavourably. For instance, it is generally agreed that Keats intended the irregular stanzas of 'To Psyche', with their inserted

---

1 An expression borrowed from Robert Bridges.
2 pp. 172–3.

shorter lines, to produce loosely the effect of a 'Pindaric' ode, and it seems to me that this effect is obtained (the unrhyming lines are not much more noticeable than in 'Lycidas'). It is only if we become preoccupied with Keats's experiments with the sonnet-form in this ode—experiments which Messrs. Garrod and Ridley have shown to be connected with the evolution of the stanza used in the other odes (a ten-line stanza except in 'To Autumn,' which adds an eleventh line)—that we are likely to think that 'To Psyche' gives 'an uneasy impression of trying to be recurrent and failing'.[1] It does not in fact give such an impression unless we have stopped reading the poem as a poem and are looking at it instead as a stepping-stone to a later metrical perfection.

Most readers of 'To Psyche' will feel that they can safeguard their experience of the poem from a simple injustice of this sort, but a more insidious type of misunderstanding with a similar origin in the grouping of the odes can be illustrated from Dr. Garrod's account of the ode's last stanza. Keats has promised to serve Psyche as a priest and to dress a sanctuary for her in a corner of his mind. He concludes triumphantly and, I should have thought, unambiguously:

> And there shall be for thee all soft delight
> That shadowy thought can win,
> A bright torch, and a casement ope at night
> To let the warm Love in!

Psyche is in possession of the 'rosy sanctuary' and the torch is to direct her lover Cupid or Eros to her. The reference is, of course, to Cupid's visits by night in the legend as told by Apuleius (now that Psyche is deified and knows her lover for a god there is no further need for them to meet in darkness). The capital letter of 'Love' would seal this interpretation if there were any real doubt, and the human warmth of the quatrain may remind us that Keats was living next door to Fanny Brawne in April 1819 and probably kept an eye on her window when it was lit at night. Keats is vicariously gratifying a natural wish.

Dr. Garrod reads the quatrain very differently.

There shall be a 'bright torch' burning for her, and the casement shall be open to let her in at night. I do not find that any commentator has seized the significance of this symbolism. The open window and the

---

1 Ridley, *Keats's Craftsmanship* (1933), p. 205.

 *personification*

lighted torch—they are to admit and attract the timorous *moth-goddess*, who symbolizes melancholic love . . . Keats has in fact identified the Psyche who is the soul (love's soul) with the Psyche which means moth.

It is a strange goddess whom he has brought from her native unrealities into the reality of the imagination. But her identity is certain—we encounter her again, brought into darker shadow, in the *Ode on Melancholy*.[1]

I submit that this is a howler. Professor Finney and the late Ernest de Selincourt, however, describe it as a valuable comment, and more recently Mr. John Holloway in his essay on Keats's odes in *The Charted Mirror* (1960)[2] implicitly approves of it when he borrows from Garrod to say of 'To Psyche', 'The stress falls largely on the melancholic aspects of Psyche the Love-goddess (she is called "mournful Psyche" in *On Melancholy*).' To all this the temperate reply is:

1. Psyche is not a goddess in 'On Melancholy'

In its context the plea 'Nor let the beetle, nor the death-moth be/Your mournful Psyche' is simply Keatsian for 'Do not let your soul be so mournful that all the most gloomy things you can think of (beetles, death-moths, etc.) become fit images for your mood'. It is clear that Keats knew that Psyche could mean both soul and butterfly (or moth), but there is no sign at all that he was thinking of Psyche, the woman or goddess of the legend. 'Veil'd Melancholy' is the only goddess in the poem.

2. There is no melancholy in 'To Psyche'.

The nostalgia of the central section of the ode is a different emotion, and it is resolved comfortably in the last stanza with the indulged expectation of the re-enactment of Psyche's happiness. She is seen blissfully contented in the first stanza—neither timorous nor mournful. 'To Psyche' is a happy poem—in the sense of the expression, 'This is a happy ship', which does not mean that all personal problems have been solved for the crew.

What Dr. Garrod is at is a rapid sleight-of-mind by which he first deceives himself and then others; and he is disposed to this error by the assumption that links of thought and feeling between the odes must exist. There is certainly some truth in this assumption, but my example shows that it may be inexpedient to dwell on it.

1 *Keats* (1926), pp. 98–9.   2 pp. 40–52.

Mr. Holloway might have noticed Dr. Garrod's mistake if it had not helped him to grind an axe of his own. Speaking empirically, the danger of 'general theories' of the odes is that they encourage careless handling of the evidence, and, though Mr. Holloway tries to be scrupulous, he pushes some of his evidence too far. I digress—and I think it will not prove to be a pointless digression—to deal with his suggestive argument because it has not been controverted, because I had to come to terms with it in my own attempt to read 'To Psyche', and because I believe that it could be restated in an acceptable form.

Mr. Holloway holds that the odes collectively are 'a psychological document . . . of unique interest' because they 'prove to be a complex and detailed poetic revelation of what Keats knew himself as the creative mood', and he finds the main evidence for this view in certain repetitions of phrase which in his opinion establish a distinctive unity for the six poems (he includes 'On Indolence'). With the help of the *Letters* the creative mood of the odes is then revealed as a drowsy, luxurious indolence, a visionary ecstasy in which consciousness struggles with insight on the very edge of oblivion. I object in reply that the value of the odes as a 'psychological document' is questionable, that the poetic revelation of the nature of Keats's creative mood is not to be found in all the odes, or in any of them, perhaps, quite so clearly as Mr. Holloway argues, and that in the sense in which it is to be found in several of the odes (including 'To Psyche') it is also to be found in much else of Keats's poetry. Mr. Holloway claims both too much and too little. He claims too much in insisting that the odes provide unambiguous psychological evidence—the 'creative mood' is partly a literary fabrication by Keats—and, again, in his assertion that his own viewpoint makes for 'a more sensitive, balanced, comprehensive interpretation of each poem by itself'. Here I merely note that it does not help with 'To Autumn' at all and that Mr. Holloway nearly admits as much when he says that this poem 'may well have arisen from a quite independent poetic impulse'. He claims too little when he fails to see that in 'Sleep and Poetry', *Endymion*, 'Lamia', and 'The Fall of Hyperion', for example, it is possible to discover with varying degrees of directness the same expectant passiveness in which pain and pleasure are relaxed neighbours (there are sexual overtones where sexuality is not overt). Mr. Holloway has not looked far enough afield and he should have remembered an acute remark by Robert Graves: 'Keats's chief interest was the poet's relations with poetry, and the imagery he chose was predominantly sexual.'[1] The repetition of phrases from ode to ode is extremely interesting, but, if verbal correspondences are sought beyond the odes, a few hours with a text and a concordance should convince the most sceptical that the accumulated evidence does not suggest an isolated character for the odes: it shows, rather, how coherent and crammed with particulars—and, we must recognize, how inescapably literary—was Keats's poetic world throughout.

This brings me back to the 'psychological evidence' of the odes. I am surprised that Mr. Holloway should be so unsuspicious. Keats's extraordinary ability to assimilate to his own poetic needs whatever he picked up from his reading is a strong hint that the evidence may be doctored. For example, Mr. Holloway argues that

> Surely I dreamt to-day, or did I see
> The winged Psyche with awaken'd eyes?

exemplifies the 'suspension between sleeping and waking' described in 'On Indolence', and he might have quoted a further corroborative echo from 'To a Nightingale':

> Was it a vision, or a waking dream?
> Fled is that music:—Do I wake or sleep?

Now this may be a circumstantial clue to the nature of Keats's creativeness, but it hardly seems possible to take it at its face value if we are aware that as an opening the quoted lines would be conventional (i.e. without direct psychological significance) in an Elizabethan poem—see Spenser, *Amoretti*, LXXVII:

> Was it a dreame, or did I see it playne
> a goodly table of pure yvory . . .

—or, more importantly, that Hazlitt had said in his *Lectures on the English Poets* (1818), some of which Keats had attended (he had read and weighed them all):

Spenser was the poet of *our waking dreams*; and he has invented not only a language, but a music of his own for them . . . *lulling the senses into a deep oblivion* of the jarring noises of the world, from which we have no wish ever to be recalled.[2]

1 *The Common Asphodel* (1949), p. 245.
2 Lecture II. My italics here and in the Hazlitt quotations below.

This is not an isolated example of a literary debt. Hazlitt touches several times in different lectures on various characteristics of the creative mood that Mr. Holloway finds idiosyncratically projected in the odes. I allow space for a further illustration, which suggests a literary element in Keats's Pleasure–Pain equivalence. He wrote:

> My heart aches, and a drowsy numbness pains
>   My sense . . .
>
> 'Tis not through envy of thy happy lot
>   But being too happy in thine happiness . . .[1]

and again:

> She dwells with Beauty—Beauty that must die;
>   And Joy, whose hand is ever at his lips
> Bidding adieu; and aching Pleasure nigh . . . [2]

What he had heard Hazlitt say or had read in his printed lectures was this:

The poetical impression of any object is that *uneasy, exquisite sense of beauty* . . . that strives . . . to relieve *the aching sense of pleasure* by expressing it in the boldest manner . . . [3]

and, with reference to Milton, this (Keats would certainly pick up the echo of *Othello*):

He refines on his descriptions of beauty; *loading sweets on sweets, till the sense aches* at them.[4]

II

If we try to forget the other odes and look at 'To Psyche' freshly, two immediate impressions seem normal. The first is that the poem opens badly but warms up rapidly after a weak start; the second is that, while the poem is a happy one, its tone is more exactly described if the happiness is thought of as defensive or defiant.

Robert Bridges observed that 'the beginning of this ode is not so good', and it needs no special insight to see that Keats could have produced a more arresting opening by deleting his first

---

1 'To a Nightingale.'   2 'On Melancholy.'
3 Lecture I.   4 Lecture III.

quatrain with its tasteless echo of 'Lycidas' and the displeasing phrase 'soft-conched ear' (Elizabethan for the cliché 'shell-like ear'). Again, later in the first stanza, the repetition of 'grass' in lines 10 and 15 is clumsy, and the reader is nagged by the distracting survival of the rhymes for a further two lines after the sense has closed in:

A brooklet, scarce espied.

Some of these faults probably came from working over the poem too often and at first, perhaps, too coolly—the price that Keats paid for his 'peaceable and healthy spirit' may have been that his 'pains' fixed his first stanza against further correction while its elements were still imperfectly combined (the version of the ode in the Pierpont Morgan Library, apparently the earliest that we have, is certainly not a first draft). Here the practical result is that several layers of composition appear to be cobbled together, not inexpertly, but without the ruthlessness of exclusion of otherwise acceptable phrase or rhyme that would have been given by a firm sense of poetic direction. The weakness disappears after the first stanza, which seems to confirm that Keats discovered his real subject in the process of writing—the rise in poetic temperature at the beginning of the third stanza ('O brightest! though too late for antique vows') may announce his full awareness of this discovery. I differ from Bridges about the value of this central section of the ode. He considers that the poem climbs with a steady improvement towards its conclusion and that its middle is only 'midway in excellence'. I find the first half of the third stanza at least the equal in excellence of the final stanza so admired by Bridges, particularly if his comment is kept in mind that 'the imagery is worked up to outface the idea' in the ode's last section. The observation has, of course, a wider and more general application to Keats's poetry—it is simplest to ascribe the 'outfacing' to his infatuation with a luxurious Elizabethan diction (as Lady Chatterley remarked to her husband, whom circumstances compelled to prefer Art to Life, 'The Elizabethans are so upholstered'). Against the overloaded imagery of the fourth stanza and some weak phrasing earlier, it is fair to set the successful rhyming. 'To a Nightingale', for example, has a bad rhyme in stanza six and forced expressions for the sake of rhyming in the first and last stanzas.

The other immediate impression, that of the ode's defensive happiness, is not easy to pin down, but Keats seems to be rejoicing because of

> . . . having to construct something
> Upon which to rejoice.

There is a defiant assertion that unaided he can put the clock back, that the ode itself proves that his is 'a fond believing lyre' in spite of an age

> . . . so far retir'd
> From happy pieties . . .

Positively, one relates this conviction to the nearness of Fanny Brawne—Keats is in love and for lovers 'happy pieties' are still possible.

In any move to go beyond these immediate impressions it is natural to examine carefully the serial letter to George and Georgiana Keats (Letter 123) in which an unrevised version of 'To Psyche' is copied out. It cannot, surely, be an accident that this copy of the ode should closely follow Keats's reflections on the world as 'vale of Soul-making'. 'Do you not see', says Keats, 'how necessary a World of Pains and troubles is to school an Intelligence and make it a Soul?' We can hardly fail to link the intelligent 'Spark' struggling to become a soul as a result of a 'World of Pains and troubles' with the Psyche who achieves apotheosis and happiness after long wanderings and sufferings in search of Cupid. Keats had met the legend in Mrs. Tighe's fantasticated Spenserian version as early as 1817, and he mentions Psyche's woes and her reward in 'I stood tip-toe' (ll. 141–50), but the reference to Apuleius in Letter 123 (see below) implies that by 1819 he had looked at a translation of *The Golden Ass*. For Keats the obvious translation was William Adlington's Elizabethan one of 1566, and C. L. Finney has noted verbal parallels between it and the ode.[1] Whether Keats's reflections on soul-making came directly out of his experience of life, and then, remembering that Psyche was the soul, he decided to read Apuleius in Adlington's version, or whether it was a reading of Adlington's account of Psyche's expiatory wanderings that prompted the famous description of soul-making in his letter, cannot be settled and perhaps is

1 *The Evolution of Keats's Poetry* (1936), vol. ii, pp. 614–15.

not very important. What can be shown convincingly is that the following passage was in his mind when he was writing 'To Psyche':

Thus poore Psyches being left alone, weeping and trembling on the toppe of the rocke, was blowne by the gentle aire and of shrilling Zephyrus, and caried from the hill with a meek winde, which retained her garments up, and by little and little brought her downe into a deepe valley, where she was laid in *a bed of most sweet and fragrant flowers.*

Thus faire Psyches being sweetly couched among the soft and tender hearbs, as in a bed of sweet and fragrant floures, and having qualified the thoughts and troubles of her restlesse mind, was now well reposed. And when she had refreshed her selfe sufficiently with sleepe, she rose with a more quiet and pacified minde, and fortuned to *espy a pleasant wood invironed with great and mighty trees. Shee espied likewise a running river as cleare as crystall*: in the midst of the wood well nigh at the fall of the river was a princely Edifice, wrought and builded not by the art or hand of man.[1]

Professor Finney asks us to set the italicized phrases beside the picture of Cupid and Psyche in the first stanza of the ode (' . . . couched side by side/In deepest grass . . . where there ran/A brooklet, scarce espied:/ 'Mid hush'd, cool-rooted flowers, fragrant-eyed. . . . They lay calm-breathing on the bedded grass . . . '), but these verbal correspondences, though telling, are not more so than the way in which the landscape of Keats's fourth stanza reproduces the Apuleius–Adlington setting—in both descriptions a mountain wall and great trees shut off a flower-strewn valley containing a retreat or sanctuary. It also weighs a little with me that Adlington's ' . . . she rose with a more quiet and pacified minde . . . ' seems to be crookedly echoed in a passage, already quoted, from Letter 123 (' . . . to write other things in even a more peaceable and healthy spirit . . . ').

How did Keats first hear of Apuleius? There can be no certainty, but Lemprière's *Classical Dictionary* (1788) may have been his source. It is certain that Keats referred to the dictionary —the entry under 'Psyche' is drawn on in his explanation of the ode in Letter 123. In Lemprière we are told that Psyche is 'a nymph whom Cupid married and conveyed to a place of bliss. . . . The word signifies *the soul,* and this personification of Psyche, first mentioned by Apuleius, is consequently posterior to the Augustan age, though it is connected with antient

1 Finney's italics. Text from C. Whibley's reprint of the 1639 edition.

mythology . . .', and again, a little below this, that Cupid's divinity 'was universally acknowledged, and vows, prayers, and sacrifices were daily offered to him'. Keats repeats some of the information for his brother and sister-in-law:

> You must recollect that Psyche was not embodied as a goddess before the time of Apulieus (*sic*) the Platonist who lived after the A[u]gustan age, and consequently was never worshipped or sacrificed to with any of the ancient fervour—and perhaps never thought of in the old religion —I am more orthodox that [*for* than] to let a heathen Goddess be so neglected.[1]

The similarity of these two accounts is less interesting than the differences between them. It is Keats who calls Apuleius a Platonist, which may strengthen the connection between 'To Psyche' and the reflections on soul-making. It is Keats, again, who puts together the two facts of Psyche's late personification and of the daily worship of Cupid in earlier times in order to insist in his letter that the goddess 'was never worshipped or sacrificed to with any of the ancient fervour'. Apparently this was what struck him most forcibly in Lemprière, so that the dull phrases of the dictionary may be said to govern the form taken by the ode's second stanza with its catalogue of imagined rites and devotions. 'This personification . . . is consequently posterior to the Augustan age' is therefore the improbable germ of the apostrophe with which the second stanza opens:

> O latest born and loveliest vision far
> Of all Olympus' faded hierarchy! . . .

Psyche is the 'loveliest vision far', lovelier than the Moon or Venus, because she is a love-goddess with an understanding of troubled human experience, because she has known in her own person—as no true Olympian could ever know—suffering and seemingly hopeless longing. She is 'loveliest' because she is 'latest' (there is much in 'Hyperion' and 'The Fall of Hyperion' obviously relevant to this identification)—not an early and therefore simple personification of such forces of nature as the wind or the sea, but a late and more sophisticated personification of human nature subjected to an inevitable and cruel process of growing up and growing old. The impatient dismissal of perfectibility (' . . . the nature of the world will not admit of it . . . ')

1 *Letters*, p. 340.

with which Keats introduces his sermon on soul-making reveals the passion behind his perception that life is cruel and that to understand it is to be disenchanted. Man, he affirms, is 'destined to hardships and disquietude of some kind or other' (Tom had died of tuberculosis only four months earlier). It is this conviction, joined with his awareness of the existential pathos of the human soul (the tragic hero is any man, however fortunate), that makes the celebration of Psyche more than a piece of mythological embroidery; and in Psyche's final apotheosis there may be dimly expressed Keats's longing, which was now almost without hope, for some kind of personal immortality.

We need to be aware how closely ideas on the meaning and function of myth were bound up with Keats's attempt to make sense of the human situation. He tells George and Georgiana that his system of soul-making 'may have been the Parent of all the more palpable and personal Schemes of Redemption, among the Zoroastrians the Christians and the Hindoos' (Letter 123). That is to say, in these intimate speculations Psyche has for him much the same degree of reality and unreality as 'their Christ their Oromanes and their Vishnu'. Figures drawn from religious myths —and to Keats Christianity was simply the last of the great mythologies—may be understood sympathetically, he thinks, as personifications of certain kinds of human need or self-knowledge (people 'must have the palpable and named Mediator and Saviour'). This is Keats's personal extension of a mode of mythological explanation then a commonplace. It has been conveniently summarized by Hazlitt.

If we have once enjoyed the cool shade of a tree, and been lulled into a deep repose by the sound of a brook running at its foot, we are sure that whenever we can find a shady stream, we can enjoy the same pleasure again, so that when we imagine these objects, we can easily form a mystic personification of the friendly power that inhabits them, Dryad or Naiad, offering its cool fountain or its tempting shade. Hence the origin of the Grecian mythology.[1]

Keats first met these ideas powerfully in Book IV of Wordsworth's *The Excursion* (see, especially, ll. 847–87), a poem which in one mood he hailed as among the 'three things to rejoice at in this Age' (Letter 36). Though Wordsworth's influence on Keats's

1 *Lectures on the English Poets*, Lecture I.

thought has not been fully traced—Book IV of *The Excursion* is quarry for much more in the odes than is generally realized—it is, of course, accepted that Keats expounded Greek myths with a Wordsworthian accent in much of his early poetry, including *Endymion.*

Echoes of Milton's 'On the Morning of Christ's Nativity' have been noted in the second stanza of 'To Psyche'. De Selincourt, followed by Finney and others, cites the nineteenth stanza of the hymn:

> The Oracles are dumm,
> No voice or hideous humm
>   Runs through the arched roof in words deceiving.
> *Apollo* from his shrine
> Can no more divine,
>   With hollow shreik the steep of *Delphos* leaving
> No nightly trance, or breathed spell,
> Inspire's the pale-ey'd Priest from the prophetic cell . . .

and finds a parallel in the ode's

> No voice, no lute, no pipe, no incense sweet
>   From chain-swung censer teeming;
> No shrine, no grove, no oracle, no heat
>   Of pale-mouth'd prophet dreaming.

This, however, does not quite do justice to Keats's memory. Milton's influence is active earlier in stanza two and also extends more subtly to the first half of the ode's third stanza. Thus one line from the twenty-first stanza of the hymn—

> The *Lars*, and *Lemures* moan with midnight plaint . . .

—should be set beside Keats's

> Nor virgin-choir to make delicious moan
> Upon the midnight hours;

and Milton's two preceding lines—

> In consecrated Earth,
> And on the holy Hearth . . .

—lend the force of 'consecrated' and 'holy', as applied to the elements of earth and fire, to reinforce 'haunted' in his twentieth stanza:

> From haunted spring, and dale
> Edg'd with poplar pale,
> The parting Genius is with sighing sent . . .

—and so, I believe, help to inspire Keats's nostalgic

> When holy were the haunted forest boughs,
> Holy the air, the water, and the fire.

It is all much simpler than it sounds in the telling. Only three stanzas of Milton's hymn are involved and their splintering and telescoping in recollection suggest that Keats was not conscious of pastiche.

The chief Miltonic echoes have been recorded, but nobody has stopped to explain why Keats thought of Milton at this point in his poem. Clearly what happened was that 'faded' in line 25 started a train of thought—to which a strong feeling-tone of regret was compulsively attached—about the end of the old Greek world with its 'happy pieties' (thought and feeling become explicit in the poem some ten lines later at the beginning of the third stanza). By literary association ideas of the fading of belief in the Olympian gods and of a lost numinous nature recalled Milton's description of the departure of the heathen deities of the Mediterranean world at the birth of Christ. The difference in tone between the two poems could hardly be wider. Milton writes of the end of heathendom with an almost fierce satisfaction (though it is certainly possible to detect an undercurrent of tenderness for the 'parting Genius' and 'Nimphs in twilight shade' of the classical world). Keats's tone is throughout one of unmixed regret for 'the fond believing lyre', for primitive times with their supposed simplicity and wholeheartedness of feeling. 'To Psyche' is now becoming something more than the celebration of a neglected goddess—it projects a nostalgia for an imagined wholeness of being once possible:

> Le squelette était invisible
> Au temps heureux de l'art païen—

but now, it would seem, impossible (except at lucky moments for the poet and lover). The nostalgia has also a direct personal application. Keats's regret for the realm of Flora and old Pan is at the same time a regret for an earlier phase of his own mental growth before the disenchantment produced by reflection on a darkening experience of the world. A critic should move as delicately in these matters as if he were treading on eggshells, but this double reference is unmistakable. It would be an over-simplification to think of Keats's attitude as 'purely escapist'. By the spring of 1819 he was not trying to avoid thoughts of 'Whirl-pools and volcanoes'—he had worked his way through at least to a theoretical acceptance of the value of heartbreaking experience: what he found it hard to bear was that moments of joy and well-being should be poisoned by self-consciousness.

> The point at which Man may arrive is as far as the paral[l]el state in inanimate nature and no further—For instance suppose a rose to have sensation, it blooms on a beautiful morning it enjoys itself—but there comes a cold wind, a hot sun—it cannot escape it, it cannot destroy its annoyances—they are as native to the world as itself.[1]

Men ought not to be less happy than roses, Keats might have said; and he believed that those who had—in a phrase from *Endymion*—'culled Time's sweet first-fruits' had been able to live in the immediate present and were much to be envied. His own power to live in the present, which lay close to the sources of his poetry, depended for survival, as he knew, on his skill in pre-venting the withering of instinctive enjoyment by reflection.

If Keats thought that sun was exchanged for shadow at some necessary stage in the development both of the individual and of human society as a whole, what was it on the universal plane that corresponded in his view to the over-balance of the reflective power that he feared in himself? The answer is to be found in 'Lamia'—the dangerous respect given to science (natural philo-sophy) at the expense of the imagination.

> Do not all charms fly
> At the mere touch of cold philosophy? . . .
> Philosophy will clip an Angel's wings,
> Conquer all mysteries by rule and line,
> Empty the haunted air, and gnomed mine—
> Unweave a rainbow . . .[2]

It is known that this passage leans heavily on a paragraph in the first of Hazlitt's *Lectures on the English Poets*. The paragraph concludes:

1 *Letters*, p. 335.   2 Part II, ll. 229-30 and 234-47.

... the history of religious and poetical enthusiasms is much the same; and both have received a sensible shock from the progress of the experimental philosophy.

Keats was less simple-minded than Hazlitt, but he accepted this judgement in essence. I do not think he was ever interested in discovering when this historical change had taken place or begun to take place; and, in saying so, I do not forget in how many ways he was a child of the Enlightenment or how mutually antagonistic were some of the 'prose' feelings with which he saluted the March of Mind. But Keats could not doubt that the poetic experience was valuable, or fail to suppose that in forgetting Pan men had lost something which they would not find in the *Transactions* of the Royal Society (the 'Fall' had taken place somewhere between the days of 'the fond believing lyre' and the present). He felt that currents of thought, among the most reputable and influential of his age, were inimical to the kind of poetry that he was writing and perhaps to all poetry; and that he needed to develop his resistance to their influence, and to the influence of the reflective traitor within himself, if he was to remain wholehearted, i.e. keep his capacity for responding poetically to experience.

These ideas and feelings seem relevant to the fourth stanza of 'To Psyche'. Against the background that I have sketched the

> ... fane
> In some untrodden region of my mind

becomes the 'Great Good Place' where the experimental philosophy rumbles as harmlessly as distant thunder. Keats is constructing a mental landscape for wholehearted enjoyment, and it is fitting that the scenery should recall the natural setting of the Pan festival in *Endymion* and 'Time's sweet first-fruits' under the side of Latmos. The similarity of setting can be shown by quotation.

> Far, far around shall those dark-cluster'd trees
>   Fledge the wild-ridged mountains steep by steep;
> And there by zephyrs, streams, and birds, and bees,
>   The moss-lain Dryads shall be lull'd to sleep;
> And in the midst of this wide quietness
> A rosy sanctuary will I dress[1]

1 'To Psyche', stanza 4.

Upon the sides of Latmos was outspread
A mighty forest . . .
And it had gloomy shades, sequestered deep,
Where no man went . . .

. . . Paths there were many,
Winding through palmy fern, and rushes fenny,
And ivy banks; all leading pleasantly
To a wide lawn, whence one could only see
Stems thronging all around between the swell
Of turf and slanting branches: who could tell
The freshness of the space of heaven above,
Edg'd round with dark tree tops? . . .

Full in the middle of this pleasantness
There stood a marble altar, with a tress
Of flowers budded newly . . . [1]

In this 'green remote Cockagne', which mixes the scenery of
Latmos with the delectable valley in Apuleius, Keats will be able
to preserve the visionary poetic experience from marauding
analysis—the 'shadowy thought' expended for Psyche's delight is
the gardener's creative reverie, opposed antithetically to the
matter-of-fact operations of scientific logic. And Keats recognizes
that keeping one part of the self simple and direct in its receptive-
ness is a matter intimately linked with the experience of love—
the soul's sanctuary is rosy, Milton's 'celestial rosie red, love's
proper hue'. We may note here that both the meeting of Cupid
and Psyche in the first stanza and the description of the sanctuary
in the fourth stanza have diffuse echoes of Spenser's Garden of
Adonis (*Faerie Queene*, Book IV, canto vi) and of the nuptial bower
in Eden in *Paradise Lost*.

Since we have to do with a mental landscape, the introduction
of Fancy as the gardener is apt enough (though it jars many readers
at first). It follows easily as an idea from the Renaissance and neo-
classic doctrine that fancy has the power of 'retaining, altering
and compounding' the images supplied by the senses. The phrase
quoted is from No. 411 of *The Spectator*, and in another paper
Addison comes very close to thinking of fancy as a gardener
when he says that the poet 'has the modelling of nature in his

1 *Endymion*, Book I, ll. 63–4, 65–6, 79–86, 89–91.

own hands' (No. 418). The same doctrine of art's ability to improve on nature may be found earlier in Sidney, Bacon, and others; and Puttenham invents his own gardener:

... arte is not only an aide and a coadiutor to nature in all her actions, but an alterer of them, and in some sort a surmounter of her skill, so as by meanes of it her owne effects shall appeare more beautifull or straunge or miraculous ... the Gardiner by his arte will not onely make an herbe, or flowr, or fruite, come forth in his season without impediment, but will also embellish the same ... that nature of her selfe woulde never have done. ...[1]

Puttenham, Sidney, Bacon, and Addison express a stock idea—they are not, of course, in any sense sources of Keats's image, though I suspect that 'feign' in

> With all the gardener Fancy e'er could feign

may be a generalized Elizabethan echo. For example, Burton's discussion of Phantasy in *The Anatomy of Melancholy* mentions that it 'feigns infinite other unto himselfe' from the images furnished by daily experience. It is an amusing coincidence that Burton should choose 'Psyche's palace in Apuleius' as one example of fancy's power. I do not want to make too much of a last remark about 'the gardener Fancy', but I think it probable—since Fancy is the true creator of the mental landscape in this stanza—that Keats is glancing at the idea of God as the gardener who designed Eden. Indeed the association seems inevitable if we remember that Adam and Eve cull Time's first-fruits and that 'To Psyche' is about a kind of Fall.

If this attempt to understand 'To Psyche' is correct in outline, the poem moves through three stages. In the first stage (stanza 1, ll. 1–23) Keats sets out to praise Psyche as the neglected goddess whose sufferings and mistakes represent the inevitable conditions of human experience. She has achieved 'identity' and lasting happiness. Love is her companion. Keats uses the convention of a sudden vision or waking dream, which comes to him when he is wandering 'thoughtlessly', because he had learned to speak in one breath of 'the most thoughtless and happiest moments of our Lives' (Letter 183), because Spenser's mythological poetry seemed to him a kind of waking dream, and because he knew that

---

[1] *The Arte of English Poesie*, lib. III, ch. xxv.

poetic experience was to be wooed by opening the mind recep-
tively, not by concentrating its conscious powers. The vision
of Psyche and 'the winged boy' in their Eden-like retreat draws
some of its richness, as I have said, from descriptions of em-
bowered lovers in Spenser and Milton. The tone of this first
stanza is contented, even cool, except for the touch of feeling
conveyed by the repetition 'O happy, happy dove', which
measures the irksome distance between the actual world and the
happiness that Psyche has already won.

The second stage of the poem spreads itself over the second and
third stanzas (ll. 24–49). Keats passes easily from the neglect of
Psyche (born as a goddess too late for the fervours of primitive
worship) to the fading and wearing-out of belief in the Olympians,
and then to a nostalgic outpouring of feeling for the magnanimity
of life in an age when all nature was still 'holy' (full of the anthro-
pologist's *mana*), all enjoyment wholehearted, and every herds-
man or shepherd the poet of his own pleasure. The contrast is not
with the age of Apuleius, but with a present which is a twilight
for poetic and mythological modes of thought—the March of
Mind has upset the balance of our natures, making the simple
enjoyment of an experience in an 'eternal moment' an almost
heroic achievement. Keats's regret embraces his own loss of an
earlier innocence. After the first quatrain of the third stanza we
have his defiance of these tendencies and changes in the age and
in himself ('Yet even in these days . . . I see, and sing, by my
own eyes inspired'). At this point the repetition of the catalogue
of worship from the ode's second stanza is a way of suggesting
the poet's firmness or obstinacy. Psyche's worship will not be
skimped or abbreviated by him in an age of unbelief.

The third and final stage of the poem consists of the fourth
stanza (ll. 50–67). Here Keats gets his second wind. The movement introduced by the emphatic

Yes, I will be thy priest . . .

represents an accession of strength. The tread is more measured
than in anything that has gone before, but there is no loss of
smoothness or pace, and the whole stanza, consisting of a single
long but quite coherent sentence, develops its momentum quietly
at first, then confidently, and finally with exultation at its climax
in the last quatrain. The defiance of the third stanza gives way to

confidence as Keats comes to see how he can worship Psyche (the repetition of 'shall' and 'will' is extraordinarily positive). Briefly, he will do so by keeping 'some untrodden region' of his mind as a safe refuge where Psyche or the soul may unfold all her powers in a landscape and climate wholly benign and friendly. The stanza constructs the remoteness and peaceful seclusion of a valley:

> Far, far around shall those dark-cluster'd trees
> Fledge the wild-ridged mountains steep by steep;
> And there by zephyrs, streams, and birds, and bees,
> The moss-lain Dryads shall be lull'd to sleep.

The succession of pictorial details moves in and down from the dark mountains and forests to the humming warmth of the valley floor with its streams and pastoral drowsiness, and the description comes to a focus on Psyche's refuge or shrine:

> And in the midst of this wide quietness
> A rosy sanctuary will I dress . . .

A complex image, accumulated from these details, is being offered as the equivalent of a mental state, which may be negatively defined by what it excludes. Calculation, anxiety, and deliberate activity are shut out. The 'wide quietness' of the valley symbolizes a mood in which the soul will be able to breathe freely, and in which poetry, here defined as 'the wreath'd trellis of a working brain' may be coaxed to put forth its buds and bells and nameless stars. The soul is promised a rich indolence which will safeguard its natural gift for delight and restore to wholeness whatever the world beyond the mountains has broken down. In this luxurious sanctuary, a place made lovely and inviting with all the resources of a poetic imagination—and these resources are infinite, for Fancy

> . . . breeding flowers, will never breed the same . . .

—Psyche will be disposed to welcome the visits of love (whose 'soft delight' was still for Keats the soul's 'chief intensity'). Perhaps the final implications are that wholeheartedness can never be lost while Psyche is willing to welcome love in at her casement, and, less directly, that love, poetry, and indolence are the natural medicines of the soul against the living death it must expect from 'cold philosophy'.

6

A Note on 'To Autumn'

ARNOLD DAVENPORT

CRITICAL COMMENT ON 'To Autumn' has generally agreed that it is the most mature and satisfying of the odes; and it is pretty generally agreed that it is the most objective and impersonal of them. It is commonly regarded as an evocation of the sounds and sights of Autumn, expressive of placid fulfilment, and having no further suggestion. C. H. Herford's paragraph on the poem in the *Cambridge History* represents the general view:

> In *Autumn*, finally, written after an interval of some months, the sense that beauty, though not without some glorious compensation, perishes, which, in varying degrees, dominates these three odes, yields to a serene and joyous contemplation of beauty itself. The 'season of mellow fruitfulness' wakens no romantic vision, no romantic longing, like the nightingale's song; it satisfies all senses, but enthralls and intoxicates none; everything breathes contented fulfilment without satiety, and beauty, too, is fulfilled and complete. . . . Keats feels here no need either of prophecy or of retrospect. If, for a moment, he asks 'Where are the songs of Spring?' it is only to reply 'Think not of them, thou hast thy music too'. This is the secret of his strength, if, also, of his limitation—to be able to take the beauty of the present moment so completely into his heart that it seems an eternal possession.

This reading is obviously possible, or it would not be so widely accepted; and it is apparently supported by Keats's own reference to the poem in his letter to J. H. Reynolds of 21 September 1819:[1]

> How beautiful the season is now—How fine the air. A temperate sharpness about it. Really, without joking, chaste weather—Dian skies —I never lik'd stubble-fields so much as now—Aye better than the

---

1 *Letters*, p. 384.

chilly green of the Spring. Somehow a stubble-plain looks warm—in the same way that some pictures look warm—This struck me so much in my Sunday's walk that I composed upon it.

Yet there are details in the poem that suggest something that is hardly compatible with a simple mood of satisfied fulfilment. 'Where are the songs of Spring? Ay, where are they?'—that has an indisputable note in it of the sad longing for what was lovely and is gone; the 'wailful choir' of gnats that 'mourn', the light wind that 'lives and dies', the day which, though bloomed, is 'soft-dying', the sleeper 'drows'd with the fume of poppies'—these are touches that come closer to the world of the 'Ode to a Nightingale' than to happy fulfilment, and suggest that there is more in the poem than the naïve celebration of fruitfulness. The fact is also worth considering that we all know 'To Autumn' by heart, whereas the beautiful, exact, and sensitive descriptions of nature in, say, Clare, we have admired and enjoyed but not remembered. Possibly 'To Autumn' imprints itself on our verbal memories not only because it is a beautiful picture of a season but because it comes home to us in a more important way. It is in fact my purpose to suggest that readings of the Herford kind are seriously wrong and do not do justice to the poem. As I read it,

> Where are the songs of Spring? Ay, where are they?
> Think not of them, thou hast thy music too

is not a momentary intrusion but the point of the whole poem.

The central element in the concept of Autumn created by the poem is that the season is a boundary, a space between two opposite conditions, a moment of poise when one movement culminates and the succeeding movement has scarcely begun. Keats begins deftly touching in these opposites from the first line: 'mists' and 'mellow fruitfulness'; 'bosom-friend, conspiring'; 'load, bless'; and the desirable apples nevertheless 'bend' the old ('moss'd') trees that bear them. Then follow three lines that appear to me univalent evocations of simple ripeness and fruitfulness, but the ambivalent note recurs in 'set budding, later flowers', collocating beginnings and endings; and there is suggestion of fulness and of loss together in 'until they think warm days will never cease . . . o'er-brimm'd', while 'warm days, summer, clammy cells' echo the initial contrast of mists and mellowness.

97

The two ideas of pause and of opposites continue in the next stanza. The hook 'spares the next swath' for a moment. Since one does not *spare* anybody something pleasant but only something painful, it is inevitably suggested that while from one point of view the reaping of the grain may be a good, from another it is not—in fact it involves the destruction of the 'twined flowers'. The furrow is 'half-reap'd', the brook is a boundary over which a figure is seen in the poised act of stepping. But in this stanza the foreground is filled with Autumn seen as a woman in four postures of repose in harvest: sitting relaxed in a granary, sleeping in the midday break in the harvest field, keeping steady her head beneath her load of gleanings, and watching the final oozings of the cider press. It is inconceivable that Keats could in this year have had in his mind the images of harvest fields and a gleaner without also having in mind somewhat the image of Ruth whose sad heart among the alien corn provided one of his most memorable passages in the 'Ode to a Nightingale'. It is worth remembering, in connection with 'To Autumn', that Ruth lay down at Boaz' feet in the *threshing floor* where, after *winnowing*, he 'lay at the end of the heap of corn' (Ruth 3 : 2–7); that she 'sat beside the reapers' at the mealtime break (2 : 14); and that she 'gleaned in the field' and Boaz filled her veil with six measures of barley and 'laid it on her' (2 : 17, 3 : 15). Compare 'granary floor, winnowing wind, half-reap'd furrow, gleaner . . . laden head'. Ruth had left her own country and now lived in a foreign land; she had lost her husband and was now a widow, though in due course she was to become the wife of Boaz. The point of pause and the opposites are there in the biblical story, and offered to Keats's imagination associative links with the context in 'To Autumn'. But in the 'Ode to a Nightingale' Keats had established a strong association between Ruth and the 'hungry generations' that tread down the human individual who must die and give place to them. There, Ruth stands as an example of the transient individual, consoled in her grief by the unchanging song of the nightingale. The three quasi-Ruth figures in 'To Autumn' may well have had in Keats's imagination associations harmonizing with the reaping hook that both harvests and destroys, with the fruit that blesses but loads the vines, with the apples that ripen and flourish but bend the bearing tree, with the press that squeezes the last oozing drops from the apples themselves. The reader may not have the same spontaneous associations, but it seems likely that under the surface of the poem there has by this point developed not only the concept of Autumn as the place between the desirable and the undesirable, between warmth and chill, between summer and winter, but also as the pause between the generation that has been fruitful and the rising of the generation which is its fruit. And it seems likely that most readers have reached in some way to these concepts, for it feels imaginatively right that the third stanza of the poem should bring this bittersweet out into the open, with the songs of Spring lost and replaced by the music of Autumn.

The music of Autumn which ends the poem is a music of living and dying, of staying and departure, of summer–winter. The wailful choir of small gnats rises and falls as the gusts of the light wind live or die—a beautiful symbol of the generations that fall and rise and in Autumn yield place, the old to the young. (In the context of the ideas that I suggest the poem contains, the reading 'sallows'—willows, with their connotations of sorrow, loss, and bereavement—seems a more appropriate word than the 'shallows' which is printed by Garrod in his edition.) The 'full-grown lambs' is a phrase that has been objected to on the common-sense grounds that a full-grown lamb is not a lamb any longer, but is either a ewe or a ram. But it is a phrase that is fully justified on this reading of the poem: that which was a lamb in the Spring is now full grown and on the point of superseding the generation of its begetters. It bleats from 'hilly bourn' which is an ambiguous phrase. It might mean 'hilly brook' but it more likely means 'hilly boundary'. Shakespeare's use of the word in that sense rather than the Scottish tour of 1818 would, one guesses, be dominant on Keats, and besides, 'To Autumn' was composed at Winchester, where, as Keats remarks in a letter to John Taylor of 5 September 1819, 'there is on one side of the city a dry chalky down'. But whether 'bourn' means brook or boundary, it still connotes a place between two areas, and the full-grown lamb, poised between two phases of life, is appropriately situated. 'Hedge-crickets' are grasshoppers. Why then did Keats not say 'Grasshoppers sing'? Possibly, in part, because a hedge also is a boundary, but possibly, too, because he had already seen the grasshopper and the cricket as types of the music of summer and winter:

A voice will run
From hedge to hedge about the new mown mead;
That is the Grasshopper's . . .
When the frost
Has wrought a silence, from the stove there shrills
The Cricket's song . . .

By using the alternative name, hedge-cricket, Keats manages to suggest in one word both the singer of the past summer and the singer of the coming winter. The redbreast that whistles from the garden-croft is characteristically a winter bird and remains in England; the swallow is proverbially the bird of summer and leaves the country when summer is over: its departure is the signal for the beginning of winter.

This final image of the swallows is of special interest. We know that Keats translated the *Aeneid* while he was still a schoolboy; and in the sixth book there is the striking and memorable description of the souls of the dead on the banks of the river of the underworld. It is a crowd in which the generations come together, and Virgil mentions matrons and men, heroes, young boys and unwedded girls, and youth taken to the pyre before the eyes of their sorrowing parents; and of this crowd, some *pass on* over the *river* into a new state of existence and some must *remain* on the hither bank. The general links with the contents of 'To Autumn' are clear. But more interesting are the two similes Virgil uses to describe the throng. They are, first, 'as many as the leaves that fall *in the first cold of Autumn*' and, second, 'as many as the *birds that gather* (*glomerantur*) *when the cold year drives them across the sea*'.[1] Birds gathering for migration have links, in fact, with both the decay of autumn and with the dead generations of mankind. The wailful choir of gnats may also be linked with Virgil's account of the souls who must stay on the hither bank and for a hundred years 'wander' and 'float hovering' (*volitant*) about 'these shores' until they are permitted to return to the still and fenny waters (*stagna*) that they yearn for (*exoptata*).[2]

[1] The same passage contains a description of the ills that dwell in the porch of the underworld, and this has some parallels with stanza 3 of the 'Ode to a Nightingale'.

[2] It is worth noting, perhaps, that in the Homeric equivalent of the *Aeneid*, vi (*Odyssey*, end of Book x and Book xi) Chapman makes Circe direct Odysseus to seek a place where grow '*sallows* that their fruits soon lose' (noted by de Selincourt), and puts into the mouth of the ghost of Odysseus' mother the words: 'When the

A NOTE ON 'TO AUTUMN'

I have not so far asked whether there is, apart from the gleaning Ruth, any evidence outside the poem that such an interpretation as I suggest accords with Keats's imagination. There are indications that it does. The main point of the poem as I see it is, after all, the main subject of 'Hyperion' in which the glory of the new Gods shines out to eclipse the Titans, the loss of whose old grandeur is the price that must be paid for the new beauty. As for the details of the interpretation, one might refer to the letter to Reynolds describing the walk that prompted the composition of 'To Autumn', where Keats goes on immediately to say, 'I always somehow associate Chatterton with autumn'. If we turn up the early sonnet to find out what Chatterton meant to Keats we find Keats seeing in him, as in Autumn, a juxtaposition of opposites, a junction of endings and beginnings, and a youthful music silenced and replaced by another, different, music:

> How soon thy voice, majestic and elate
> Melted in dying numbers! Oh! how nigh
> Was night to thy fair morning. Thou didst die
> A half-blown flow'ret which cold blasts amate.
> But this is past: thou art among the stars
> Of highest Heaven: to the rolling spheres
> Thou sweetly singest . . .

Some details of 'To Autumn' may originate in Coleridge.[1] There are notable parallels to the final paragraph of 'Frost at Midnight':

> Therefore all *seasons* shall be sweet to thee,
> Whether the *summer* clothe the general earth
> With greenness, or the *redbreast* sit and *sing*
> Betwixt the tufts of snow on the bare branch

[1] We know that Keats wrote for a copy of *Sibylline Leaves* in Nov. 1817, and there are several echoes of Coleridge in his poetry. Thus, for instance, the relationship between Coleridge's 'Love' and 'La Belle Dame sans Merci' has been commented on; there is a possibly significant parallel between Coleridge's
> Each matin bell, the Baron saith
> Knells us back to a world of death
and Keats's
> Forlorn! the very word is like a bell
> To toll me back from thee to my sole self . . .
and 'The Frost performs its secret ministry . . . extreme silentness . . .' may lie behind Keats's 'When the frost Has wrought a silence . . .'.

Summer came/And Autumn all fruits ripen'd with his flame,/Where grape-charged vines made shadows most abound.'

Of *mossy apple-tree,* while the nigh *thatch*
Smokes in the *sun*-thaw; whether the *eave*-drops fall
Heard only in the trances of the blast,
Or if the secret ministry of frost
Shall hang them up in silent icicles,
Quietly shining to the quiet moon.

If Coleridge's poem were indeed stirring in Keats's memory, it would harmonize well with 'To Autumn', for 'Frost at Midnight' is about Coleridge the parent regretting his frustrated and lost youth but determined that his baby son should have a fuller and more natural life: out of the parent's spoiled life should come a new and better being.

I would argue, then, that Herford was wrong in saying that 'To Autumn', unlike 'To a Nightingale' and 'On a Grecian Urn', does not include the 'sense that beauty, though not without some glorious compensation, perishes'. On the contrary, central to the poem is the sense that a new good is purchased only at the price of the loss of a former good. Far from being an objective, self-sufficient evocation of the 'beauty of the present moment' it is, as Mr. J. M. Murry once suggested, a projection in image and symbol of the calm Shakespearian vision: 'Man must abide his going hence, even as his coming hither. Ripeness is all.' It is in 'To Autumn' rather than in the sonnet 'On sitting down to read King Lear once again' that Keats realizes 'The bitter-sweet of this Shakespearian fruit.'

7

The Meaning of 'Hyperion'

KENNETH MUIR

THE FACTS about the composition of 'Hyperion' are now fairly
well established. Keats began thinking of the subject soon after
the publication of *Endymion*. He prepared himself for his task by
the study of *Paradise Lost* and of Cary's translation of Dante,
which he took with him on his walking-tour in Scotland. He
returned from that tour, with an ominous sore throat, to watch
by the bedside of his dying brother, Tom; and though he had
intended to study for a longer time before beginning his poem,
he found himself obliged to 'write, and plunge into abstract
images to ease' himself of Tom's 'countenance, his voice and
feebleness'. He had told Woodhouse that he would write no
more; but this was a momentary mood, for he was 'at very
instant . . . cogitating on the characters of Saturn and Ops'. By
the time Tom died, on 1 December 1818, Keats had finished the
first two books of the poem. Freed from his responsibility to
Tom, he became attracted by Fanny Brawne; but it was under the
influence of Mrs. Isabella Jones that he wrote 'The Eve of St.
Agnes'. Just before, or just after, writing this poem, he abandoned
'Hyperion' in the middle of Book III.[1] After a period of indolence,
a fallow period, Keats spent the spring and early summer of 1819
in writing five of his odes. Then, during the composition of *Otho
the Great* and 'Lamia', he took up 'Hyperion' again, recasting it
as 'The Fall of Hyperion'. This he abandoned on 21 September;
and during the autumn, he seems to have been preparing the original 'Hyperion' for the press, revising it with the help of 'The Fall
of Hyperion'. Brown's statement that Keats devoted his autumn

[1] It is possible, as Murry argues, that the Mnemosyne scene was written in
Mar. 1819, immediately after the soul-making parable.

evenings to the writing of 'Hyperion' has been taken to mean that he had gone back on his resolution to abandon 'The Fall of Hyperion'. But this can hardly be since the lines quoted in the letter of 21 September are near the end of the poem; and what followed, even if it had not then been written, was an adaptation with the minimum of alteration of the corresponding lines of the first 'Hyperion'. The composition to which Brown refers must have been confined to a few verbal changes, in either of the two versions. Indeed, from a comparison of the manuscript with the 1820 text, it can be seen that some readings of 'The Fall of Hyperion' were incorporated in the earlier poem.

This account of the composition of the two versions would now be accepted, without much modification, by all critics; but on the interpretation of the poem, on the reasons why Keats finally abandoned it, and on the relative merits of the two versions something may still be said.

I

To understand the full meaning of the first 'Hyperion' it is expedient to read the second. In the summer of 1819 Keats was able to interpret the earlier poem with the help of what he had learned in the interval; and the second poem, precisely because it embodied this new knowledge, is both different from the first, and indispensable to its interpretation. Even during the actual composition of 'Hyperion' Keats was developing rapidly, and the original conception was altered and deepened as he wrote. It is probable that the poem was conceived, at least vaguely, before the completion of *Endymion*, and that Keats's original intention was merely to fill out the old myth with poetical ornament: he trusted that the theme would acquire significance as he wrote, as had happened with *Endymion* itself. But in the year that elapsed before he began the poem he had learnt to tell a story more effectively by writing 'Isabella'; he had studied and thought deeply; he had been reading Milton and Wordsworth, and from them and from Dante he had derived some valuable lessons. He had decided that ideas could be better expressed in poetry by embodying them in narrative form, than by using the more direct method of *The Excursion*—a poem he had regarded not long before as the poetic masterpiece of his time. He was determined to attempt the epic form, and for that purpose blank verse was the obvious choice of a medium. He knew that he could write better blank verse than Cary; and he hoped to excel that of *The Excursion*, with *Paradise Lost* as his nearest model.

As he brooded on his subject it began to acquire a contemporary significance. At the time when he began to write the first 'Hyperion', and again when he abandoned the second, Keats's mind turned to the subject of politics. 'As for Politics', he wrote in October 1818,

> They are in my opinion only sleepy because they will soon be too wide awake—Perhaps not—for the long and continued Peace of England itself has given us notions of personal safety which are likely to prevent the re-establishment of our national Honesty—There is of a truth nothing manly or sterling in any part of the Government. There are many Madmen in the Country, I have no doubt, who would like to be beheaded on Tower Hill merely for the sake of eclat, there are many Men like Hunt who from a principle of taste would like to see things go better . . . but there are none prepared to suffer in obscurity for their Country. . . . We have no Milton, no Algernon Sidney. . . . Notwithstanding the part which the Liberals take in the Cause of Napoleon I cannot but think he has done more harm to the life of Liberty than any one else could have done.

It is clear from this that Keats disliked the reactionary government of his day; that he realized that 'a principle of taste' was not a satisfactory foundation for political action—a lesson some have still to learn; and that he disagreed with English Bonapartists such as Hazlitt.

Eleven months later, in the very letter which announced the abandonment of 'Hyperion', Keats returned to the subject of politics:

> In every age there has been in England for some two or three centuries subjects of great popular interest on the carpet: so that however great the uproar one can scarcely prophesy any material change in the government, for as loud disturbances have agitated this country many times. All civilized countries become gradually more enlighten'd and there should be a continual change for the better.

He goes on to describe how the tyranny of the nobles was gradually destroyed, and how in every country the kings attempted to destroy all popular privileges:

The example of England, and the liberal writers of France and England sowed the seeds of opposition to this Tyranny—and it was swelling in the ground till it burst out in the French Revolution. That has had an unlucky termination. It put a stop to the rapid progress of free sentiments in England; and gave our Court hopes of turning back to the despotism of the 16(th) century. They have made a handle of this event in every way to undermine our freedom. They spread a horrid superstition against all innovation and improvement. The present struggle in England of the people is to destroy this superstition. What has rous'd them to do it is their distresses—Perhaps on this account the present distresses of this nation are a fortunate thing—tho so horrid in their experience. You will see I mean that the French Revolution put a temporary stop to this third change, the change for the better. Now it is in progress again and I think it an effectual one. This is no contest between whig and tory—but between right and wrong.

That is why Keats hoped before he died 'to put a Mite of help to the Liberal side of the Question'.

I am not suggesting that Keats's political views found direct expression in 'Hyperion', and still less that it is an allegory of the French Revolution. But it is not fanciful to suggest that the revolutionary climate of the time contributed to, if it did not suggest, the subject of the poem. It is, on one level, a poem on Progress. Keats's desire for an England in which the progress interrupted by the Tory reaction after the revolution in France would be resumed and accelerated is reflected in the poem. The great speech of Oceanus expresses Keats's belief in progress. The Titans

> cower beneath what, in comparison,
> Is untremendous might,

even as the tyrants of the world would cower before those who strove for freedom; and Saturn himself cries to Thea—

> Tell me, if thou seest
> A certain shape, or shadow, making way
> With wings or chariot fierce to repossess
> A heaven he lost erewhile; it must, it must
> Be of ripe progress.

But to discover the deeper meaning of the poem it is necessary to consider Keats's idea of progress, and the difference between the new gods and the old. It is here that Keats most obviously developed during the composition of the poem. Until he reached the end of the second book, he had intended to make Apollo merely more beautiful than Saturn and Hyperion. The speeches of Clymene and Oceanus make it clear that the law of progress envisaged by Keats was a development towards a greater perfection of beauty, in accordance with the eternal law—

That first in beauty should be first in might;

but when he wrote the third book his conception of beauty had deepened. Already, in the first two books, Keats was groping towards the conception of Apollo expressed in Book III. In Thea's face sorrow had made

Sorrow more beautiful than Beauty's self;

and the 'living death' in Apollo's music had made Clymene sick 'Of joy and grief at once'. We can trace the germs of this conception to passages in *Endymion,* and to letters written after the completion of that poem. Keats had declared that 'what the imagination seizes as Beauty must be truth', and that 'Sorrow is Wisdom'; and he had spoken of his 'mighty abstract Idea . . . of Beauty in all things'—in sorrow, as well as in joy. Beauty, wisdom, and sorrow he had accepted as correlatives.

Before he began the composition of 'Hyperion', Keats had been considering what he called 'Men of Achievement' and 'Men of Power'. Men of genius, he wrote,

are great as certain ethereal Chemicals operating on the Mass of neutral intellect—but they have not any individuality, any determined Character—I would call the top and head of those who have a proper self Men of Power.

A few weeks later, he declared that the quality which 'went to form a Man of Achievement, especially in Literature', was Negative Capability. He returned to the subject in October 1818, when he told Woodhouse that the poetical character

is not itself—it has no self—it is everything and nothing—It has no character—it enjoys light and shade; it lives in gusto, be it foul or fair, high or low, rich or poor, mean or elevated—It has as much delight in conceiving an Iago as an Imogen. What shocks the virtuous philosopher, delights the camelion Poet.

This idea of the poetical character was partly derived from some of Hazlitt's essays in *The Round Table*; and from Hazlitt, too, Keats took the term *identity*:

A poet is the most unpoetical of any thing in existence; because he has no identity—he is continually informing and filling some other Body—The Sun, the Moon, the Sea and Men and Women who are creatures of impulse are poetical and have about them an unchangeable attribute—the poet has none; no identity—he is certainly the most unpoetical of all God's creatures.

Keats was aware of the defects and dangers inherent in negative capability. He felt that the poet's personality was liable to be 'incoherent' and disintegrated:

It is a wretched thing to confess; but it is a very fact that not one word I ever utter can be taken for granted as an opinion out of my identical nature—how can it, when I have no nature?

Tom's identity pressed upon him so much that sometimes he was obliged to go out. He became the person contemplated, and suffered with him—just as he was able to identify himself with a sparrow pecking about the gravel, or even a billiard ball:

The identity of every one in the room begins to press upon me that I am in a very little time annihilated—Not only among Men; it would be the same in a Nursery of children.

In view of these quotations, it is noteworthy that Saturn and the other Gods of the old dispensation possess identities. Saturn speaks of his 'strong identity', his 'real self'; but Apollo has no identity. He possesses to a supreme degree the negative capability that Keats had laid down as the prime essential of a poet. In other words, the old gods are men of power, the new gods are men of achievement. The poem describes the victory of the men of achievement. That is its primary meaning; linked with it, and almost equally important, is the account of the price that must be paid for being a man of achievement.

It is sometimes said that Keats could not finish the poem because he had expended all his powers in describing the nobility and beauty of the old gods, so that he was unable, as the poem demanded, to make the new gods superior to them. The criticism is not valid because, unless Saturn had been made noble, Oceanus genuinely wise, and Hyperion beautiful, the poem would have lost half its tragic beauty. The old order is great and beautiful—otherwise its downfall would have lacked significance. The best of the past must be conquered by the new gods. In a similar way, Blake in his poem on the French Revolution did more than justice to his representatives of the *ancien régime*.

In the first two books of 'Hyperion' we are given to understand that Apollo is superior in beauty and wisdom to the old gods, but on his first appearance in Book III we find him overcome with sorrow. Oceanus had declared that the 'top of sovereignty' was

> To bear all naked truths,
> And to envisage circumstance, all calm.

But such a stoical submission to nature's law was not enough. Keats wished to show that sorrow could be creative; and it has even been said[1] that his whole poetic output can be regarded as an attempt to find a justification for suffering. Apollo, with no personal reasons for grief, takes upon himself the sorrows of mankind, and by so doing he is deified. He is superior to Oceanus in much the same way as Jesus, in Keats's opinion, was superior to Socrates; and he is superior to Hyperion in the same way that the poet is superior to the great heroes of which he writes. Although Keats may not at the time have been fully conscious of the identification, there is no doubt that his account of the deification of Apollo by disinterested suffering is a symbolic presentation of the 'dreamer' becoming a great poet. But the reference is wider. Keats, in his famous parable, wrote of the world, not as a vale of tears, but as a vale of soul-making; so that the deification of Apollo is symbolic of the birth of a soul in all who are thus reborn. The vale of god-making in 'Hyperion' is the same as the vale of soul-making; and since, as Blake put it, 'The Poetic Genius is the true man', Keats, in describing his own conversion from dreamer to poet, was writing of the birth of the soul in all men. Apollo, though ostensibly a god, has to be deified because he represents both the poet and man:

> Knowledge enormous makes a God of me.
> Names, deeds, grey legends, dire events, rebellions,
> Majesties, sovran voices, agonies,
> Creations and destroyings, all at once

1 Stephen Spender, *Forward from Liberalism*, p. 31.

> Pour into the wide hollows of my brain
> And deify me, as if some blythe wine
> Or bright elixir peerless I had drunk
> And so become immortal.

This new knowledge Apollo learns from the silent face of Mnemosyne, who is the personification of the vision and understanding of human history, and a mirror of the inescapable suffering inherent in historical change and in the human condition itself.

This description of 'dying into life' is the conclusion of the poem. When Keats had written so far he handed the manuscript to Woodhouse, realizing that he had reached the limit of his experience. He may have intended, as de Selincourt thought, to write another book and a half, in order to describe the submission of the old gods to the new; but any such ending would have been merely formal, since the old and new had already been contrasted.

Even *Endymion* had been something more than a mythological narrative: Keats had used it to express a personal dilemma. 'Hyperion', in which he had once again 'touched the beautiful mythology of Greece', is only superficially about the ancient gods: its real subject, as we have seen, is human progress; and the new race of men imagined by the poet were not stronger or cleverer than their predecessors, but more sensitive and vulnerable—not characters, but personalities.[1]

The weaknesses of the poem, apart from its too Miltonic style, are that Keats's narrative power is only intermittently displayed; the rhythmical impetus frequently exhausts itself at the end of a paragraph; and the fable itself is not perfectly adapted to the meaning Keats tried to impose on it. It was in an attempt to remedy these faults that he began to recast the poem in the summer of 1819.

II

Between the two versions of 'Hyperion' several months elapsed; and we can trace Keats's development during this time, not

---

[1] Keats seems also to imply by deification through creative suffering that supernatural religion would be superseded by the natural religion of a love of one's fellow-men; but he did not share Hunt's rather shallow Abou-Ben-Adhemism.

merely in the narrative poems, sonnets, and odes, but also in his letters, particularly in the long journal-letter to George and Georgiana, begun in February and finished in May. He is led from the news of the approaching death of Haslam's father to a consideration of disinterestedness. He points out that 'very few men have ever arrived at a complete disinterestedness of Mind'; but that though we are involved, with the animals, in a struggle for survival, 'we have all one human heart', and can rise to deeds of heroism and self-sacrifice. A few weeks later, Keats, who had been reading Robertson's *America* and Voltaire's *Siècle de Louis XIV*, discusses the lamentable plight of the common people in a civilized as well as in an uncivilized society:

Man is originally a 'poor forked creature' subject to the same mischances as the beasts of the forest, destined to hardships and disquietude of some kind or other. If he improves by degrees his bodily accommodations and comforts—at each stage, at each ascent there are waiting for him a fresh set of annoyances—he is mortal and there is still a heaven with its stars above his head.

Even if Godwinian perfectibility were possible—and Keats regards it as a Utopian illusion—man would still die; and the more unalloyed his worldly happiness, the bitterer death would be. This leads Keats to his parable of the world as a vale of soul-making, which is in a sense an interpretation, or a forerunner, of the third book of 'Hyperion'. A world of pains and troubles is necessary 'to school an intelligence and make it a Soul'. Here Keats was trying to find a purpose in human suffering, and setting up as an ideal the disinterested and sympathetic sharing of the sorrows of others. The climax of his poem, he realized, was not merely the deification of Apollo, but, compressed into a single experience, his own acceptance of human suffering. One other passage in the same letter is significant for our present purpose:

Though a quarrel in the Streets is a thing to be hated, the energies displayed in it are fine. . . . By a superior being our reasonings may take the same tone—though erroneous they may be fine—This is the very thing in which consists poetry; and if so it is not so fine a thing as philosophy.

On the surface Keats is saying that philosophy is finer than poetry; but he probably meant merely that poetry, to be great, must be an image of truth. It is a reaffirmation at a deeper level of his former intuition that what the imagination seizes for beauty must be truth; and it looks forward to the 'Ode on a Grecian Urn'.

The significance of these passages in the journal-letter is that Keats, by accepting suffering, had transcended it. The 'dark passages' of which he had written in May 1818 he had now been exploring. He was able to face the 'eternal fierce destruction' from which he had recoiled in March 1818. Now in the odes he wrote before turning again to 'Hyperion' after contrasting the immortality and joy of poetry with the miseries of this mortal life (in the 'Ode to a Nightingale'), he accepted the inseparability of joy and sorrow (in the 'Ode on Melancholy'), and concluded not by escaping from life into art, but by contemplating life as though it were a work of art (in the 'Ode on a Grecian Urn'), and finding that there too the disagreeables evaporate:

> Rein ist im heiteren Geist,
> was an uns selber geschieht.

III

'The Fall of Hyperion' is cast in the form of a dream or vision, and J. L. Lowes has demonstrated the pervasive influence of Dante's *Purgatorio*.[1] It is very much a purgatorial poem, and the steps symbolize, as they do in Dante, the striving of the Dreamer towards the truth. We may agree, too, with Bridges who remarked that Keats had now 'added to his style a mastery of Dante's especial grace'.

The first 280 lines of the poem are new; the remainder is a recast of the earlier version. In the 'induction' Keats distinguishes between the fanatics, who 'weave a paradise for a sect', and the poets who alone are able to tell their dreams by means of 'the fine spell of words'. There is an implied contrast between the true poet, who reveals the meaning of life, and those who propagate a false view of life, just as in Coleridge's 'Allegoric Vision', to which Keats was also indebted,[2] superstition is contrasted with religion.

The landscape described in the next section of the poem (ll. 12–60) corresponds closely both to Keats's first period of poetry

1 J. L. Lowes, *T.L.S.* (11 Jan. 1936) and *P.M.L.A.* (1936), pp. 1098 ff.
2 J. L. N. O'Loughlin, *T.L.S.* (6 Dec. 1934).

that culminated in 'Sleep and Poetry', and also to the Chamber of Maiden Thought. The draught with which the Dreamer pledges the living and the renowned dead symbolizes poetry—the poetry Keats has used in order to escape from 'the weariness, the fever, and the fret' and from the consciousness that 'the world is full of misery and heartbreak, pain, sickness and oppression'. The wine is both the 'dull opiate' and the 'draught of vintage' of the 'Ode to a Nightingale'; and the Dreamer 'started up As if with wings' just as Keats in the ode had been borne on the 'viewless wings of poesy'. The Dreamer finds himself in an old sanctuary, the Temple of Saturn, which has been interpreted as 'the temple of knowledge' and as 'the temple of life becomes conscious of itself in man'. Whatever it represents, there is a certain ambiguity in Moneta's position, for she had been the priestess of Saturn and also the foster-parent of Apollo. Apparently Keats intended her to be the priestess of Truth, who had outlived the various manifestations of truth in different ages of the world. She tells the Dreamer that he has felt 'what 'tis to die and live again before' his fated hour; and she explains that he has been 'favoured for unworthiness' because he is one of

> those to whom the miseries of the world
> Are misery, and will not let them rest.

She tells him, nevertheless, that he is less worthy than those

> Who love their fellows even to the death,
> Who feel the giant agony of the world,
> And more, like slaves to poor humanity,
> Labour for mortal good.

Keats is careful not to claim for himself, what could only be known after his death, that he is a poet rather than a dreamer. The lines that follow (187–210) were apparently meant to be deleted, and in the Houghton transcript they are omitted. De Selincourt, however, claims that they are necessary to complete the argument about the difference between the poet and the dreamer: without these lines Moneta would appear to condemn all poets. Keats wrote the passage in order to make the distinction; but he may have felt it was untrue to his real conviction to class himself categorically with the dreamers, and also that the attack on Byron was irrelevant and uncontrolled. He therefore repeated the words 'Majestic shadow, tell me', rewrote the lines describing how Moneta's breath moved the linen folds about a golden censer, and continued with the poem—meaning, perhaps, to rewrite the dialogue on the poet and the dreamer, or else to salvage some of its lines for a later part of the poem. Murry argues forcibly that the lines should be deleted; and in view of the repetitions they should at least be relegated to a footnote.

The unveiling of Moneta is a repetition of the scene in the first 'Hyperion' in which Apollo gazes into the eyes of Mnemosyne; and this fact is the strongest argument for the indentification of Keats and Apollo, and for Murry's assumption that the deification of Apollo represents the transformation of a romantic dreamer into a great poet:

> Then saw I a wan face,
> Not pin'd by human sorrows, but bright blanch'd
> By an immortal sickness which kills not;
> It works a constant change, which happy death
> Can put no end to; deathwards progressing
> To no death was that visage; it had pass'd
> The lilly and the snow; and beyond these
> I must not think now, though I saw that face—
> But for her eyes I should have fled away.
> They held me back, with a benignant light,
> Soft mitigated by divinest lids
> Half closed, and visionless entire they seem'd
> Of all external things—they saw me not,
> But in blank splendor beam'd, like the mild moon,
> Who comforts those she sees not, who knows not
> What eyes are upward cast.

There is nothing Miltonic about these lines. In them, and in many others in the first canto of 'The Fall of Hyperion' Keats is writing in a style peculiarly his own. This blank verse—and the maturity it expresses—was perhaps Keats's greatest achievement as a poet.

H. W. Garrod has argued that allegory is the natural refuge 'of timid minds brought up against facts, and too conscientious to ignore them altogether';[1] and that Keats printed the first 'Hyperion' rather than the second, to 'save his work of allegory'. But it should be sufficiently clear that it was from no 'shyness of the

1 *Keats*, p. 68.

actual' that Keats wrote in an allegorical form. The second
'Hyperion' is more allegorical than the first, and yet it is obviously
more courageous and more direct in the way it faces life. What
Keats had to say could not have been more directly expressed
than in the vision of Moneta. It is even arguable that the expression is too direct for the highest poetry. Spenser constructed
a complicated system of belief, which he converted into allegory;
Keats, on the other hand, expressed his own experience as directly
as possible. 'The Fall of Hyperion' is an attempt to express an
intuition about the ultimate nature of reality in the only way
possible, the parabolic.

The contrast between the poet and the dreamer, which is the
real theme of the poem, is a final expression of a conflict which
had agitated Keats as early as 'Sleep and Poetry'. 'The strife and
agonies of human hearts', of which he speaks in that poem, may
indeed refer to his ambition to write tragedies; but this ambition
was closely connected with his desire to write poetry which
would not be merely the opium of the middle classes or the expression of personal emotions. In *Endymion* the same conflict is
symbolized by the hero's love for Diana and the Indian Maiden:
and it is there resolved by the conviction that a poet will best
help humanity by his poetry. But from his letters in the autumn
of 1818 and the spring of 1819, we know how cruelly the miseries
of humanity pressed in upon Keats. By the time he conceived
Moneta he had come to think not only that the very condition of
writing great poetry is that the poet should feel the miseries of
the world as his own, but that ordinary good men and women
are more valuable than 'romantic' poets.

We need not agree with Keats's condemnation of his own
earlier poetry, though his judgement should warn us against the
temptation to read too much into it. Yet it may be admitted that
if the odes remain great in spite of Keats's criticism, they are,
compared with what he was ambitious to write, comparatively
minor poetry.

IV

The second half of the poem is adapted from the first 'Hyperion':
and in the opinion of most critics, Murry and Ridley being
honourable exceptions, Keats has done little but maim the

original. To discover whether in fact his powers were already beginning to show a decline, it will be necessary to examine several passages in some detail. In 'Hyperion', Thea is thus described:

> She was a Goddess of the infant world;
> By her in stature the tall Amazon
> Had stood a Pigmy's height: she would have ta'en
> Achilles by the hair and bent his neck,
> Or with a finger eas'd Ixion's toil.
> Her face was large as that of Memphian Sphinx
> Pedestal'd haply in a Palace court
> When Sages look'd to Egypt for their lore.
> But oh! how unlike Marble was that face:
> How beautiful, if sorrow had not made
> Sorrow more beautiful than beauty's self.

In 'The Fall of Hyperion' the corresponding lines are:

> 'That divinity
> Whom thou saw'st step from yon forlornest wood,
> And with slow pace approach our fallen King,
> Is Thea, softest-natur'd of our Brood.'
> I mark'd the goddess in fair statuary
> Surpassing wan Moneta, by the head,
> And in her sorrow nearer woman's tears.

The Amazon, the pigmy, Achilles, and Ixion, even the Memphian Sphinx and the last two lovely lines, all are gone. The reasons are apparent. The Amazon–pigmy comparison was a deliberate echo of Milton, and the whole passage has too obviously a Miltonic ring. The passage disturbs the balance of the poem, for the reader's interest should here be concentrated on Saturn. The essence of the last two lines had already been used to describe Moneta, and it was impossible to leave them in without repetition.

The next passage is an interesting example of the way Keats endeavoured to eliminate his exclamations. In 'Hyperion' it reads:

> O aching time! O Moments big as years,
> Each as ye pass swell out the monstrous truth
> And press it so upon our weary griefs
> That unbelief has not a space to breathe.
> Saturn sleep on: O thoughtless, why did I . . .

The rhythm of these lines is slightly monotonous, and Keats was right to condense them into the three lines of the later version:

> With such remorseless speed still come new woes
> That unbelief has not a space to breathe.
> Saturn, sleep on:—Me thoughtless, why should I . . .

The new line, with its Shakespearian echo, effectively conveys
the essence of the previous passage, though, as Bridges observed,
'Me thoughtless' is more Miltonic than the expression it replaces.

The famous simile of the trees, as Ridley has shown, is
improved rather than weakened in the later version—

> As when upon a tranced summer night
> Those green rob'd Senators of mighty woods
> Tall Oaks, branch-charmed by the earnest Stars,
> Dream and so dream all night without a stir
> Save from one sudden solitary gust
> Which comes upon the silence and dies off
> As if the ebbing Air had but one wave:
> So came these words and went . . .

The second of these lines, beautiful as it is, has to go, because it
distracts attention from the purpose of the simile, which is to
describe the *sound* of Thea's words. The oaks are changed to
forests, so that we hear them, rather than see them. *Stir* is likewise changed to *noise*, a word which reproduces the sound of the
wind and concentrates our attention on that, rather than on the
movement of the trees. The regular rhythm of the sixth of these
lines is changed into one which suggests what it describes—

> Swelling upon the silence; dying off.

The changes in this passage alone would serve to show that Keats's
power as a poet had suffered no decline, or at least that he was
still able to improve on his earlier work.

The lines describing Saturn and Thea—

> And still these two were postur'd Motionless
> Like natural Sculpture in cathedral cavern

—were altered to what Ridley calls 'a rather awkward conceit'—

> Long, long, those two were postured motionless,
> Like sculpture builded up upon the grave
> Of their own power.

Exception has been taken to 'up upon';[1] but in other respects the

---

1 If the line is read with a caesura after *up* the juxtaposition need not offend.

new version is an improvement. It is superior to the first from
the point of view of euphony; and the image is more relevant than
that of the cathedral cavern to the theme of the poem. It springs
from and illuminates the subject—it is not a decorative addition.
To find a parallel to it one would have to go to one of
Shakespeare's best images—

> Yet thou doest looke
> Like patience, gazing on Kings graues, and smiling
> Extremitie out of act.

As a last comparison, we may take the two versions of Saturn's
speech—

> O tender spouse of gold Hyperion
> Thea I feel thee ere I see thy face—
> Look up and let me see our doom in it.
> Look up and tell me if this feeble shape
> Is Saturn's, tell me if thou hear'st the voice
> Of Saturn, tell me if this wrinkling brow
> Naked and bare of its great Diadem,
> Peers like the front of Saturn! What dost think?
> Am I that same—O chaos who had power
> To make me desolate? Whence came the Strength
> How was it nurtur'd to such bursting forth
> While fate seem'd strangled in my nervous grasp?
> But it is so; and I am smothered up
> And buried from all godlike exercise
> Of influence benign on Planets pale,
> Of admonitions to the Winds and Seas,
> Of peaceful sway above Man's harvesting,
> And all those arts[1] which Deity supreme
> Doth ease its heart of Love in—I am gone
> Away from my own Bosom—I have left
> My strong Identity—my real self
> Somewhere between the Throne, and where I sit
> Here on this bit of earth—Search Thea search!
> Open thine eyes eterne, and sphere them round
> Upon all space: space starr'd and lorn of light,
> Space region'd with life air; and barren void—
> Spaces of fire, and all the yawn of Hell—
> Search Thea search! and tell me if thou seest
> A certain Shape or Shadow making way

1 Keats probably intended to write *acts*, which is the reading of the 1820 volume.

With wings or chariot fierce to repossess
A heaven he lost erewhile—it must, it must
Be of ripe progress—Saturn must be King—
Yes, there must be a golden Victory;
There must be gods thrown down, and trumpets blown
Of Triumph calm; and hymns of festival
Upon the gold clouds metropolitan—
Voices of soft proclaim and silver stir
Of strings in hollow shells; and there shall be
Beautiful things made new, for the surprise
Of the Sky-children—I will give command—
Thea! Thea! Thea! where is Saturn?

'Moan, brethren, moan; for we are swallow'd up
And buried from all godlike exercise
Of influence benign on planets pale,
And peaceful sway above man's harvesting,
And all those acts which Deity supreme
Doth ease its heart of love in. Moan and wail.
Moan, brethren, moan; for lo! the rebel spheres
Spin round, the stars their antient courses keep,
Clouds still with shadowy moisture haunt the earth,
Still suck their fill of light from Sun & Moon,
Still buds the tree, and still the sea-shores murmur.
There is no death in all the universe
No smell of Death—there shall be death—Moan, Moan;
Moan, Cybele, moan, for thy pernicious babes
Have chang'd a God into a shaking Palsy.
Moan, brethren, moan; for I have no strength left,
Weak as the reed—weak—feeble as my voice—
O, O, the pain, the pain of feebleness.
Moan, Moan, for still I thaw—or give me help:
Throw down those Imps and give me victory.
Let me hear other groans, and trumpets blown
Of triumph calm, and hymns of festival
From the gold peaks of Heaven's high piled clouds;
Voices of soft proclaim, and silver stir
Of strings in hollow shells; and let there be
Beautiful things made new for the surprize
Of the sky children'—So he feebly ceas'd,
With such a poor and sickly sounding pause,
Methought I heard some old Man of the earth
Bewailing earthly loss.

The radical changes in Saturn's speech have been variously lamented. The orthodox opinion would seem to be that 'as poetry the second version is hardly comparable with the first'. Yet it is not difficult to see the reason for all the alterations. The speech is no longer addressed to Thea, because all her sympathy can avail him nothing. His power is gone; and most of the changes were made to enable the speech to reflect his fallen state. The oft repeated moans exhibit his impotence. The reference to progress has to be cut since it is the new gods alone who stand for progress. Saturn is no longer obeyed, so the final resolution, 'I will give command', is omitted. Keats in the first version had described Saturn as speaking with a palsied tongue; these words are now inserted in the text of the speech, and its tone is altered to suit the description. Saturn is humanized, because in the plan of the poem his sorrows are a reflection of the sorrows of humanity. He now seems like

> some old Man of the earth,
> Bewailing earthly loss.

The hope that animated the first version is expunged, since those who retain hope have not plumbed the depths of despair. In the first version, both of this speech and of the next, Saturn still hopes to be able to create:

> Cannot I form? Cannot I fashion forth
> Another World, another Universe,
> To overbear and crumble this to naught?

In the second version, by a stroke that is both psychologically and poetically truer, Saturn can only think of destruction: since he cannot create, he will destroy—

> There is no death in all the universe,
> No smell of death—there shall be death.

So the passage relating to the stars is changed from a description of the heavens, where Thea is to watch for the approach of Hyperion, to a dramatic use of the same properties: the fact that the stars no longer obey Saturn leads directly to his desire for destruction. Other changes in the speech are more obviously improvements. Keats wisely eliminated the ugly phrase and jingle—

> Where I sit
> Here on this bit of earth

and he changed a Miltonic to a Keatsian phrase;

> Upon the gold clouds metropolitan

becoming—

> From the gold peaks of Heaven's high piled clouds.

Keats's motives for altering the speech are therefore clear. If the two versions are considered in isolation divorced from their contexts, the first may well seem to be poetically superior; but its Miltonic grandeur is obtained at the expense of characterization and dramatic appropriateness. The statement that the revision is a product of Keats's failing powers cannot be substantiated.

Nevertheless Keats was right to print the first version. It was more likely to be acceptable to the public taste; it was more complete than the revision; it was more polished; and it was less vulnerable to the sneers of the reviewers, to whom the soul-searching of the second version would have been an easy target.

The decision to abandon the second 'Hyperion' was taken on 21 September. The reason given by Keats is that there were too many Miltonic inversions in it:

The Paradise Lost though so fine in itself is a corruption of our Language—it should be kept as it is unique—a curiosity—a beautiful and grand Curiosity. The most remarkable Production of the world. A northern dialect accommodating itself to greek and latin inversions and intonations. . . . I have but lately stood on my guard against Milton. Life to him would be death to me.

On the same day, he was telling Reynolds—

I have given up Hyperion—there are too many Miltonic inversions in it—Miltonic verse cannot be written but in an artful or rather artist's humour. I wish to give myself to other sensations. English ought to be kept up.

He goes on to ask Reynolds to mark in the manuscript lines which illustrate 'the false beauty proceeding from art' and others which display 'the true voice of feeling'. As Reynolds did not have the manuscript of 'The Fall of Hyperion', we must suppose that Keats was referring to a copy of the first version. This would seem to imply that he had abandoned both poems. He had realized that he could never finish 'The Fall of Hyperion', for a reason obvious enough but never mentioned by him: he had already used up the climax of the first poem in the first canto of the second version. Apart from this, he had found that he could not entirely eliminate the Miltonic influence from it. Driven back to the first version, he found that the new verse he had achieved in the other made him profoundly dissatisfied with the artificiality of the verse of the first. Murry, indeed, has argued that the rejection of Miltonic verse symbolized also the rejection of an attitude to life; and it is true that the financial difficulties of his brother had made Keats decide to come to terms with the public. Yet the fact that he had been writing *Otho the Great* during the summer with a reasonable hope of its being performed, means that we should not over-emphasize the mood of withdrawal. His primary reason for getting away from London—and from Fanny—was so that he could write without distraction. It is significant that he wrote nothing of importance in the five months that remained to him before his first haemorrhage.

The conflict apparent in 'The Fall of Hyperion' was not re-solved: but it was allayed by being faced. If Keats had not been compelled to abandon the poem, there would still have been only an arbitrary solution to its central problem. This could be solved only in action, by an integration of theory and practice—in other words, by writing the kind of poetry of which Moneta would have approved. 'To Autumn', written immediately afterwards, shows that Keats had attained, if only for a few days, to a mood of grave serenity. He was at last able to reconcile beauty and truth in a vision in which imaginative understanding reveals reality as a whole of significance and value, satisfying both to the man and to the poet. In the meeting with Moneta imagination and reality have been reconciled; and the way to reconciliation had lain through the vale of soul-making. 'To Autumn' represented the first fruits, and the last fruits, of Keats's new understanding.

Some critics have regretted that Keats was not contented to be a 'romantic' poet, the Dreamer of 'The Fall of Hyperion'. Garrod's witty but misleading book was written to show that Keats's best work was written only when he escaped from philosophy, politics, action, and character, into 'the world of pure imaginative forms'. A more subtle variation of this error is to be found in de

Selincourt's view[1] that Keats escaped from life into nature:

> The supreme truth to the poet is not to be found in the lessons of
> nature, but in her mysterious beauty, and in her never failing power,
> whencesoever it may spring, to respond to every mood of the changing
> heart of man. . . . Here lies the mystery: here, too, in a world of barren
> facts, of arid controversies, of idle speculations, the irresistible appeal.

That Keats sometimes sought relief from the fever and fret of
existence in the beauty of nature is not to be denied; but in his
greatest poetry the moon beams in blank splendour, and he describes autumn objectively. Indeed, only by extreme sensitivity to
the external world is it possible to be objective.

Whatever our views on the relative merits of the odes and the
two 'Hyperions', it is impossible to accept Garrod's theory that
Keats was continually being led away from poetry by his thirst for
'reality'; for he could not have written 'The Eve of St. Agnes'
and 'To Autumn' if he had not elsewhere attempted to
philosophize. The determination to be faithful to his own experience and his sensitive recording of the external world were really
inseparable. If he had not sought truth, he could not have written
great poetry.

1 *Poetical Works*, p. lxvii.

8

Some Ideas and Usages

R. T. DAVIES

IN A NOTE TO CHAPTER THREE of his *Keats and Shakespeare*, Mr. J. M. Murry recommends, 'to anyone who desires to do a valuable piece of literary research', the close study of Keats's use of such 'peculiar and personal words' as 'identity', 'intense', 'sensation', and 'philosophy'. An analysis of six such words is offered here, preceded by some preliminary observations about the nature and scope of Keats's criticism and ideas in general. These observations are partly the result of rumination and impression and only partly of a systematic collation of the evidence, so that they may be said to complement, unsystematically, the more impersonal analysis of the selected words.

I

Until he wrote to Bailey on 22 November 1817 Keats appears to have expressed most of his critical ideas in verse. These, however, are not of the first class. With the exception, perhaps, of the long comment in a letter, again to Bailey, of October 1817 on Hazlitt's criticism of Wordsworth's 'Gipsies', and the description of poetry in 'Sleep and Poetry' as 'might half slumb'ring on its own right arm', there are no ideas in the earlier letters and poems with the strength of those that suddenly bubble over in the letter of 22 November 1817 about the lack of determined character in men of genius, about the holiness of the heart's affections and Keats's longing for sensations rather than thoughts. This letter also reports that to finish the composition of *Endymion* 'there are wanting 500 lines',[1] and no more; so that, what-

1 *Letters*, Letter 31, p. 69.

ever speculation we may make on the reason for it, about the time that he finished *Endymion* Keats began to enjoy a vigour and fecundity of critical thinking such as he had not known before.

It is the beginning of the great period of his critical utterances. To it belong the handful of magazine reviews, the letters on the absence of determined character from men of genius, on the holiness of the heart's affections, on negative capability, on how a 'consequitive man' will think parts of Keats's poetry mere words, on Wordsworth's obtrusive egotism, and how poetry should come naturally or not at all; as well as the letter confessing a conflict between the poet's sense of the luxurious and his love for philosophy, and the further letter on the mansion of many apartments.[1] This last was written in May 1818, and in the following month Keats began his tour of the Lakes and of Scotland. Though he wrote many letters on this strenuous holiday, none is of great critical interest.

He returned to London during August, and, while he was nursing his brother, Tom, in the last stages of consumption, began with 'Hyperion' a period of great poetical creativity which included 'The Eve of St. Agnes', the odes, 'Lamia' and 'The Fall of Hyperion', and ended in September 1819. This great creative period is not without its critical letters, just as the great critical period is not without its poetry. In October 1818 there is the letter to Woodhouse on the chameleon poet and the letter to George and Georgiana quietly asserting, 'I think I shall be among the English Poets after my death.' In the February part of the journal-letter, George and Georgiana are told that Shakespeare led a life of allegory, and in August Bailey learns that 'a fine writer is the most genuine Being in the World'. As the period ends there are three letters in September criticizing his own poetry and what has influenced it; and then, apart from an odd letter to Brown not long before he left for Italy acknowledging that women are classed in his 'books with roses and sweetmeats', there is in November 1819 the last literary letter[2] addressed to Taylor. It is constructive and on his ambition to write 'a few fine plays' because now 'Wonders are no wonders to me. I am more at home amongst Men and Women'.

1 *Letters*, pp. 67, 72, 91, 96, 108, 135, 143.
2 Ibid., pp. 227, 232, 305, 368, 516, 440.

Apart from what is in the handful of reviews—in quantity and quality almost negligible—the primary evidence of Keats's critical ability is in poems, marginal jottings, and casual letters. Formal criticism such as that of Johnson, Coleridge, Arnold, and Mr. Eliot is not to be found, and yet from some points of view Keats as a critic is their equal.

Another preliminary consideration in assessing Keats as a critic is that he was no older than twenty-four when he made his finest critical remarks. He matured extraordinarily fast and he wrote some of the wisest things ever said, but he was a young man and with his young man's daring went a young man's callowness. He wrote with a character forming—so that half our interest is in observing it—but as yet unformed.

By temperament Keats was unlikely to be monumentally dogmatic like Johnson or nicely tentative like Mr. Eliot. He was essentially impulsive, an enthusiast whom ideas struck. They took shape on paper before the heat of their impact cooled. He writes of 'showing a thought which has struck me' and refers[1] to his enjoyment of Shakespeare in the same terms: 'the following, from the Tempest, never struck me so forcibly as at present'. For Keats the sudden intensity with which an idea overwhelmed his consciousness was almost a guarantee of its rightness. Whereas Keats himself very often doubted whether the ideas that came into his mind could be proved or were in any way true, if he sometimes trusted his intuitions, while acknowledging them for what they were, we must, then, respect them as such, so that it is only after every attempt at sympathetic understanding that we have any right to lament that his not using traditional currency in his philosophical transactions may have caused him to waste some of his time and ours. He was fully aware that his thoughts were not consecutive but, rather, 'attracted by the Loadstone Concatenation'.[2] He was cheerfully aware that he was not a formal reasoner, despite his repeated speculation and his manner that is frequently like that of one reasoning.

He was essentially a poet and without a philosophical training. He shows no knowledge, for example, of Plato or Berkeley, who might have helped him to say more (or less) about Beauty and Truth. It was his realization of his own ignorance that made him

1 *Letters*, Letters 123, and 13, pp. 336 and 21. Cf. p. 337 and Letter 156, p. 401.
2 Ibid., Letter 57, p. 123.

ask Hazlitt for advice on what philosophy to read. But if he could not be an academic thinker, if he had not the latter's deliberate and rigorous scepticism, nor his learned perspective, nor his technical language, he enjoyed the freshness, intensity, and lack of inhibition which the academic thinker correspondingly lacks. A further consideration, then, is that Keats is clearly not a trained or systematic critic, and our surprise should be not that there are mistakes and inconsistencies, but that there are so few.

He enjoyed having ideas. With typically forthright and innocent relish he indulged his 'speculations', whether they were about literature or life, and he was not always concerned primarily or at all about their correspondence with objective reality. The poet who enjoyed fine phrases like a lover might easily throw out a brilliant observation about poetry without intending its meaning to be too closely scrutinized. 'I am sometimes so very sceptical as to think Poetry itself a mere Jack-a-lanthen to amuse whoever may chance to be struck with its brilliance.'[1] What satisfied the moment was enough, and as poetry it may still satisfy, but not as criticism. An image suddenly swimming into a mind attending critically to some object might so catch a poet's eye that he would pursue it for his own imaginative satisfaction rather than for the help it could give in exploring the truth. I doubt, for example, whether there is anything specially significant in Keats's distinction between the poetic faculties in terms of sailing a boat.[2] Keats liked throwing out exciting ideas just as he liked coining fine phrases.

He tended to think in 'character', as if he were this person or that and not John Keats. With natural courtesy he adapted his style to his correspondents—'I wish I knew always the humour my friends would be in at opening a letter of mine, to suit it to them as nearly as possible',[3]—and it may be also that different correspondents drew out of him contradictory ideas. Certainly he himself confesses to Bailey, after throwing out several 'speculations' and 'maxims', that 'I must once for all tell you I have not one Idea of the truth of any of my speculations'.[4] He continues in a frivolously gay vein so that we may suspect the validity of even this disclaimer, and, clearly, there is a great deal more to be said than this about Keats's relativism. But the importance of

1 *Letters*, Letter 53, p. 111.   2 Ibid., Letter 25, p. 53.
3 Ibid., Letter 76, p. 176.   4 Ibid., Letter 53, p. 112.

bearing the point in mind as a preliminary consideration is further suggested by the end of a letter to Reynolds, written a month or so before, advocating a sort of wise passiveness: 'I am sensible all this is a mere sophistication [i.e. piece of sophistry] (however it may neighbour to any truths), to excuse my own indolence. . . . It is no matter, whether I am right or wrong, either one way or another, if there is sufficient to lift a little time from your shoulders.' He ends the letter to Woodhouse about the chameleon poet: 'even now I am perhaps not speaking from myself: but from some character in whose soul I now live.'[1] The student of Keats's critical ideas has no general guarantee at any particular instant that the chameleon poet is not also the chameleon critic.

There are, however, four respects in which Keats shows his capability as a critic. The first is in his expression of several important ideas about poetry, the poetic nature, and the different meanings of knowledge: such ideas as those of negative capability, the naturalness of great verse,[2] and the importance, in apprehending truth, of the 'nerves' and the 'pulses'. If some of the ideas are a little lumpish and gawky, that is only through Keats's want of proper training: that they come dripping fresh and eager from his own experience is a good part of their appeal. There are other ideas of this sort which are not in the first class because they are only half true or seem to be true only after they have been either filled out or pinched in: such an idea is one that has various formulations in the letters and poems but may be most easily remembered as 'Beauty is truth'. Ideas like this, though inadequate as they stand, stimulate thought.

The second respect in which Keats is a valuable critic is in his enthusiastic commendation of what he enjoys. After reading him on Kean's acting or Shakespeare's 'cockled Snails' we want to taste for ourselves. He also helps us—and this is the third respect—to see more clearly and feel more sensitively the quality of particular authors and, less frequently, of particular passages. Some of the few things he has to say about Milton or Wordsworth are of major importance.

The fourth respect in which he shows his critical stature is in his understanding of himself as a growing poet and in his laying bare this understanding to his friends. It is more for this

---

1 *Letters*, Letter 48, p. 105; and Letter 93, p. 229.
2 Ibid., Letters 44, 51, and 90, pp. 96, 108, and 223.

than for anything else that we read Keats's letters. Not even Wordsworth's deliberate portrayal of the growth of his poetic mind in *The Prelude* can compare in interest and reality with these informal and incidental revelations, for through them we know Keats as intimately as his friends knew him, and with immediacy, that is to say without the change that must have taken place in Wordsworth's memories of his development as they matured before their inclusion in his poem. Through these letters we gain an inner understanding of what it is to be such a poet as Shakespeare.

II

In contrast with the general observations in the first part of these contributions to the study of John Keats as a critic and man of ideas an analysis is made, in this second part, of six words which are conspicuous in his poetry and prose by their frequency and apparent idiosyncrasy. They are, I believe, focal points of Keats's vision. The lexicographical method that I have used underlies Mr. N. F. Ford's close scrutiny of particular aspects of Keats's thought in *The Prefigurative Imagination of John Keats* (1951), but he does not present his analyses as formally as those here offered and subordinates them to the elucidation of his chosen theme, sometimes selecting only the immediately relevant uses of the words. My primary intention has not been to draw general conclusions. Where I have disagreed with Mr. Ford I have said so incidentally, but no thorough attempt has been made to check all that he says: each analysis is freshly made and at least one word, *sublime*, has not concerned Mr. Ford at all.

1. *Speculation (speculating)*

Keats once or twice uses *speculation* in the sense of 'risky business venture',[1] and this may colour some of his other uses of the word. In his poetry the word is twice used in the sense of 'contemplation', 'looking', 'sight'.[2] In prose he frequently uses it in the sense of 'thought'. For example, it is apparently used as a synonym for cogitating,[3] to mean fantasies or imaginings,[4] the

---

1 *Letters*, pp. 437, 41.   2 'Isabella', l. 183 'I stood tip-toe', l. 189.
3 *Letters*, p. 228.   4 Ibid., pp. 421, 476-7. Cf. pp. 112-13.

thoughts inspired by painting and music,[1] and 'inspired guesses or conjectures'. This last is Keats's most significant use of the word, as in the passage about Wordsworth:[2] 'Every man has his *speculations*, but every man does not brood and peacock over them', but wants 'confidence to put down his half-seeing'. This is connected with 'half-knowledge' with which Coleridge is not content, his 'fine isolated verisimilitude caught from the Penetralium of mystery'.[3] Sometimes Keats contrasts speculation with superficial thinking. One of his correspondents was 'without a thought of . . . the deeps of good and evil—you were at the moment estranged from speculation'.[4] Hence the word comes to mean 'idea entertained as a result of an intuition of reality'. Writing of a passage in *Endymion* he tells Bailey:[5]

you may know my favourite *Speculation* . . . I am the more zealous in this affair, because I have never yet been able to perceive how any thing can be known for truth by consequitive reasoning.

But elsewhere he says he has not 'one Idea of the truth of any of my speculations—I shall never be a Reasoner'.[6] As examples of such speculations, guesses at truth, we may mention the comparison of human life 'to a large Mansion of Many Apartments',[7] and his account of the world as a 'vale of Soul-making'.[8] Although Keats does sometimes appear to reason, he is aware that such typical speculations, as intuitions of reality, represent only a half-seeing; but he also knows that as a chameleon poet, gifted with negative capability and determined to make his mind a thoroughfare for all thoughts, such speculations are the very stuff from which his poems are made.

2. *Truth* (*true*)

Keats uses Truth in the sense of an idea or representation corresponding with reality.[9] It is distinguished from 'a mere sophistication'—a clever bit of sophistry the immediate purpose of which is merely to make an excuse.[10] Truth is verifiable by the senses[11] or by experience. Keats tells us that he has resolved 'never to take any thing for granted—but even to examine the *truth* of the commonest proverbs',[12] because, as he says later, 'Nothing ever

1 *Letters*, pp. 71, 68.   2 Ibid., p. 96.   3 Ibid., p. 72.
4 Ibid., p. 84.   5 Ibid., p. 67. Cf. p. 374.   6 Ibid., p. 112.
7 Ibid., pp. 143-4.   8 Ibid., pp. 335-6.   9 e.g., ibid., p. 145.
10 Ibid., p. 105.   11 'Sleep and Poetry', l. 294.   12 *Letters*, p. 259.

becomes real till it is experienced—Even a Proverb is no proverb to you till your Life has illustrated it.'[1] He recognized that it must be possible to know truth 'by consequitive reasoning'[2] but, since he knew he would never be a reasoner himself,[3] he believed that there were other ways of arriving at truth. 'The only means of strengthening one's intellect is to make up one's mind about nothing . . . Dilke will never come at a *truth* . . . because he is always trying at it.'[4]

Truth, therefore, could be apprehended by the imagination, as some lines in *Endymion* were 'a regular stepping of the Imagination towards a Truth'.[5] Keats confessed that he could not 'feel certain of any *truth* but from a clear perception of its Beauty'.[6] He told Bailey that he thought enjoyment in the hereafter would befall 'those who delight in Sensation, rather than hunger as you do after *Truth*'[7] and declared on several occasions that reasoning brought him no conviction. He was continually seeking 'truth', and continually speculating about reality and how to live, though he was often sceptical of the value of the normal instruments of thinking, logic and evidence, fact and reason. Wishing to make his mind 'a thoroughfare for all thoughts, not a select party',[8] he was not over-anxious to be in the right, even in matters of religion.[9]

Keats' distrust of 'consequitive reasoning' made him suppose that 'even the greatest Philosopher' only 'arrived at his goal' after 'putting aside numerous objections. However it may be, O for a Life of Sensations rather than of Thoughts.'[10] In other words he thought he was more likely to arrive at Truth by feeling than by thinking, because thought, in its necessary process of selection and ordering, omitted some of the richness and complexity of experience. 'Axioms in philosophy are not axioms until they are proved upon our pulses.'[11]

In one famous passage in the *Letters*[12] Keats came near to expressing the message of the Grecian Urn:

What the imagination seizes as Beauty must be *truth*—whether it existed before or not—for I have the same Idea of all our Passions as of Love they are all in their sublime, creative of essential Beauty.

1 *Letters*, p. 318.   2 Ibid., p. 68.   3 Ibid., p. 112.   4 Ibid., p. 426.
5 Ibid., p. 91. Cf. p. 56, where Wordsworth's 'Gipsies' is criticized because it is 'not a search after truth'.   6 Ibid., p. 259. Cf. p. 71.
7 Ibid., p. 68.   8 Ibid., p. 426.   9 Ibid., pp. 111–12.
10 Ibid., p. 68.   11 Ibid., p. 142.   12 p. 67.

Here by *truth* Keats means 'what has objective reality', not only foreseen by the imagination but created by it. It is not an image or idea in the mind eventually found to correspond with already existing external reality, but external reality brought into existence by the image or idea in the mind.

The shifting nature of Keats's ideas can be illustrated by the fact that between the time he wrote this letter and his statement in the ode on the identity of beauty and truth—in one sense, a regression—he appears to put truth above beauty and philosophy above poetry:[1]

> By a superior being our reasonings may take the same tone—though erroneous they may be fine. This is the very thing in which consists poetry, and if so it is not so fine a thing as philosophy—For the same reason that an eagle is not so fine a thing as a truth.

It would give a misleading account of Keats's ideas to ignore their developing and dialectic nature.

3. *Spirit (spiritual; spiritualize)*

The word *spirit* is used by Keats in a number of ordinary senses: as a particular quality or character;[2] as a frame of mind;[3] as a person considered in relation to his character,[4] particularly as a synonym for 'genius';[5] as a synonym for 'soul'.[6] Keats speaks of a man as 'trying the resources of his spirit';[7] and his system of 'spirit-creation' is identical with his system of 'soul-making'.[8] 'Soul' is distinguished from 'mind' or 'intelligence'. 'Intelligences' are identified with 'sparks which are God', which 'are not Souls till they acquire identities, till each one is personally itself'. Personal identity is acquired by the suffering of the heart: 'a World of Pains and troubles' schools an Intelligence and makes it a Soul. Thus 'does God make individual beings, Souls, Identical Souls by the Sparks of his own essence'.[9]

Spiritual is opposed to 'worldly' and associated with 'disinterestedness':[10] it is contrasted with 'material', and associated with 'ethereal finger-pointings';[11] it is applied to the heavenly state of the immortals, free from the limitations of time and space, but not exclusive of bodily pleasures;[12] and it is applied to

1 *Letters*, p. 317. 2 Ibid., p. 414. 3 Ibid., p. 340.
4 Ibid., p. 151. 5 *Endymion*, II. 250. 6 *Letters*, p. 68.
7 Ibid., p. 69. 8 Ibid., p. 336. 9 Ibid., p. 336.
10 Ibid., pp. 233, 80. 11 Ibid., pp. 122, 103. 12 Ibid., p. 95; *Endymion*, II. 906.

moral values.[1] In his essay on Edmund Kean, Keats distinguishes between sensual and spiritual pleasures, the appeal made by poetry to the senses, and that which it makes to the imagination.

In one passage already alluded to, Keats speaks of the 'Spiritual repetition' of human life in the hereafter, earthly happiness being 'repeated in a finer tone'. What appears beautiful to the imagination will then actually exist, as Adam awoke to find his dream of Eve was true.[2] In another passage Keats clearly distinguishes between the intercourse of spirits, which is 'a direct communication of Spirit', and the intercourse of separated human beings, which is in their imaginations and as intimate only as the memory is vivid:[3]

Sometimes I fancy an immense separation, and sometimes, as at present, a direct communication of Spirit with you. That will be one of the grandeurs of immortality—There will be no space and consequently the only commerce between spirits will be by their intelligence of each other.

Finally Keats uses spirit as a synonym for ghost,[4] and to signify a being other than human.[5] His use of *spiritualized* is discussed under *sublime*.

4. *Sublime* (*sublimity*)

Keats uses this word with the general sense of 'high', 'exalted', and 'grand', the antithesis of 'low'.[6] He applies it to people, to immortals,[7] to impressive natural phenomena,[8] to the solitude devoted to epic creation ('my Solitude is *sublime* . . . there is a *Sublimity* to welcome me home'),[9] and to some kinds of poetry, Wordsworth's genius being characterized in a famous phrase as the 'egotistical *sublime*'.[10] Occasionally Keats seems to use the word in the Miltonic sense of 'uplifted':[11]

> faeries stooping on their wings *sublime*
> To kiss a mortal's lips.

But here and in several other places it may be used to mean 'pertaining to the immortals'. In one interesting passage sublimity is contrasted with mere greatness:[12]

1 *Letters*, p. 233.   2 Ibid., p. 68.   3 Ibid., p. 246.
4 'Isabella', XLI. 1.   5 'Lamia', I. 280.   6 'The Fall of Hyperion', I. 173.
7 *Endymion* III. 965.   8 *Letters*, p. 175; 'Epistle to Reynolds', l. 69.
9 *Letters*, pp. 240–1.   10 Ibid., p. 227. Cf. 'sublime pathetic' applied to Milton.
11 'The Cap and Bells', XI.   12 *Letters*, p. 235.

a philosophical Quaker full of mean and thrifty maxims, the other sold the very Charger who had taken him through all his Battles. Those Americans are great but they are not *sublime* Man—the humanity of the United States can never reach the *sublime*.

Two images are of particular interest. Keats thought that human passions 'are all in their *sublime* creative of essential Beauty',[1] a sentence which links up with his belief that the excellence of every art is its intensity. In the other passage[2] Keats speaks of being 'self spiritualized into a kind of *sublime* Misery'. Here, and probably in the former passage, the word carries an overtone of 'sublimated'—of course in the chemical not in the modern psychological sense.

5. *Sensation*

The commonest meanings of the word are 'feeling', 'emotion', 'sense datum', 'state of consciousness'.[3] In one instance—'all your sensations and symptoms concerning the Palpitation'[4]—it appears to be synonymous with symptom. In another it means 'sexual desire':[5]

I am ... too much occupied in admiring to be awkward or on a tremble. I forget myself entirely because I live in her ... I like her and her like because one has no *sensations*—what we both are is taken for granted.

In view of the exceptional impact which the external world made on Keats, *sensation* would sometimes appear to mean 'impression', 'an effect made on the feelings', though in the context of the last quotation he distinguishes between *impression* and sensation. The woman who aroused no sensations in him 'When she comes into a room ... makes an impression the same as the Beauty of a Leopardess.' In referring to the impact on his consciousness of objects in the external world and in his mind, Keats uses the peculiar expression 'press upon' on six occasions.[6] The exceptional intensity and vividness of Keats's feelings, and the value he placed on them, have caused Colvin, de Selincourt, Thorpe, and Murry to interpret sensation as 'intuition'.

1 *Letters,*, p. 67.   2 Ibid., p. 56.
3 Ibid. pp. 55, 178, 42, 465, 315, etc.   4 Ibid., p. 74.
5 Ibid., p. 233. But cf. p. 520: 'I am in a state at present in which woman merely as woman can have no more power over me than stocks and stones, and yet the difference of my sensations with respect to Miss Brawne and my Sister is amazing.'
6 Ibid., pp. 216, 228, 230, 247, 314.

There does not, however, seem to be any context where Keats used *sensation* with that precise sense. He used it as a synonym for creative experience, as when he abandoned Miltonic verse because, as he said, 'I wish to devote myself to other sensations';[1] or as a synonym for a more general literary—a reader's—experience, as when he said that the public would get 'sensation of some sort' from 'Lamia',[2] or asked 'With what sensation do you read Fielding?'[3] More often the word means simply 'experience' or 'feeling'. He contends, for example, that poetry[4]

cannot be matured by law and precept, but by sensation & watchfulness in itself.

This is paralleled by the saying that 'Nothing ever becomes real till it is experienced'.[5] In the famous exclamation, quoted above, 'O for a Life of Sensations rather than of Thoughts!',[6] Keats meant by sensations not intuitions, but sense-experiences and feelings about them, or perhaps just feelings. He refers in one letter to 'high Sensations'.[7] He complains of *Don Juan*[8] that

Byron's perverted education makes him assume to feel, and try to impart to others, those depraved sensations which the want of any education excites in many.

In contrast to these depraved sensations, Keats speaks earlier, in a passage of some obscurity, of 'undepraved sensations':[9]

O for a recourse somewhat human independant of the great Consolations of Religion and undepraved Sensations—of the Beautiful—the poetical in all things—O for a Remedy against such wrongs within the pale of the World! Should not those things be pure enjoyment?

This passage is clearly linked with 'the mighty abstract Idea' Keats had 'of Beauty in all things'.[10] It appears also to be linked with his declaration that he was[11]

certain of nothing but of the holiness of the Heart's affections and the truth of the Imagination—What the Imagination seizes as Beauty must be Truth.

The 'undepraved sensations' are apparently the same as the normal affections which Keats affirms to be holy; and just as the

---

1 *Letters*,, pp. 384, 425.   2 Ibid., p. 402.
3 Ibid., p. 258. Cf. p. 324, where Keats reported that Coleridge talked on 'Poetical Sensation'.
4 Ibid., p. 223.   5 Ibid., p. 318.   6 Ibid., p. 68.   7 Ibid., p. 140.
8 Ibid., p. 521,   9 Ibid., p. 60.   10 Ibid., p. 241.   11 Ibid., p. 67.

normal imagination seizes upon beautiful images that must be
true, so also these sensations are apprehensions of the Beautiful.
Keats is consoling Bailey because he had been badly treated by a
bishop. He wishes that he could obtain some cruder satisfaction
for his wrongs, and not have to seek consolation in undepraved
sensations of the beautiful, or to wait for the consolations of
another world.

6. *Ethereal (etherially; etherialized)*

Keats uses ethereal in a variety of senses. When applied to
physical things and actions it can mean 'having the insubstan-
tiality and rarity of *ether*, delicate, refined, volatile'. It seems to
be derived from Keats's medical studies in which he would have
found ether contrasted with heavy spirits. He says, for example,
that 'the more ethereal Part' of Claret 'mounts into the brain'.[1]
Sometimes it means spirit-like, aerial, heavenly.[2] When applied
to human beings it can express ecstasy, heavenly feelings of delight, as at the climax of 'The Eve of St. Agnes':[3]

> Beyond a mortal man impassion'd far
> At these voluptuous accents, he arose,
> Ethereal, flush'd, and like a throbbing star.

The word may be applied to poetry to suggest that it transcends
the earthly. In one passage there is a submerged metaphor suggested by the poet's training as an apothecary:

I shall learn poetry here and shall henceforth write more than ever,
for the *abstract* endeavor of being able to add a mite to that *mass* of
beauty which is harvested from these grand *materials*, by the finest
spirits, and put into *etherial* existence for the relish of one's fellows.[4]

In another passage Keats speaks of[5]

looking upon the Sun the Moon the Stars, the Earth and its contents
as materials to form greater things—that is to say ethereal things.

Here the phrase means little more than 'things of the imagination'. In a later passage the universe and poetry are put in the
same category. Keats says that 'Ethereal things may at least be
thus real'; and he gives as examples of 'Things real', 'existences
of Sun, Moon & Stars and passages of Shakespeare'.[6]

---

1 *Letters*, p. 302.
2 Ibid., pp. 192, 94–5. Cf. *Endymion*, III. 25, IV. 420.
3 'The Eve of St. Agnes', XXXVI.   4 *Letters*, p. 157. My italics.
5 Ibid., p. 31.   6 Ibid., p. 112.

Another passage in which the word occurs has, I think, been misinterpreted by N. F. Ford. Keats tells Bailey that[1]

a complex Mind—one that is imaginative and at the same time careful of its fruits—who would exist partly on Sensation partly on thought . . . such an one I consider your's and therefore it is necessary to your eternal Happiness that you not only drink this old Wine of Heaven, which I shall call the redigestion of our most ethereal Musings on Earth, but also increase in knowledge.

Even if we allowed that 'ethereal musings' was 'pretty surely a synonym for passages of poetry', the emphasis is not on the 'sensational' as essential in a complex mind for eternal happiness, as Ford says, but on the place in such a mind that must be held by 'knowledge'. The emphasis is more on thought than on sensation. 'Redigestion' is another chemical word. To 'Digest' means to extract an essence either by heat or by dissolving in, for example, spirits. So 'ethereal Musings' are the essences extracted from experience; in heaven these essences are 'extracted' to a still further stage of purity and 'etheriality'. That 'ethereal musings' has a wider significance than poetry is, in fact, shown by the context. Keats has been talking of the rewards obtained by the simple mind. These are

in the repetition of its own silent Working coming continually on the Spirit with a fine Suddenness . . . have you never by being Surprised with an old Melody—in a delicious place—by a delicious voice, felt over again your very Speculations and Surmises at the time it first operated on your Soul—do you not remember forming to yourself the singer's face more beautiful than it was possible and yet with the elevation of the Moment you did not think so—even then you were mounted on the Wings of Imagination so high—that the Prototype must be here after.

So in another letter Keats explains how 'one grand and spiritual passage' of prose or poetry, should one 'muse upon it, and reflect upon it', will start a 'voyage of conception', so that 'a nap upon Clover engenders ethereal finger-pointings'.[2]

Finally, there are two or three passages in which *ethereal* is used in metaphorical expressions describing the effect of men of genius, and of their literary works, on mankind. 'Men of Genius are great as certain ethereal Chemicals operating on the Mass of neutral

1 *Letters*, p. 68.   2 Ibid., p. 103.

intellect.'[1] They are like the chemical liquid, ether, which will extract valuable and active substances from the chemically inert mass over which it is poured. In the next passage Keats suggests that it is better to use a book rather as a starting-point for one's own reflections than as a thing to imitate:[2]

> Now it appears to me that almost any Man may like the spider spin from his own inwards his own airy Citadel—the points of leaves and twigs on which the spider begins her work are few, and she fills the air with a beautiful circuiting. Man should be content with as few points to tip with the fine Web of his Soul, and weave a tapestry empyrean full of symbols for his spiritual eye, of softness for his spiritual touch, of space for his wandering, of distinctness for his luxury.

Keats next considers the objections that such a tapestry would have only a personal significance:

> But the Minds of Mortals are so different and bent on such diverse journeys that it may at first appear impossible for any common taste and fellowship to exist between two or three under these suppositions.

Keats answers this difficulty by saying that on the contrary,

> Minds would leave each other in contrary directions, traverse each other in numberless points, and at last greet each other at the journey's end.

He then turns to the objectionable 'obtrusiveness' of Words-worth's poetry:

> Man should not dispute or assert but whisper results to his neighbour and thus by every germ of spirit sucking the sap from mould ethereal every human might become great, and Humanity instead of being a wide heath of Furze and Briars with here and there a remote Oak or Pine, would become a grand democracy of Forest Trees!

N. F. Ford takes 'mould ethereal' to be a synonym for poetry, as it well may be;[3] but it may be taken to include also the thoughts and musings suggested by 'any one grand and spiritual passage' of poetry and prose.

---

1 *Letters*, p. 67.   2 Ibid., pp. 103–4.
3 *Keats's Pre-figurative Imagination*, p. 35.

9

Keats and Hazlitt

KENNETH MUIR

MOST BIOGRAPHERS of Keats and Hazlitt have discussed the relationship between the two men, and Professor C. L. Finney has pointed out a large number of parallels between Hazlitt's views and those of Keats; but no one, I believe, has fully demonstrated the way in which almost all Keats's critical opinions originated in Hazlitt's essays. Most of the evidence I shall bring forward, in approximately chronological order, will be found in H. W. Garrod's book,[1] in de Selincourt's edition,[2] and, above all, in Finney's *Evolution of Keats's Poetry*;[3] and I make this general acknowledgement of indebtedness to avoid a multiplicity of footnotes.[4]

Keats met Hazlitt at Leigh Hunt's in the winter of 1816–17. Hazlitt was 38 years of age, and though he had published seven books, he was only beginning to make his name as an essayist by his contributions to *The Examiner*. One of Keats's sonnets had been printed in the same journal, and Hunt had shown his manuscript poems to Hazlitt. By the time Keats's 1817 volume was published, he knew Hazlitt well enough to echo his conversational mannerisms, and in September of the same year he expressed admiration for the essays, collected from *The Examiner* under the title of *The Round Table*. 'How is Hazlitt?', Keats asked Reynolds.[5]

We were reading his Table last night. I know he thinks himself not estimated by ten People in the World—I wish he knew he is.

1 *Keats* (1926).   2 1935.   3 Cambridge (Mass.), 1936.
4 Cf. H. E. Briggs, *P.M.L.A.* (1944), pp. 596–8, and C. D. Thorpe, ibid. (1947), pp. 487–502.
5 *Letters*, p. 48.

A month later, Keats referred in a letter to Bailey[1] to two of *The Round Table* essays—one 'On Common-Place Critics', in which Hazlitt speaks of the people who adopt the views of the *Edinburgh Review* and *Quarterly Review*; and the other, 'On Manner', in which Hazlitt had criticized Wordsworth's poem on gipsies. Bailey, a devout Wordsworthian, had apparently been pained by Hazlitt's gibes at one of Wordsworth's feeblest poems:

Mr. Wordsworth, who has written a sonnet to the King on the good that he has done in the last fifty years, has made an attack on a set of gipsies for having done nothing in four-and-twenty hours. 'The stars have gone their rounds but they had not stirred from their place.' And why should they, if they were comfortable where they were? We did not expect this turn from Mr. Wordsworth, whom we had considered as the prince of poetical idlers, and patron of the philosophy of indolence, who formerly insisted on our spending our time 'in a wise passiveness'. Mr. W. will excuse us if we are not converts to his recantation of his original doctrine; for he who changes his opinions loses his authority. We did not look for this Sunday-school philosophy from him. What had he himself been doing in these four-and-twenty hours? Had he been admiring a flower, or writing a sonnet? We hate the doctrine of utility, even in a philosopher, and much more in a poet— for the only real utility is that which leads to enjoyment, and the end is, in all cases, better than the means.[2]

Keats was torn between his admiration for Wordsworth and his desire to placate Bailey on the one hand, and his admiration for Hazlitt's critical power on the other:

Now with respect to Wordsworth's Gipseys, I think he is right and yet I think Hazlitt is right, and yet I think Wordsworth is rightest. Wordsworth had not been idle, he had not been without his task—nor had they Gipseys—they in the visible world had been as picturesque an object as he in the invisible. The Smoke of their fire—their attitudes—their Voices were all in harmony with the Evenings—It is a bold thing to say and I would not say it in print—but it seems to me that if Wordsworth had thought a little deeper at that moment he would not have written the Poem at all—I should judge it to have been written in one of the most comfortable Moods of his Life—it is a kind of sketchy intellectual Landscape—not a search after Truth—nor is it fair to attack him on such a subject—for it is with the critic as with the poet; had Hazlitt thought a little deeper and been in a good temper he would never have spied an imaginary fault there.[3]

1 *Letters*, p. 56. 2 Hazlitt, *Works*, ed. P. P. Howe, iv. 45. 3 *Letters*, p. 56.

Keats criticizes the tone of Hazlitt's remarks, though he does not really differ from him about the feebleness of the poem. Yet his remarks are subtler and deeper than Hazlitt's, and they exhibit, notwithstanding his reverence for Wordsworth at this time and his admiration for Hazlitt, a genuine independence of judgement. It was about this time that he told Haydon[1] that there were three things to rejoice at in 1818—*The Excursion*, Haydon's pictures, and 'Hazlitt's depth of taste'.

In December 1817, after a visit to Hazlitt's favourite haunt at Burford Bridge, Keats deputized for Reynolds as dramatic critic of *The Champion*, and the articles he wrote are obvious imitations of Hazlitt's. In his essay on Edmund Kean he mentions the 'indescribable gusto in his voice',[2] when speaking Shakespeare's verse; and a week later he remarks that 'the acting of Kean is Shakespearean—he will fully understand what we mean'. Hazlitt's favourite word was *gusto*, and his favourite actor was Kean. In the same essay Keats discusses the way in which Shakespeare's genius was fettered in the Histories, and he adds:

The poetry of Shakespeare is generally free as the wind—a perfect thing of the elements, winged and sweetly coloured. Poetry must be free! It is of the air, not of the earth; and the higher it soars the nearer it gets to its home.[3]

Hazlitt had made the same point in his essay, 'On Poetical Versatility'. Poetry, he says, 'when it lights upon the earth . . . loses some of its dignity and its use. Its strength is in its wings; its element the air. Standing on its feet, jostling with the crowd, it is liable to be overthrown, trampled on and defaced.'[4] Keats, in the same article, remarks that 'the English people do not care one fig about Shakespeare'. So Hazlitt, in his essay, 'On Posthumous Fame' asks, 'what is the amount of Shakespeare's fame?' and answers 'that in that very country which boasts his genius and his birth, perhaps not one person in ten had ever heard of his name, or read a syllable of his writings'.[5]

About this time Keats went to see 'Death on the Pale Horse', a picture by the aged President of the Royal Academy, Benjamin West. He remarked in a letter to his brothers:

It is a wonderful picture when West's age is considered. But there is nothing to be intense upon; no woman one feels mad to kiss, no face

---

1 *Letters*, p. 79.   2 *The Champion* (21 Dec. 1817).
3 Ibid. (28 Dec. 1817).   4 *Works*, iv. 151.   5 Ibid. iv. 124.

swelling into reality—The excellence of every art is its intensity, capable of making all disagreeables evaporate, from their being in close relationship with Beauty and Truth. Examine *King Lear*, and you will find this exemplified throughout; but in this picture we have unpleasantness without any momentous depth of speculation excited, in which to bury its repulsiveness.[1]

Hazlitt, in his essay, 'On Gusto', in *The Round Table*, had said that the infinite quantity of dramatic invention in Shakespeare takes from his gusto. The power he delights to show is not intense, but discursive.[2]

At first sight, Keats seems to contradict Hazlitt; but on closer examination it will be seen that the contradiction is more apparent than real. Keats is using the word *intensity* almost in the sense of Hazlitt's *gusto*. Hazlitt had defined gusto in these words:

Gusto in art is power or passion defining any object. . . . In one sense, however, there is hardly any object entirely devoid of expression, without some character of power belonging to it, some precise association with pleasure or pain; and it is in giving this truth of character from the truth of feeling, whether in the highest or lowest degree, but always in the highest degree of which the subject is capable, that gusto consists.[3]

Keats's phrase, 'Capable of making all disagreeables evaporate', makes explicit what is perhaps implied by Hazlitt.

I am not suggesting that Keats was a slavish imitator of Hazlitt, but rather that many of his most famous critical remarks were crystallized from his consideration of Hazlitt's opinions. Nothing better demonstrates the independence and subtlety of Keats's mind than the way he refined on Hazlitt's stimulating but cruder theories. Hazlitt wrote on the nature of poets and poetry from the outside. Keats looked within, and compared what he found there with Hazlitt's theories. He never accepted a theory about poetry unless he could support it from his own experience. Axioms were not axioms with him till they were proved upon his pulses. 'We read fine things', he told Reynolds, 'but never feel them to the full until we have gone the same steps as the Author.'[4]

In the letter in which he mentions West's painting, Keats makes his famous distinction between Shakespeare and Coleridge. As he walked home with Brown and Dilke from the pantomime, they discussed various subjects:

1 *Letters*, p. 71. 2 *Works*, iv. 79. 3 Ibid. iv. 77. 4 *Letters*, p. 142

Several things dove-tailed in my mind, and at once it struck me what quality went to form a Man of Achievement, especially in Literature, and which Shakespeare possessed so enormously—I mean *Negative Capability*, that is, when a man is capable of being in uncertainties, mysteries, doubts, without any irritable reaching after fact and reason —Coleridge, for instance, would let go by a fine isolated verisimilitude caught from the penetralium of mystery, from being incapable of remaining content with half-knowledge. This pursued through volumes would perhaps take us no further than this, that with a great poet the sense of Beauty overcomes every other consideration, or rather obliterates all consideration.[1]

This penetrating criticism of Coleridge may have been suggested by Hazlitt's review of the *Biographia Literaria*, which had appeared four months previously.

Reason and imagination are both excellent things; but perhaps their provinces ought to be kept more distinct than they have been lately . . . Mr. Coleridge, with great talents, has by an ambition to be everything, become nothing. His metaphysics have been a dead weight on the wings of his imagination—while his imagination has run away with his reason and common sense.[2]

Once again Keats strikes deeper than Hazlitt. The idea of *Negative Capability* really illuminates the difference between Shakespeare and Coleridge; and whereas Hazlitt declares that Coleridge's metaphysics have interfered with his poetry, Keats, with greater understanding, shows that his interest in metaphysics is only a symptom of his failure to trust his poetic intuitions.

On 13 January 1818, Hazlitt began his series of lectures on the English poets. Keats mistook the hour of the first or second lecture, and arrived at the Surrey Institution just as the audience were leaving;[3] but he attended the remainder of the course. In his lecture on Shakespeare and Milton, Hazlitt repeated a sentence from his essay on Milton's Versification (in *The Round Table*):

Dr. Johnson and Pope would have converted his (Milton's) vaulting Pegasus into a rocking-horse.[4]

1 *Letters*, p. 72.   2 *Works*, xvi. 137.

3 Writing on 23 Jan. 1818, Keats says, 'I went last Tuesday, an hour too late, to Hazlitt's lecture on Poetry, got there just as they were coming out.' If Keats had been to Hazlitt's first lecture it is surprising that he did not mention it, and more surprising that he should arrive an hour late for the second.

4 *Works*, iv. 40.

Keats had already echoed this sentence in 'Sleep and Poetry', the poem in which he had attacked Pope's followers:

> with a puling infant's force
> They sway'd about upon a rocking horse,
> And thought it Pegasus.[1]

In the lecture on Dryden and Pope, which Hazlitt delivered on 3 February, he said that Dryden's

> Tales have been, upon the whole, the most popular of his works; and I should think that a translation of some of the other serious tales in Boccaccio and Chaucer, as that of Isabella, the Falcon, of Constance, the Prioress's Tale, and others, if executed with taste and spirit, could not fail to succeed in the present day.[2]

Mr. Garrod has suggested that this remark of Hazlitt's gave Keats the idea of writing 'Isabella', which he began shortly afterwards.[3] Indeed, he and Reynolds agreed to collaborate in a volume of metrical versions of Boccaccio; but when Reynolds read 'Isabella', he urged Keats to publish it alone. His own versions of Boccaccio were published soon after Keats's death. Barry Cornwall, who also wrote a poem about Isabella—a poem which was preferred to that of Keats by the contemporary public—may likewise have taken the hint from Hazlitt's lecture.

Keats thought that Hazlitt gave Crabbe 'an unmerciful licking'[4]; he admired his discriminating criticism on Swift, Voltaire, and Rabelais; but he was very disappointed at the way Hazlitt spoke of Chatterton. It was probably due to Keats's remonstrances that Hazlitt began his next lecture with an apology:

> I am sorry that what I said in the conclusion of the last Lecture respecting Chatterton should have given dissatisfaction to some persons, with whom I would willingly agree on all such matters. What I meant was less to call in question Chatterton's genius, than to object to the common mode of estimating its magnitude by its prematureness.[5]

Hazlitt's lectures were published soon after they were delivered, and there is abundant evidence that Keats studied them carefully. In his first lecture, for example, Hazlitt had said:

> It cannot be concealed, however, that the progress of knowledge and refinement has a tendency to circumscribe the limits of the imagination,

1 ll. 185-7.   2 *Works*, v. 82.   3 *T.L.S.* (19 Mar. 1925).
4 *Letters*, p. 101.   5 *Works*, v. 123.

and to clip the wings of poetry. . . . Hence the history of religious and poetical enthusiasm is much the same; and both have received a sensible shock from the progress of experimental philosophy.[1]

In his essay on Kean, Keats had lamented that 'the goblin is driven from the hearth, and the rainbow is robbed of its mystery.'[2] A week later, at Haydon's immortal dinner-party, Keats agreed with Lamb that Newton 'had destroyed all the poetry of the rainbow by reducing it to the prismatic colours'.[3] When he came to write 'Lamia' in the summer of 1819, Keats combined the attack on Newton with an echo from Hazlitt's remarks:

> Do not all charms fly
> At the mere touch of cold philosophy?
> There was an awful rainbow once in heaven:
> We know her woof, her texture; she is given
> In the dull catalogue of common things.
> Philosophy will clip an Angel's wings, . . .[4]

Another passage which may have influenced Keats is the eloquent peroration to Hazlitt's fifth lecture, in which he speaks of the illusion of identity of flowers seen at different times:

> The daisy that first strikes the child's eye in trying to leap over his own shadow, is the same flower that with timid upward glance implores the grown man not to tread upon it.[5]

Hazlitt refers to the passage in Rousseau's *Confessions* describing how he found a periwinkle on one of his botanical excursions. Then he continues:

> The cuckoo, 'that wandering voice', that comes and goes with the spring, mocks our ears with one note from youth to age; and the lapwing, screaming round the traveller's path, repeats for ever the same sad story of Tereus and Philomel![6]

Several critics have pointed out that when in the penultimate stanza of the 'Ode to a Nightingale', Keats cries:

> Thou wast not born for death, immortal Bird!
> No hungry generations tread thee down;
> The voice I hear this passing night was heard
> In ancient days by emperor and clown: . . .

1 *Works*, v. 9.   2 *The Champion* (21 Dec. 1817).
3 Haydon, *Autobiography* (1927), p. 360.
4 II. 229 ff.   5 *Works*, v. 103.   6 Ibid. v. 103–4.

he may have been remembering Hazlitt's words. In his final sentence Hazlitt had quoted from Wordsworth's lines to the Cuckoo and ended with a reference to the Nightingale. It is certainly striking that in the first draft of the poem, Keats began the next line with the words 'perhaps the self-same voice . . . ' He altered *voice* to *song*, so as to avoid a repetition of the word; but the repetition itself suggests Wordsworth's poem 'To the Cuckoo'—especially as Wordsworth's poem, like Keats's stanza, ends with a reference to faeryland.

Meanwhile, on 3 February 1818, Keats had written to Reynolds, criticizing Wordsworth. Less than a month had elapsed since he had praised *The Excursion* extravagantly. The change in his views was ascribed by Lord Houghton to the fact that Wordsworth had called the 'Hymn to Pan' 'a pretty piece of paganism'. But it should be remembered that whereas Bailey and Haydon were Wordsworthians, Reynolds, who was later to write an ante-natal parody of 'Peter Bell', was inclined to be irreverent; and Keats varied his moods to suit those of his correspondents. He told Reynolds:

> It may be said that we ought to read our Contemporaries—that Wordsworth, etc., should have their due from us. But, for the sake of a few fine imaginative or domestic passages, are we to be bullied into a certain philosophy engendered in the whims of an Egotist—Every man has his speculations, but every man does not brood and peacock over them till he makes a false coinage and deceives himself. Many a man can travel to the very bourne of Heaven, and yet want confidence to put down his half-seeing.[1]

The last sentence links up with Keats's former criticism of Coleridge. He believed that Coleridge and Wordsworth were different aberrations from the Shakespearian ideal, the norm of poetry. The great poet records his intuitions, but does not try and make them fit into a philosophic system. A lesser poet, Coleridge, wastes his intuitions because he will not remain content with half-knowledge—he wants them to fit into a system which he has not yet constructed. Another lesser poet, Wordsworth, builds a philosophy with his intuitions, and in so doing, blunts them or buries them in a tumulus of theories. Keats at this time felt that it was a betrayal of poetry to use it to prove some-

1 *Letters*, p. 96.

thing, to regard it as a means rather than as an end. The letter to Reynolds continues:

Poetry should be great and unobtrusive, a thing which enters into one's soul, and does not startle it or amaze it with itself, but with its subject—How beautiful are the retired flowers! how would they lose their beauty were they to throng into the highway crying out, 'admire me, I am a violet!—dote upon me, I am a primrose!' Modern poets differ from the Elizabethans in this . . . I don't mean to deny Wordsworth's grandeur and Hunt's merit, but I mean to say we need not be teazed with grandeur and merit when we can have them uncontaminated and unobtrusive.[1]

The attack on Wordsworth's egotism may well have been suggested by Hazlitt's essay in *The Round Table*, 'On Mr. Wordsworth's Excursion', in which he declared:

An intense intellectual egotism swallows up everything. Even the dialogues introduced in the present volume are soliloquies of the same character, taking different views of the same subject. . . . The power of his mind preys upon itself. It is as if there were nothing but himself and the universe. He lives in the busy solitude of his own heart, in the deep silence of thought. . . . He sees all things in himself. . . . He only sympathises with those simple forms of feeling, which mingle at once with his own identity, or with the stream of general humanity.[2]

A few days later, Keats again wrote to Reynolds to develop his ideas about poetry:

Now it appears to me that almost any Man may like the spider spin from his own inwards his own airy Citadel—the points of leaves and twigs on which the spider begins her work are few, and she fills the air with a beautiful circuiting. Man should be content with as few points to tip with the fine Web of his Soul, and weave a tapestry empyrean full of symbols for his spiritual eye, of softness for his spiritual touch, of space for his wandering, of distinctness for his luxury.[3]

Keats next considers the difficulty that such a tapestry will have only a personal significance. He answers it by saying:

Minds would leave each other in contrary directions, traverse each other in numberless points, and at last greet each other at the journey's end.[4]

1 Ibid., p. 96.   2 *Works*, iv. 113.
3 *Letters*, p. 103.   4 *Letters*, p. 103.

He then returns to the question of the obstrusiveness of Words-worth's poetry:

> Man should not dispute or assert but whisper results to his neighbour and thus by every germ of spirit sucking the sap from mould ethereal every human might become great, and Humanity instead of being a wide heath of Furze and Briars, with here and there a remote Oak or Pine, would become a grand democracy of Forest Trees![1]

He concludes that we should not attempt to emulate the busy bee. 'It seems to me that we should rather be the flower.'

Keats, in this letter, was giving a metaphorical and subtler expression to the views on poetry which Hazlitt had expressed in *The Round Table*. In the essay 'On Poetical Versatility', for example, Hazlitt had remarked:

> Poetry dwells in a perpetual Utopia of its own. . . . It cannot be 'constrained by mastery'. It has the range of the universe; it traverses the empyrean, and looks down on nature from a higher sphere. . . . Its strength is in its wings; its element the air. . . . Poets live in an ideal world, where they make everything out according to their wishes and fancies. They either find things delightful or make them so. . . . They are naturally inventors, creators of truth, of love and beauty.[2]

This passage, ending with a reference to Keats's three absolutes—Beauty, Love, and Truth—finds an echo in more than one of his letters, and Hazlitt's description of poetry as an escape into an ideal world finds expression again in a letter written to Bailey in which Keats declares that he is sometimes

> so very sceptical as to think Poetry itself a mere Jack-a-lanthen to amuse whoever may chance to be struck with its brilliance.[3]

Keats sometimes reacted against Bailey's humourless insistence on the poet's mission.

At the end of February, Keats sent his publisher, Taylor, the famous axioms of poetry[4] which were suggested to him by a comparison of *Endymion* with his poetic aims, and which are a brilliant condensation of his thoughts about poetry during the past months. He stresses the importance of naturalness, the organic nature of imagery, and the necessity of spontaneity. Wordsworth had stated or implied all these things in the preface to the second

1 *Letters*, pp. 103–4.   2 *Works*, iv. 151–2.
3 *Letters*, p. 111.   4 Ibid., p. 108.

edition of the *Lyrical Ballads*; and Hazlitt, whose theories of poetry owed more to Wordsworth and Coleridge than he was always willing to admit, lays stress on the necessity of naturalness and spontaneity. The value of Keats's axioms depends not on their originality, but on the fact that they flowered naturally from his own experience.

The letters Keats wrote in 1818 are filled with references to Hazlitt. He speaks of Hazlitt as 'your only good damner',[1] and describes him playing with Miss Edgeworth's cat.[2] He told Reynolds that he was proposing to learn Greek and Italian, 'and in other ways prepare myself to ask Hazlitt in about a year's time the best metaphysical road I can take'.[3] A week later, in crossing another letter to Reynolds, Keats remarked:

> This crossing a letter is not without its association—for chequer work leads us naturally to a Milkmaid, a Milkmaid to Hogarth, Hogarth to Shakespeare, Shakespeare to Hazlitt—Hazlitt to Shakespeare, and thus by merely pulling an apron string we set a pretty peal of Chimes at work—.[4]

Keats was probably referring to Hazlitt's *Characters of Shakespeare's Plays*, which were published about this time. Keats's copy is extant, and it contains some interesting annotations. Hazlitt concludes his essay on *King Lear* by putting down four things that have struck him in reading the play. Keats seems to have been particularly interested in the last two of these remarks. Hazlitt declares:

> 3. That the greatest strength of genius is shewn in describing the strongest passions; for the power of the imagination; in works of invention, must be in proportion to the force of the natural impressions, which are the subject of them.[5]

Keats added this note:

> If we compare the passions to different tuns and hogsheads of wine in a vast cellar—thus it is—the poet by one cup should know the scope of any particular wine without getting intoxicated—this is the highest exertion of Power, and the next step is to paint from memory the gone self storm.[6]

---

1 Ibid., p. 119.   2 Ibid., p. 125.   3 Ibid., p. 137.
4 Ibid., p. 143.   5 *Works*, iv. 271.
6 Another reading of the last four words is, 'Of gone self storms'. I have not been able to see the original.

Even this annotation seems to have been suggested by Hazlitt's remarks in his first lecture 'On the English Poets', in which he speaks of the dramatic representation of passion:

The storm of passion lays bare and shews us the rich depths of the human soul; the whole of our existence, the sum total of our passions and pursuits, of that which we desire and that which we dread, is brought before us by contrast; the action and re-action are equal; the keenness of immediate suffering only gives us a more intense aspiration after, and a more intimate participation with the antagonist world of good; *makes us drink deeper of the cup of human life*; tugs at the heart-strings; loosens the pressure about them; and calls the springs of thought and feeling into play with ten-fold force.[1]

Hazlitt's third note corresponds to Keats's earlier statement that 'the excellence of every art is its intensity'. The fourth note is as follows:

4. That the circumstance which balances the pleasure against the pain in tragedy is, that in proportion to the greatness of the evil, is our sense and desire of the opposite good excited; and that our sympathy with actual suffering is lost in the strong impulse given to our natural affections, and carried away with the swelling tide of passion, that gushes from and relieves the heart.[2]

The second part of this sentence is reminiscent of Keats's phrase, 'capable of making all disagreeables evaporate', though he added the characteristic words 'from their being in close relationship with Beauty and Truth'. In reading *Characters of Shakespeare's Plays*, Keats sometimes found that his own intuitions were supported by Hazlitt—unless, indeed, Hazlitt himself owed something to Keats's conversation.

Keats had a deeper understanding of *King Lear* than Hazlitt himself. This can be seen both from his sonnet on the play and also from his other note on Hazlitt's essay. The critic, in speaking of the function of the Fool, remarks that

The contrast would be too painful, the shock too great, but for the intervention of the Fool, whose well-timed levity comes in to break the continuity of feeling when it no longer can be borne, and to bring into play again the fibres of the heart just as they are growing rigid from over-strained excitement.[3]

Keats demurs. 'And is it really thus?' he asks:

1 *Works*, v. 6.   2 Ibid. iv. 271.   3 Ibid. iv. 260.

Or as it has appeared to me? Does not the Fool by his very levity—give a finishing touch to the pathos; making what without him would be within our heart-reach nearly unfathomable. The Fool's words are merely the simplest translation of poetry as high as Lears.

After his walking tour in the summer of 1818, Keats returned to London, where he learnt that Hazlitt was prosecuting Blackwood for a libellous attack on *Characters of Shakespeare's Plays*, which had appeared in the same issue of *Blackwood's Edinburgh Magazine* as the notorious attack on Keats. Keats, in his letter to Dilke, makes no mention of his own cause for complaint:

> I suppose you will have heard that Hazlitt has on foot a prosecution against Blackwood. I dined with him a few days since at Hessey's—there was no word said about it, though I understand he is excessively vexed.[1]

Towards the end of October, Keats told Woodhouse in conversation that he 'thought there was now nothing original to be written in poetry; that its riches were already exhausted, and all its beauties forestalled, and that he would therefore write no more'. Hazlitt had ended his course of lectures on the English poets with an apology:

> I have felt my subject gradually sinking from under me as I advanced, and have been afraid of ending in nothing. The interest has unavoidably decreased at almost every successive step of the progress, like a play that has its catastrophe in the first or second act. This, however, I could not help.[2]

Woodhouse wrote a letter to Keats urging him not to give up writing; and the poet, in reply, explained the inconsistency of the poetical character:

> As to the poetical Character itself . . . it is not itself—it has no self—it is every thing and nothing—it has no character—it enjoys light and shade; it lives in gusto, be it foul or fair, high or low, rich or poor, mean or elevated—it has as much delight in conceiving an Iago as an Imogen. What shocks the virtuous philosopher, delights the cameleon Poet. It does no harm from its relish of the dark side of things any more than from its taste for the bright one; because they both end in speculation. A Poet is the most unpoetical of any thing in existence; because he has no Identity—he is continually informing and filling some other Body—The Sun, the Moon, the Sea, and Men and Women who are creatures of impulse are poetical and have about them an unchangeable

1 *Letters*, p. 215.   2 *Works*, v. 168.

attribute—the poet has none; no identity—he is certainly the most un-poetical of all God's Creatures. If then he has no self, and if I am a Poet, where is the Wonder that I should say I would write no more? . . . It is a wretched thing to confess; but it is a very fact that not one word I ever utter can be taken for granted as an opinion growing out of my identical nature—how can it, when I have no nature? When I am in a room with People, if I ever am free from speculating on creations of my own brain, then not myself goes home to myself; but the identity of every one in the room begins to press upon me that I am in a very little time annihilated—not only among Men; it would be the same in a Nursery of children; I know not whether I make myself wholly under-stood; I hope enough so to let you see that no dependence is to be placed on what I said that day.[1]

Most readers, I suppose, tend to think Keats was exaggerating the fluidity of the poet's character. Perhaps he was; but he told Woodhouse that he could conceive

of a billiard ball that it may have a sense of delight from its own round-ness, smoothness and volubility and the rapidity of its motion.[2]

and he told Bailey in November 1817—

The setting Sun will always set me to rights—or if a Sparrow come before my window I take part in its existince and pick about the Gravel.[3]

In the same letter to Bailey, Keats made his first distinction be-tween men of genius and men of power:

Men of Genius are great as certain ethereal Chemicals operating on the Mass of neutral intellect—but they have not any individuality, any determined Character—I would call the top and head of those who have a proper self Men of Power.[4]

His idea of the poetical character had been in his mind for nearly a year when he analysed it for Woodhouse.

It can be shown that Hazlitt's idea of the poetical character is very similar. In June 1815, he had written an essay in *The Examiner*, in which he distinguished between Milton and Shakespeare:

The genius of Milton was essentially undramatic; he saw all objects from his own point of view, and with certain exclusive preferences. Shakespeare, on the contrary, had no personal character, and no moral

1 *Letters*, pp. 227–8. 2 Cited D. Hewlett, *Adonais* (1937), p. 124.
3 *Letters*, p. 69. 4 Ibid., p. 67.

principle, except that of good nature. He took no part in the scene he describes, but gave fair play to all his characters, and left virtue and vice, folly and wisdom, right and wrong, to fight it out between themselves.[1]

In the essay 'On Posthumous Fame', reprinted in *The Round Table*, Hazlitt again stressed the idea that the great poet has no identity:

> He seemed scarcely to have an individual existence of his own, but to borrow that of others at will, and to pass successively through 'every variety of untried being'.[2]

In another essay in the same book, 'On the Literary Character', he dealt with the same subject from a less flattering angle:

> Indeed, after all, compared with the genuine feelings of nature, 'clad in flesh and blood', with real passions and affections, conversant about real objects, the life of a mere man of letters and sentiment appears to be at best but a sort of living death; a dim twilight existence; a sort of wandering about in an Elysian Fields of our own making; a refined, spiritual, disembodied state, like that of the ghosts of Homer's heroes, who we are told, would gladly have exchanged situations with the meanest peasant upon earth!
>
> The moral character of men of letters depends very much upon the same principles. All actions are seen through that general medium which reduces them to individual insignificance. Nothing fills or engrosses the mind—nothing seems of sufficient importance to interfere with our present inclination. Prejudices, as well as attachments, lose their hold upon us, and we palter with our duties as we please.[3]

Finally, in his lecture on Shakespeare and Milton, Hazlitt described Shakespeare's ability to identify himself with his characters:

> The striking peculiarity of Shakespeare's mind was its generic quality, its power of communication with all other minds—so that it contained a universe of thought and feeling within itself, and had no one peculiar bias, or exclusive excellence more than another. He was just like any other man, but that he was like all other men. He was the least of an egotist that it was possible to be. He was nothing in himself; he was all that others were, or that they could become. He not only had in himself the germs of every faculty and feeling, but he could follow them by anticipation, intuitively, into all their conceivable ramifications, through every change of fortune or conflict of passion or turn of thought. . . . There was no respect of persons with him. His genius shone equally on the evil and on the good, on the wise and foolish, the monarch and the

---

1 *The Examiner* (11 June 1815).   2 *Works*, iv. 23.   3 Ibid. iv. 135.

beggar. . . . He had only to think of any thing in order to become that thing, with all the circumstances belonging to it. . . . That which, perhaps, more than anything else, distinguishes the dramatic productions of Shakespeare from all others, is this wonderful truth and individuality of conception. Each of his characters is as much itself, and as absolutely independent of the rest, as well as of the author, as if they were living persons, not fictions of the mind. The poet may be said, for the time, to identify himself with the character he wishes to represent, and to pass from one to another, like the same soul successively animating different bodies. By an art like of the ventriloquist, he throws his imagination out of himself, and makes every word appear to proceed from the mouth of the person in whose name it is given. . . . One might suppose that he had stood by at the time, and overheard what passed.[1]

The resemblance between Keats's idea of the poetical character and Hazlitt's cannot be fortuitous; but it will be apparent that Keats has made Hazlitt's thoughts his own. Hazlitt's essays on poetical versatility and the literary character were written partly as a counterblast to Hunt's views on the latter subject, which were also published in *The Round Table*, and he was being deliberately provocative. Now his chief defect as a critic of his contemporaries is a certain captiousness which was partly due to his disappointment at his own creative achievements and partly to his dislike of the political apostasy of Wordsworth, Coleridge, and Southey. It is therefore remarkable that the sardonic, almost satirical, opinions of Hazlitt concerning his fellow-writers could be applied by Keats to himself, even though he combined them with Hazlitt's analysis of the nature of Shakespeare's genius. Keats used Hazlitt's theories to explore his own personality; and his own account of the poetical character is so coloured by his own experience that it is subtler and truer than Hazlitt's.

Keats at this time was writing 'Hyperion', and his ideas on the nature of the poet were reflected in the theme of the poem. We have seen that he contrasted men of achievement with men of power. The poem, as we have shown, describes the victory of the men of achievement.

Meanwhile, in December 1818, Keats told Haydon:

I feel in myself all the vices of a Poet, irritability, love of effect and admiration—and influenced by such devils I may at times say more ridiculous things than I am aware of—.[2]

1 *Works*, v. 47–50.   2 *Letters*, p. 271.

He may have been thinking of a passage in Hazlitt's essay, 'On Poetical Versatility':

> The object of poetry is to please; this art naturally gives pleasure and excites admiration. Poets, therefore, cannot do well without sympathy and flattery. It is accordingly very much against the grain that they remain long on the unpopular side of the question. . . . Truth alone does not satisfy their pampered appetites without the sauce of praise.[1]

The next important reference to Hazlitt in Keats's letters is when he copied out long extracts from the *Letter to William Gifford* for George and Georgiana and added the admiring comment:

> The manner in which this is managed; the force and innate power with which it yeasts and works up itself—the feeling for the costume of society; is in a style of genius—He hath a demon, as he himself says of Lord Byron.[2]

Later in the same journal-letter, Keats wrote a bogus petition to the governors of St. Luke's Hospital, in which he asserts that he does not admire Hunt, Moore, Southey, and Rogers, 'and does admire Wm. Hazlitt'. Soon afterwards Keats described the mood in which he was later to write the 'Ode on Indolence':

> I am in a sort of temper indolent and supremely careless. I long after a stanza or two of Thompson's *Castle of Indolence*. My passions are all asleep from my having slumbered till nearly eleven and weakened the animal fibre all over me to a delightful sensation about three degrees on this side faintness. . . . In this state of effeminacy the fibres of the brain are relaxed in common with the rest of the body, and to such a happy degree that pleasure has no show of enticement and pain no unbearable frown.[3]

Hazlitt had said that Thomson, in his *Castle of Indolence*, had

> poured out the whole soul of indolence, diffuse, relaxed, supine, dissolved into a voluptuous dream; and surrounded himself with a set of objects and companions, in entire unison with the listlessness of his own temper.[4]

In his essay 'On Poetical Versatility', Hazlitt had said of poets:

> Their only object is to please their fancy. Their souls are effeminate, half man and half woman—they want fortitude, and are without

---

1 *Works*, iv. 152.   2 *Letters*, p. 310.
3 Ibid., p. 315.   4 *Works*, v. 88.

principle. If things do not turn out according to their wishes, they will make their wishes turn round to things.[1]

This may be compared with two passages in the essay 'On the Literary Character':

The defects of the literary character proceed, not from frivolity and voluptuous indolence, but from the overstrained exertion of the faculties, from abstraction and refinement.[2]

The very same languor and listlessness which, in fashionable life, are owing to the rapid 'Succession of persons and things', may be found and even in a more intense degree, in the most recluse student. . . . [3]

Neither Keats nor Hazlitt fully realized that such a mood of indolence was a necessary preparation for the writing of great poetry. Just before he wrote 'Hyperion', and again just before the period of the great odes, Keats came to what seemed a dead end, but which was in fact a prelude to creative activity.

Immediately after the passage about indolence, Keats discusses his attitude to Haslam's approaching bereavement, and he comments:

We have leisure to reason on the misfortunes of our friends; our own touch us too nearly for words. Very few men have ever arrived at a complete disinterestedness of Mind. . . . From the manner in which I feel Haslam's misfortune I perceive how far I am from any humble standard of disinterestedness. . . . I have no doubt that thousands of people never heard of, have had hearts completely disinterested.[4]

Now Hazlitt's favourite doctrine was of the 'natural disinterestedness of the human mind'. It was the subject of his first book, which Keats is known to have possessed and admired. But curiously enough, there is no evidence that Keats had studied *On the Principles of Human Action* with great attention. There is no sign in his discussion of disinterestedness that he had followed the drift of Hazlitt's argument, though he seems to have been influenced by the repetition of the word 'identity' just after the ornate passage of which the author was justifiably proud.

The reason why a man should prefer his own future welfare to that of others is, that he has a necessary, absolute interest in the one, which he cannot have in the other—and this, again, is a consequence of his being

1 *Works*, iv. 152. 2 Ibid. iv. 132–3.
3 Ibid. iv. 133. 4 *Letters*, p. 316.

always the same individual, of his continued *identity* with himself. . . .
How am I to know that I am not imposed upon by a false claim of
identity? . . . Here, then, I saw an end put to my speculations about
absolute self-interest and personal *identity*. I saw plainly . . . that my
identity with myself must be confined to the connection between my
past and present being. . . . It is this greater liveliness and force with
which I can enter into my future feelings, that in a manner identifies
them with my present being; and this notion of *identity* being once
formed, the mind makes use of it to strengthen its habitual propensity,
by giving to personal motives a reality and absolute truth which they
can never have.[1]

When, in his journal-letter, Keats continues his speculations on
human life, he seems to echo the repetition of 'identity', though
he uses the word in a slightly different sense. He describes the
world as a vale of soul-making:

There may be intelligencies or sparks of the divinity in millions—but
they are not Souls till they acquire identities, till each one is personally
itself. . . . How then are Souls to be made? How then are these sparks
which are God to have identity given them—so as ever to possess a bliss
peculiar to each one's individual existence? How, but by the medium
of a world like this?[2]

He goes on to explain that the Intelligence, the Human Heart, and
the World act upon each other for the 'purpose of forming the
Soul or *Intelligence destined to possess the sense of Identity*'. Then follows
the parable of the world as a school, the heart as the horn-book,
and the soul as the child. Keats then summarizes his argument

and what was his Soul before it came into the world and had these
provings and alterations and perfectionings? An intelligence—without
Identity—and how is this Identity to be made? Through the medium of
the heart. And how is the heart to become this Medium but in a world
of Circumstances?[3]

Now this passage on soul-making is really an interpretation of
'Hyperion' which Keats had recently laid aside. The Vale of Soul-
making is the same as the vale in which Apollo meets Mnemosyne.
But Keats's terminology is now different. In the autumn of 1818,
he had described the poet as having no identity. Apollo, being a
poet, likewise has no identity, for identity is the static character
which the poet must, at all cost, avoid. Yet—though Keats may

1 *Works*, i. 47.　　2 *Letters*, p. 336.　　3 Ibid., p. 337.

not have been aware of it at the time of composition—the deification of Apollo symbolizes not only the transformation of dreamer to great poet, but also the birth of a soul in the ordinary man by the operation of suffering. When he came to interpret his own poem in the spring of 1819, Keats made 'identity' to mean the individuality which must be added to an intelligence to make it a soul. It is apparent that he was now using the word in a different sense; and the change may be due to his reading of Hazlitt's philosophical essay.

I have tried to show that nearly all Keats's theories about poetry were developed from remarks of Hazlitt. The ideas he expresses on the poetical character, on the nature of Shakespeare's genius, and on the relative deficiencies of Wordsworth and Coleridge are very close to the views expressed by Hazlitt on the same subjects. Yet it would be a great mistake to minimize the differences between the two writers. Hazlitt is a good critic; Keats is a great one. As Mr. Eliot has said:

> There is hardly one statement of Keats about poetry, which, when considered carefully and with due allowance for the difficulties of communication, will not be found to be true; and what is more, true for greater and more mature poetry than anything Keats ever wrote.[1]

Because he accepted nothing on trust, but proved his axioms on his pulses, Keats's borrowings were all transformed and individualized, so that they came to express not merely his tastes but his deepest convictions.

Keats continued to hold a high opinion of Hazlitt's judgement. When in the autumn of 1819 he wanted to make a living as a journalist, he decided to consult his friend; and on 25 March 1820, after his fatal illness had shown itself, Keats managed to attend the private view of Haydon's painting, *Christ's Entry into Jerusalem*. Haydon records in his *Autobiography*—'Keats and Hazlitt were up in a corner, really rejoicing.'[2] It is fitting that Keats, who had earlier coupled Haydon's pictures and Hazlitt's depth of taste, should last be seen with the critic on the day of the painter's short-lived triumph.

1 *The Use of Poetry and the Use of Criticism* (1933), p. 101.
2 *Autobiography* (1927), p. 376.

10

The Keatsian Incantation

A Study of Phonetic Patterning

DAVID I. MASSON

EMBARKING UPON AN ANALYSIS of the ' "harmonies" ' of
the 'Ode on Melancholy', M. R. Ridley in his apologia observes
that nowadays we have dulled our aural perceptions and are deaf
to the ' "music of words" '; but that by expending a little pains
we can resensitize our ears 'so that all the exquisite harmonies
which the great poets can elicit from their instrument, no longer
slide past us'.[1]

The present essay is undertaken in a somewhat similar spirit.
It is an attempt to establish the characteristic music of Keats
through analysis of a number of sound-patterns in his other late
odes and in 'The Eve of St. Agnes'; and through some comparison with his first thoughts and drafts and some reference to the
patterns of a few predecessors and contemporaries.

This is not to assert that Keats was necessarily aware of such
patterns. Unless we are poseurs, our most characteristic mannerisms, in poetry as in life, are not those of which we are most
conscious. In this connection we may recall the warning of M. R.
Ridley, that the foundation of a good poet's 'music' is not any
deliberate exercise of virtuosity in pattern-building, but his half-
conscious mental 'ear'.

To make succinct reference and description possible, and to
short-circuit a quite unmanageably enormous amount of periph-
rasis, a certain minimum of special terminology and notation is
essential. This may suggest a dogmatic approach to detail, which
is quite unintended.

1 Ridley, *Keats's Craftsmanship* (1933), pp. 232–40.

Walter Jackson Bate demonstrates Keats's (conscious?) use of sound, in patterns modulating between 'short' monophthongs and 'long' or diphthongal vowels; in simple and patterned assonances; and in the use together of various labial consonants.[1] The type of pattern, however, which this essay discusses, is one which seems to be implied in parts of Ridley's analysis: a spell-like concatenation of several elements (vowel or consonant or both) in a more or less complex repetitive system. Common in European lyrical, and not uncommon in dramatic and social, poetry, this device, now conscious, now partly unconscious, had attained since the Renaissance a richness and subtlety impossible before. It is probably related to something fundamental in human nervous construction, and sounds suggestively like a refinement and elaboration upon the phonetic patterns of passion and oratory, of savage ritual and of infant babbling.[2] Indeed, the officially codified phonetic structures of poetry, such as Welsh *cynghanedd*, Germanic *Stabreim*, and all types of rhyme, may be regarded as selective formalizations of a natural human tendency, of which the device we are to discuss is the freer manifestation: a predilection for the repetition, or permutation, of tightly linked or extended chains of sound, analogous to the repetition or inversion of a melodic line in music. Such patterns, like the more often discussed patterns of rhythm, may short-circuit consciousness, while they stir the whole organism to response.

Keats is one of the best examples of a poet in whose works such a web of sound is important, and the late odes and 'The Eve of St. Agnes' exhibit a rich tapestry of free patterns: elaborately interwoven indeed, though they do not form a perfectly organized whole in each poem. Though Keats's patterns are not deliberately constructed, they were evidently of great importance to his mental ear, for it will often be found that his second thoughts in composition have greatly improved the formal beauty and suitability of the sound-patterns. Though illustration of the meaning is not their main function, his patterns often suit the general

1 Walter Jackson Bate, *The Stylistic Development of Keats* (New York: Modern Language Association of America, 1945), pp. 51-65, 134-6.

2 Leopold Stein, *The Infancy of Speech and the Speech of Infancy* (London, 1949), suggests a similarity between the origins and evolution of language and its development in the child, and finds parallels (pp. 97-104, 113-34, 158-9, 173, 184-96) between reduplicative babbling and savage repetitive patterns, both of which are originally associated with emotional satisfaction.

atmosphere, and sometimes bear a rather subtle relation to the sense. But if we compare them with the disciplined sound-patterns of the Augustans, we must conclude that Keats was using to excess the devices of his predecessors, and that in him they had become divorced from rhetorical and didactic purpose. Yet at their best they exercise a compelling magic which is their principal justification.

For the sake of conciseness, it will sometimes be necessary to speak as though Keats had chosen the words for their sound alone. But the prior claims of meaning and atmosphere, and the verbal influences of his reading, though here largely ignored, are certainly not forgotten.

As this essay deals with phonetic patterns, it is essential to state what phonetic conventions are observed, and why. We may reasonably suppose that man's *linguistic* phonetic perception is intimately bound up with his *aesthetic* phonetic perception. By the former is meant the pre-conscious cerebral activity, a pre-requisite of speech and its apprehension, which identifies each given segment of speech-sound as one of a particular class, a particular counter in communication.[1] By the latter is meant the unconscious or semi-conscious activity which recognizes repetitions of sound in poetry, etc., and acknowledges the simpler connotations of such sound, or its emotional relevance.[2] Therefore in considering the aesthetics of phonetic sound in poetry, whether programmatic or formal, we should, ideally, first establish the phonemes, and secondly, the more delicate phonetic features. The first give us the general picture of phonetic structure; but the second are also important.

It is not enough to establish the features of standard English: we should consider the individual poet, whose 'ear' was responsible for the phonetic aspects of his final choice of words. 'Received Pronunciation' English (R.P.) in Daniel Jones's sense,[3] will do fairly well for most British poetry of *c.* 1800–1950.

1 Cf. Martin Joos, *Acoustic Phonetics* (*Language*, Monograph 23, Baltimore, 1948); G. E. Peterson, 'The Phonetic Value of Vowels', *Language*, xxvii (1951), 541–53.

2 On the relation of sound to emotion (and to aesthetic delight) cf. Carroll Pratt, 'The Design of Music', *Journal of Aesthetics and Art Criticism*, xii (1954), 289–300, esp. 296: 'patterns which at the level of form are indistinguishable from the patterns of bodily reverberations. *Music sounds the way emotions feel*' (original italics).

3 Daniel Jones, *An Outline of English Phonetics*, 4th ed. (London, 1934), 6th ed. (New York, 1940), § 61, p. 12; his *An English Pronouncing Dictionary*, 9th ed. (London, 1948), pp. ix–xii.

But in the case of Keats, son of a London livery stable ostler, we must ask ourselves whether his pronunciation, even after his acquaintance with a diversity of educated men, had not perhaps a mild Cockney tinge. If Keats grew up with a 'light' Cockney accent, he must have had the equivalent 'ear', only partly modified by intercourse with others. Now it is fairly certain that London speech at the time was not unlike the Cockney of today.[1] In any case, many features of London phonology are typical of all south-eastern English semi-educated speech. No one, unfortunately, would seem to have established the phoneme system of any Cockney speaker, though the general phonology is fairly well charted.[2]

We shall attempt here to outline briefly the phoneme structure of R.P. English, with remarks on our conventions of alliteration and assonance; and to suggest possible modifications to represent Keats's pronunciation. Among English consonants the picture is tolerably clear: among vowels, agreement on R.P. has not been reached, and we must choose the system best suited to our purpose.

CONSONANTS. We recognize as separate phonemes the labials /p, b, m, f, v/, the dentals and alveolars /t, d, n, th,[3] dh,[3] s, z/, the various palatals[4] /sh,[3] zh,[3] k, g, ng[3]/, also /l, r/,[5] and /h/. In certain patterns, homorganic voiced/voiceless pairs (e.g., t/d)

---

1 William Matthews, *Cockney Past and Present: a Short History of the Dialect of London* (London: Routledge, 1938), pp. 157–80. The raised (or even conflated) simple vowels, and some of the lowered, centralized, or crossed-over diphthongs, appear from the evidence of occasional spellings to have been used as early as the fifteenth century, while *-in* for *-ing*, and confusions between *-n* and *-nd*, between voiced and unvoiced stops, and several other London pronunciations, some now obsolete, similarly show up during the last few centuries: see ibid., pp. 18–46, 162–88.

2 Ibid., pp. 76–81; Daniel Jones, *Outline*, ed. cit., §§ 58, 401, 847 (v), 876, 879.

3 For the convenience of the reader unaccustomed to phonetic symbols, digraphs are used in this essay instead of the correct single symbols.

4 These are grouped together on Jakobsonian grounds as 'compact' consonants; see Roman Jakobson, C. G. M. Fant, and M. Halle, *Preliminaries to Speech Analysis*, 2nd printing (Massachusetts Institute of Technology, May 1952), § 2.41, pp. 27–8 and Appendix, pp. 43–4; but nevertheless the common sibilance of s/z, sh/zh must be regarded as aesthetically, even if not phonemically, important.

5 This is in opposition to Jakobson, *et. al.*, *Preliminaries*, Appendix, pp. 43–4 and § 2.3111, p. 21, where R.P. 'r' is conflated with [ə], [ʌ] as a vowel; but Jakobson groups /l, r/ as liquids or semi-vowel-like in most languages (ibid., § 2.222, p. 19).

are here held capable of sub-alliteration or semi-equivalence. More rarely, the prosody of the pattern may activate a lesser degree of sub-alliteration, e.g. between *th* and *d*, or between different nasals.

The compound consonants, or affricates [t*sh*, d*zh*][1] are regarded by Daniel Jones as single phonemes, but written each with two symbols; Jakobson uses single symbols.[2] We shall represent these element-groups variously according to the phonetic patterns in which they occur, and as capable of alliteration with /*sh*, *zh*/ and of sub-alliteration with /t, d/.

The only features known about Keats's consonants are, that his -*l* appear to have been syllabic in *rumblings*, *dazzling*, etc.; and that, like Wordsworth, he rhymes *robin(s)/sobbing(s)*.[3] The latter feature is typical of both London and eighteenth-century standard speech, and we cannot be certain that Keats did not intend 'openin' on the foam', for instance; but his rhymes are often obviously imperfect by intention (*wand/hand*, *Thessaly/pie*, *possible/dispel*).

VOWELS. As a vowel is more sonorous and usually longer than a consonant, the non-phonemic affinities and distinctions of the vowels are more important. In the compound vowels,[4] their main element is here considered usually to assonate or sub-assonate with the corresponding simple vowel, and their glide-vowel occasionally to assonate with the equivalent syllabic vowel (*y/i*, *w/u*, *ə/ə*).

For R.P. English vowels we shall construct a modification of the Swadesh system,[5] as follows (unaccented variants in paren-

1 See n. 3, p. 162.

2 D. Jones, *Outline*, §§ 601, 609 (he omits from the table of English sounds, p. x); Jakobson *et al.*, *Preliminaries*, Preface, p. vi, § 2.321, p. 24, Appendix, pp. 43–4. Phonetic affricates such as /tr, dr/, /ts, dz/, which have no phonemic unity in English, will not usually be recognized; cf. D. Jones, *Outline*, §§ 617–36.

3 Amy Lowell, *John Keats* (London, 1925), vol. i, pp. 229, 266–7.

4 Literary writers, including Ridley and Bate, distinguish short and long vowels as well as diphthongs; among the phoneticians, Daniel Jones distinguished length in /i:, u:/ etc., and Etsko Kruisinga, *The Phonetic Structure of English Words* (Bern: A. Francke, 1943), speaks of free and checked vowels. Yet in 1954 at least, the 'short' vowels of *sad*, *gone*, are far longer than the 'long' vowels of *seated*, *fateful*. Swadesh and Jakobson both break up 'long' or 'free' English vowels into pairs of phonemes; see Morris Swadesh, 'On the Analysis of English Syllabics', *Language*, xxiii (1947), 137–50; Jakobson *et al.*, *Preliminaries*.

5 Swadesh, article in *Language*, xxiii (1947), § 5.1, esp. p. 145; but for /-i, -u/ he uses /-j, -w/. Though they are unfamiliar and therefore almost entirely avoided in

theses); the reference numbers are given to save unnecessary repetition of the visual pattern:

Single symbols [V] as in:

1 /i/ pit 6 /u/ put

(petition) 4 /ə/ (potato)

(patrician)

2 /e/ pet 7 /o/

(portentous)

5 /a/ putt

3 /æ/ pat 8 /å/ pot

Double [VV] [or otherwise lengthened] as in: 4 pert; 5 part, pah; 7 port, paw. *Və as in*: 1 peer; 2 pair; 4 [see VV]; 6 poor; 7 pore. *Vi/Vy as in*: 1 peat; 2 pate; 5 spite; 7 boy, poison. *Vu/Vw as in*: 5 pout; 6 boot; 7 boat. *Viə as in*: 5 pyre; 7 [coir]. *Vuə as in*: 5 power.

Thus *pate* (main vowel 2) is phonemically /peit/ or /peyt/; but in fact its /e/ could barely sub-assonate in R.P. with the slacker /e/ of *pet* or the still lower /e/ of *pair*, while its /i/ might assonate with the first two vowels of *petition*, and echo the /i/ of /spait/ (*spite*). Similarly *peat, pit, peer* (main vowel 1) do not fully assonate. Another, non-phonemic, sub-assonance connects (5) *part* /paat/ with (7) *pot* /påt/; and a non-phonemic distinction prevents *putt*/pat/ from achieving full assonance with *part*/paat/ (both 5).

Syllabic /l, m, n/, e.g., in *bottle(d)/dazzling, chasm(s), button(ed)*, are to be considered to function as vowels; the first, sub-assonating with /u/: the u-resonance was probably even stronger in the London accent of Keats. In the series *let, pelt, petal,* /l/ may be compared *functionally* with /y,i/ in the series *yet, pate, petty*.

Keats rhymes *vile/toil* in *Endymion*, and this is in line with London spellings from the fifteenth century onwards.[1] This confusion was condemned as a vulgarism in the middle eighteenth century, and Amy Lowell suggests that *vile/toil* was not intended as a perfect rhyme;[2] but although Matthews regards *oi* spellings

1 Matthews, *Cockney*, pp. 182-3, 41.   2 Amy Lowell, *John Keats*, vol. i, p. 368.

this essay, the writer finds the Jakobsonian auditory distinctive features (*Preliminaries, passim*) clarify the picture, especially where sound-connotations are involved; but more medial positions seem required than Jakobson would allow. A critical consideration of Jakobson's theories is contained in Eli Fischer-Jørgensen, 'The Phonetic Basis for Identification of Phonemic Elements', *Journal of the Acoustic Society of America*, xxiv (1952), 611-17.

of 'long *i*' as indicating a 'rounded' Cockney diphthong, it seems more probable that they represent a quite common educated pronunciation of both diphthongs as identical (approximately [ai] by this time), as shown in many Augustan rhymes. Varieties of our modern 'spelling-pronunciation' of *oi* appear, but this anomalous diphthong was not fully established for all forms normally spelt with *oi/oy*, until some time in the nineteenth century.[1] If so, Keats's *poison, toil* (if not his *boy*) should be placed, in the table above, with his *spite*. Possibly his *poor* should be placed with *pore*; and his *oft, cough* (but not *pot*) with his *port*: both rather old-fashioned R.P. pronunciations, and both also close to Cockney.

If we think of Keats's basic phoneme structure as *raised* and compressed to:

(1) i		(6) u
	(4) ë	
(2) é		(7) *é*
	(5) a	
(3) è		(8) o

but his Vi(-), Vu(-) forms as lowered and slightly *centralized* or *crossed over*, towards

(1) ii		(6) üu
	(2) əi; əu (7)	
(5) au(-)		(5) âi(-)

(with /aa/ in *part, pah* also low and equivalent to *â*), we shall be making a guess well in accordance with the general structure of south-eastern pronunciations, and supported by London 'occasional spellings' (which, of course, often illustrate a more extreme accent) since the fifteenth century.[2]

Thus in Keats's *pate* the main vowel would be more likely to sub-assonate with that of *pert* than with those of *pet, pair*. His diphthong in *boat* would be only an exaggeration of the modern R.P. diphthong in which the first element tends to resemble 'er'. As to the top pair of diphthongs (1, 6), there is indeed no spelling-evidence of their having been centralized before Bernard

1 Spelling pronunciations, etc.: the writer's interpretation from the pronunciations inferred by Constance Davies, *English Pronunciation from the Fifteenth to the Eighteenth Century* (London, 1934), p. 10.
2 Matthews, *Cockney*, pp. 157–80.

Shaw observed them;[1] except, one would suppose, in Henry Fielding, who in a comic spelling gives 'afternune' (1743);[2] in pattern-formulation we shall in fact treat Keats's /iy/, /uw/ as sub-assonant with /i, iə/ and /u, uə/ respectively, much as in R.P.

Here it will be necessary to hold back still further from consideration of the poetry itself, in order to introduce and define a number of special terms, so that the elusive phenomena we are to discuss may be more precisely handled, more firmly grasped. There is no short cut: if music deserves musical analysis, so does the music of verse.

In a given passage, we shall speak of a succession of repeated classes of sound, if they are not too scattered among irrelevant sounds to make a musically organic whole, as a *pattern* proper. A similar patterning which is significant and self-sufficient in itself, but which is an abstraction from the total musical pattern, and covers a smaller variety of sounds, we shall call a *sub-pattern*. In most poetry the sub-patterns have more significance than the patterns. Thus in William Barnes's line 'Du leän down low on Linden Leä', the vowels, or some of them, enter into the total repetitive pattern; but its consonants alone constitute a strongly marked sub-pattern.

A pattern/sub-pattern will usually be found to contain distinguishable *members*, i.e., separate successive portions, each of which has a fellow or fellows in the total. In Barnes's consonantal sub-pattern there are two such members, separated, on grounds of phonetic (not rhythmic) prosodic succession, between 'low' and 'on'. (We shall call such a two-member form a *pair*.) Each member here may be split into two *sections* of which the second, *l-nd-nl-*, is the same in each member. In some patterns, two or more larger units occur, each containing two or more recognizable members; these larger units we shall call (member-) *groups*. A member, group, or section, consists of a number of successive phonetic *components*; thus *d-l-nd-nl-* contains six components, though there are only three phonetic *elements*. An *element* is a class of sound from the standpoint of the particular pattern. A consonantal element usually corresponds to a consonantal phoneme; but with English vowels there may be more elements than relevant phonemes. In certain patterns there may be less, e.g. where the sub-assonance of *e/æ* or *é/è*, or the sub-alliteration of *t/d*, is

1 Matthews, *Cockney*, p. 179.   2 Ibid., p. 27.

activated by their position, so that they function as a single element. In this latter case, we should call the separate phonemes *allotypes* of elements *E, D* respectively.

Where pattern-transcription is really essential, it will be printed in italics, to prevent confusion with phonetic or phonemic notation. But 'element *x*' will be designated e.*x*, 'elements *x* and *y*' will be represented by ee.*x,y*. Capitalized elements represent those with several allotypes, thus e.*B*, Bilabial stop (*b/p*); e.*D*, 'Dental' stop (*d/t*); e.*G*, 'Guttural' stop (*g/k*); etc. In pattern-transcription, we shall separate groups by | | | , members by | | , sections by | . We shall use *è* for Keats's raised vowel in *pat, o* for that in *pot*, *é* for that (7, 7) in *port, oft*, and *əy, əw* for those of *pate, boat*; we shall use *a, aw* (sub-assonant, in *putt, pout*), but *â, ây* (subassonant, in *part, spite*). For all other sounds we shall use our original phonemic symbols as for R.P. English, with -*y*, -*w* for the relevant diphthongs. Note that *a, â, ô, è*, etc., have nearly *French* values.

For ease and succinctness of reference and enumeration, we shall sometimes number sub-patterns (a), (b), etc., groups I, II, etc., members 1, 2, etc., sections 1.1, 1.2, 2.1, 2.2, etc., and components 1(1), 1(2), etc. 'Component (2) of each member' will be abbreviated as n(2), and 'section 2 of each member' as n.2.

It is convenient to name certain elementary categories of pattern. Six regular types, in which each member consists of the same elements and the same number of components, are:

(i) the *series*: simple alliteration or assonance of one element;
(ii) the *couple*: a series-*pair*;
(iii) the *sequence*: repetition of elements in the same order in each member, group, or section, as in n.2 of the Barnes consonants above;
(iv) the *switch*: a sequence with some member(s) exactly reversed;
(v) the *chiasmus*: a switch-pair or complete inversion;
(vi) the *interchange*: any more irregular order of elements.

Three types with extra components are:

(vii) the *progression*: a disturbed sequence, as in Barnes's total sub-pattern and pattern;
(viii) the rare *reversion*: a disturbed chiasmus;
(ix) the *bracket*: in which an extra medial imperfect member,

167

component, or contrasting sound, acts as a central pivot for a *pair* of any type.

Where the components are adjacent in a member/members, the portion or pattern concerned will be called *tight*; a pattern/ sub-pattern may also be *tightening* or *loosening*. (A normal rhyme is a special case of tight sequence containing a stressed vowel; a one-phoneme rhyme is an assonant couple or series.) *Knotting-up*, on the other hand, describes a pattern/sub-pattern where some of the elements are not combined till the last member.

We may distinguish various subdivisions and combinations of these pattern categories, which are heard in Keats and other writers. In the interests of comparative terminology, occasional reference will be made in passing to the equivalent terms in the French prosodic classification of Jules Romains.[1] For the next few pages we shall confine ourselves to a detailed illustration of the simpler, shorter varieties, less important than the innumerable composite varieties and indeed rarely found uncontaminated in Keats or elsewhere. They exist chiefly as minor sub-patterns, and may be considered as basic types from which the composite and looser varieties proliferate. A preliminary classification of these basic types will help us to appreciate afterwards the structure of the poet's more elaborate music.

The simple consonantal series or couple may be stressed, initial, and regular, as in Teutonic *Stabreim*, or it may be irregular. It corresponds approximately to Romains's *accord imparfait* (or *pauvre*) *intérieur*. The type is C C C . . . , where C stands for a particular consonantal element. Thus in Pope, the initial couple is the most obviously patterned feature of 'What means this tumult in a *v*estal's *v*eins?' (*Eloisa to Abelard*, 4). This C C type is a simple rhetorical device, usually deliberate, which can be used to stress emotional importance or to underline syntax.[2] Shelley has the pair 'The *b*urning stars of the a*b*yss were hurled' (again contaminated by other components) ('Ode to Liberty', ll. 2). But in Keats the function seems merely lyrical and musical:[3] 'Lead'st

1 Jules Romains and G. Chennevière, *Petit traité de versification*, 12th ed. (Paris: nrf, 1923), pp. 59–80.

2 Wallace Cable Brown, *The Triumph of Form: a Study of the Later Masters of the Heroic Couplet* (University of North Carolina Press, 1948), pp. 25, 28, 43, 48, 51, 81, 88, 98–9, 152–3, 159.

3 Cf. ibid., pp. 19–20, 32, 48, 56, 151–2, for 'lyrical' alliteration in the seventeenth-eighteenth centuries.

thou that heifer lowing at the skies' ('Ode on a Grecian Urn',
IV. 3); 'Of marble men and maidens' (ibid. V. 2); 'Fade far
away . . . quite forget. . . . The weariness, the fever, and the
fret' ('Ode to a Nightingale', III. 1, 3); 'I cannot see what flowers
are at my feet' (ibid. V. 1). It appears in post-vocalic form
(Romains's *accord simple intérieur*) in the *k*-sounds of 'and his weak
spirit fails To think how they may ache' ('The Eve of St. Agnes',
II. 8–9). A mixed series in e.*p* appears in 'Until the poppied
warmth of sleep oppress'd' (ibid. XXVII. 3); here members have
been brought together which were in earlier versions further
apart.[1] A mixed series in three M's with 'syncopation' or shunting
off the stress, occurs in 'Beyond a mortal man impassion'd far'
(ibid. XXXVI. 1); the phrase was originally reversed.[2]

Accord imparfait includes combinations of two consonants
(*accord suffisant*), and we may likewise recognize a compound consonantal series or couple, type CC' CC' . . . Thus Pope: 'Not
twice a twelvemonth' ('Epilogue to the Satires', I. 1); 'By her just
standard, which is still the same' ('An Essay on Criticism', 69).
Thus Shelley: ' 'mid the steep *sk*y's *c*ommotion, Loo*se c*louds . . .'
('Ode to the West Wind', II. 1–2), (2[1] is the allotype /z/);
'Scattering contiguous far into the sky' ('Ode to Liberty', I. 4).
As might be expected, the less athletic verse of Keats provides
fewer examples of this type, but we may instance *dr* in 'drowsy . . .
drunk . . . drains . . . Dryad' ('Ode to a Nightingale', I. 1–3, 7).
In a draft, 'drowsy numbness pains' had been 'painful numbness
falls',[3] so the emendation adds an extra member.

This type of series may be also considered as a tight consonantal sequence. Thus the first example in *sk* above continues by
loosening in two subsequent members: ' 'mid the steep sky's
commotion, Loose clouds li*k*e earth'*s* de*c*aying leaves' (4[1]
being the second /z/ allotype). This sub-pattern is combined with
a loose sequence *l*-*S*/ /*l*—*S*/ /*l* . . . *S* / / . . . *l*—*S*. The second
sk example is really a 1/2/3 switch with 2 ('contiguous') loose.

The first and last members of the loose sequence above may be
called circumsyllabic (Romains's *accord riche intérieur*, an intra-
linear form of Wilfred Owen's half-rhyme), type C-C'/ / C-C' . . .

1 Ridley, *Keats's Craftsmanship* (1933), pp. 156–7; John Keats, *The Poetical Works*,
ed. H. Buxton Forman (London, 1934), p. 223.
2 Ridley, *Keats's Craftsmanship*, p. 168.
3 Keats, *Poetical Works*, ed. Forman, p. 230.

The pure circumsyllabic sequence is, like the series, a well-known rhetorical device, especially as a pair. Thus Pope: 'Why feels my *heart* its long forgotten *heat*?' (*Eloisa to Abelard*, 6) (converted to a bracket by the *t* of 'forgotten'); 'The hungry judges *soon* the *sentence sign*' (*Rape of the Lock*, III. 21) (really a 12/3/4 switch, with 3 tight, and possibly with programmatic effect). From Shelley, two typically compound instances, type CC'-C'', converted to progressions by extra components, are 'Till the thick stalk stuck like a murderer's stake' ('The Sensitive Plant', III, xvii. 2) and 'o'er Spain. . . . My soul spurn'd the chains' ('Ode to Liberty', I. 3, 5), both conveying a Shelleian fury of indignation. But Keats has the milder 'What maidens loth? What mad pursuit?' ('Grecian Urn', I. 8–9), in which the rhetorical function seems to have vanished. Another such lyrical sequence-pair is that of 'asleep in lap of legends old' ('St. Agnes', XV. 9), an important second thought of Keats which will be fully discussed below. Again, but in bracketed form, we have 'The hall door shuts a*gain*, and all the *n*oise is *gon*e' (ibid. XXIX. 9). This example is programmatic in the sense of reinforcing our impression of an opening and shutting door synchronized with the onset and cessation of the noise.

Some wider variations of consonant patterning may be mentioned here. Keats has a loosening sequence-pair in 'The lustrous salvers in the moonlight *gl*eam; Broad *gol*den fringes' ('St. Agnes', XXX. 5–6), apparently decorative in function. A tightening sequence-pair which seems to connect opposites, appears in 'Solution *s*wee*t*: meantime the fro*st*-wind blows' (ibid. XXXVI. 7); but this should perhaps be classified as a three-element interchange with e.*w*. An interval-varied 12/34 switch with incantatory effect appears in ''*t*was a *m*idnigh*t* [*ch*]ar*m* I*m*possible *to* mel*t*' (ibid. XXXII. 3–4) ['charm' equal to/ts*h*âm/]. A tightening-and-loosening progression in ee.*s,l* lends an extraordinary mystery to 'Silence and slow time, Sylvan historian' ('Grecian Urn', I. 2–3). An incantatory interchange *l* . . . *njd*/ /*l-j-nd* rubricates 'What leaf-fring'd legend' (ibid. I.5). The *again/noise/gone* bracket may be compared with Shelley's much more excited syncopated bracket in ee.*p,v*: 'Pave it; the evening sky pavilions it' ('Ode to Liberty', V. 5).

So much for the shorter consonantal forms. Assonance also has its function—the vocalic series or couple (*rime pauvre/imparfait intérieur*). Simple short vowels echo as in Pope's 'The hungry judges' (*Rape of the Lock*, III. 21), type V V; but more commonly the vowel is 'long' or 'free'. In Pope's English these were probably simple long vowels, for instance the frequent *eh*-sound:[1] 'fate . . . ray . . . away . . . pays . . . praise . . . name . . . fame' (*Imitations of Horace*, II. i. 19–20, 23–6), which includes three end-rhyme pairs; 'away The gaze of fools, and pageant of a day . . . Shade . . . unpaid. No friend's complaint . . . bless'd thy pale ghost, or grac'd thy mournful bier' ('Elegy to the Memory of an Unfortunate Lady', 43–4, 47–50), with elegiac effect. Keats and even Shelley seem to have inherited a fondness for this vowel, but in Shelley the sound is probably the modern /ey/ or /ei/, and in Keats nearly /əy/. We have, therefore, in these writers, a compound vocalic series, just as for diphthongs such as the 'long I', type VV' VV' . . . Thus Shelley: 'away . . . sustain As waves which lately paved his watery way Hiss round a drowner's head in their tempestuous play' ('Ode to Liberty', XIX. 12–13) (complicated by other tight subpatterns). Keats has 'When old age shall this generation waste, Thou shalt remain . . .' 'Grecian Urn', v. 6–7); and, as part of the total pattern evoking the sensations aroused by intense cold: 'rails . . . praying. . . . To think how they may ache in icy hoods and mails' ('St. Agnes', II. 7–9). 'They may ache' is perhaps an error in taste, and indeed Keats's use of diphthongal assonances often seems overdone and meaningless: 'the sensual ear, but more endear'd' ('Grecian Urn', II. 3).

Combinations of vowel and consonant may be noted, beginning with type VC // VC . . . and its compound forms (*rime suffisant intérieur*). In Shelley's /ey/ pattern above there is a pair in *eyv*. A compound (three-element) pair is his 'To the gate . . . I past, and there was found aghast, alone, The fallen Tyrant' (*Revolt of Islam*, v. xx 4–7). In 'The Eve of St. Agnes' we find: 'And all night kept awake, for sinners' sake to grive' (III. 9); 'The h*all* door shuts again, and *all* the noise is gone' (XXIX. 9), apparently in support of the bracket discussed above, and possibly complicated by additional instances of e.*ô* in 'door', 'gone' ('noise' is presumably /nâyz/—even Keats would hardly have perpetrated three instances of *ô* on successive accents); and 'They gl*ide*, like phan-

---

1 Helge Kökeritz, *Mather Flint on Early Eighteenth-Century English Pronunciation* (Uppsala, Leipzig, 1944), pp. 92–4, suggests a lengthened 'short *e*' rather than a long acute-*e*. The phonemic status must be left uncertain.

toms, into the w*ide* hall' (XLI. 1). In the last example, the patterning is continued in the declamatory word-repetitions of the next line, but both lines echo far less in the rejected earlier version.[1] This type of pattern makes a rather disagreeable jingle to the modern ear, when it is heavily stressed, but Keats too evidently liked it. It is, perhaps, an example of Romantic excess.

The reverse type CV // CV (and complex varieties) (cf. *rime imparfait intérieur*) is also common, e.g. Keats: 'So my soul doth ache' ('St. Agnes', XXXI. 9). A combination of CV and VC types, a 1/23 switch with looser middle member, occurs in 'In the retirèd qu*iet* of the night' (ibid. XXXI. 4), an emendation of 'Amid the quiet of St. Agnes' night'.[2] A combination with two consonants, knotted in the first member, occurs in 'glide, like . . . wide' above (ibid. XLI. 1).

Thus in 'glide' we have CVC'. The syllabic sequence, type CVC' // CVC' . . . (*rime riche intérieur*) was used, like simpler forms above, rhetorically-syntactically by the Augustans: 'Find you the virtue, and I'll find the verse' (Pope, *Epilogue to the Satires*, II. 5) where the sound probably resembled [var],[3] and the repeated verb plays a similar part. In Keats this classical device has again degenerated, and the type fulfils little function but that of general decoration; like the simpler assonance it seems to jingle. However, in 'Solution *s*(w)*eet*: meantime the frost-wind blows Like Love's alarum pattering the sharp *s*(l)*eet*/ . . . set' ('St. Agnes', XXXVI. 7–9) the assonances compensate for the dissonant rhyme 'set', and help to gloss over the word-repetition of 'sleet' in the rhyme of XXXVII 1, immediately after. For the tight progression 'Of witch. . . . Died palsy-twitch'd' (ibid. XLII. 5, 7), George Keats's copy has the version (6–7) 'Angela went off Twitch'd with the Palsy . . .' which would bring the echo crudely on to the same first beat of each line.[4] The extra *t*-sounds in 'twitch'd' recall Shelley's tight interchange-progression '*round* a *drowner's* head' quoted under *ey* patterns above. In 'fragrant boddice; by degrees Her rich attire creeps rustling' (ibid. XXVI. 4–5) we have a syllabic sequence enriched: *GriyS*/—*r*/ / . . .

1 Ridley, *Keats's Craftsmanship*, pp. 177–8; Keats, *Poetical Works*, ed. Forman, p. 228.

2 Ridley, *Keats's Craftsmanship*, p. 163; Keats, *Poetical Works*, ed. Forman, p. 224.

3 The vowel was lengthened and the /r/ may have vanished here; cf. Kökeritz, *Mather Flint*, pp. 84, 122–3, 152–8.

4 Keats, *Poetical Works*, ed. Forman, p. 229.

Griy'S/r; and preceded by the *r-Gr* of 'fragrant', and a couple of
e.*b* (the allotypes of e.*G* are of course /g,k/, those of e.*S* are
/s,z/). According to Ridley Keats had considerable difficulty with
his poem here, but it does not seem to have affected his pattern-
making.[1]

An opposite type of sequence (pair), VCV' / / VCV', also
jingles unnecessarily in Keats: 'O Attic shape! fair attitude'
('Grecian Urn', v. 1). It is less obtrusive in 'filling the chilly
room' ('St. Agnes', XXXI. 5).

Having thus limbered up, perhaps rather painfully, we are now
in a condition to run, soon more easily, through some of the
composite types of Keatsian pattern, and to consider their build-
up and their functions.

A loosening consonantal interchange-bracket in ee.*l, f, n*,
possibly accidental, heard in 'Hark! 'tis an elfin-storm from
faery-land' ('St. Agnes', XXXIX. 1), is further complicated by assonance of the vowels in the two words concerned; the next line
'Of haggard seeming . . .' forms a circumsyllabic sequence-pair
in *b-G* with 'Hark' above, which cannot be accidental; and
''tis', 'storm', 'seeming', quite apart from the vowels, produce
a tightening chiasmus in ee.*t, S* which knots with a circumsyllabic
sequence-pair in ee.*s, m* at 'storm'; in this last line too may be
noticed a tightening chiasmic bracket in ee.*d, iy* and a couple in
e.*b* ('haggard seeming, but a boon indeed'). These sub-patterns
reinforce the sense by linking 'storm' to 'seeming' and 'haggard
seeming' to 'indeed'. Another simple form, a 1/23 switch (2
tight) in ee.*l, f*, similarly forms a mere part of a more complicated
incantatory pattern of ee.*l, S, n, t, f, a, (ng?)*, in 'thy lucent fans,
Fluttering among the faint Olympians' ('Ode to Psyche', 41–2);
here Keats rejected 'above' for 'among'.[2] A knotting-up
interchange-progression in ee.*â, m, b, r, S, d* is heard in 'They lay
calm-breathing on the bedded-grass; Their arms embracèd'
(ibid. 15–16). One feels that 'calm-breathing' was an instinctive,
and 'bedded grass' a craftsmanly, sound-anticipation of 'arms
embracèd'.

A tight 3(2/3) interchange in ee.*S, l, ây* ('slide', 'chains lie',
'silent') is merely part of a larger pattern whose other notable

1 Ridley, *Keats's Craftsmanship*, pp. 154–5; converted to a progression by the /is/
of 'boddice' and by /p/ in 'creeps', if this is allowed to form an allotype of an e.*B*.
2 Keats, *Poetical Works*, ed. Forman, p. 236.

feature is the interchange-progression in ee.*S, n, t,* but which also contains ee.(*əw*), *ô, d, ch/j*:

> the bolts full easy slide:—
> The chains lie silent on the foot*wo*rn stones;—
> The key turns, and the d*oo*r upon its hinges groans.
>
> ('St. Agnes', XLI. 7–9)

The incantation persists here, although Keats seems to have found this stanza difficult in composition.[1] Similarly, the *sh-D/ / shaD / / . . . aD* of 'should shut . . . bud' is only part of a pattern which includes ee.*b, l, ây, n, d*:

> Blinded alike from sunshine and from rain.
> As though a rose should shut and be a bud again.
>
> ('St. Agnes', XXVII. 8–9)

(with tight sub-patterns in *lây, ash/sha*). Here Keats seems to have tried to eliminate the aggressive *sh-D* sequence-pair, for he crossed out 'shut' in favour of 'close' (which gives a tightening chiasmus with 'alike') but, of course, found the heavily stressed rhyming sequence-pair with 'rose' a worse alternative, and restored 'shut' before completing the line;[2] in fact, the modulation from the open, relaxed *əw* couple ('though', 'rose') to the brusque *a* couple by way of this centre-knotted 'should'/'shut'/ 'bud' sub-pattern and a couple in e.*b,* aptly and one would almost say cunningly underlines the meaning.

Again, the tightening interchange-bracket, with an intensifying function, in *in/ing, r, g, l* ('[sleep]in[g] dragons all around, At glarin[g]'), is only one sub-pattern in a total of ee.*w, S, l, i, p, n, d, r, è, g, ch, aw, əy, f*:

> were sleeping dragons all around,
> At glaring watch, perhaps, with ready spears—
> Down the wide stairs a darkling way they found.
>
> .   .   .   .   .   .
>
> A chain-droop'd lamp was flickering by each door.
>
> ('St. Agnes', XL. 2–4, 6)

So, too, a simple *m*-series already noticed above is only part of a complicated pattern in ee.*d, əy, l, S, m, n* in:

---

1 Ridley, *Keats's Craftsmanship*, p. 178; note that /ə/ probably occurs in 'bolts', 'chains', 'stones', 'turns', 'groans'; for Keats it may have enhanced the impression of the melancholy quietness of this point in his tale's conclusion.

2 Ibid., p. 157.

> dales of Arcady?
> What men or gods are these? What maidens loth?
> What mad pursuit?   ('Grecian Urn', I. 7–9)

The earlier versions reverse gods and men, and for the last three words have 'What love? what dance?'[1] a reading which would have brought the two members of the *m, n* sequence too close together, turned the *m, d* 3-member sequence into a ghostly chiasmus, and given us a crude *l*-couple. Though 'The Eve of St. Agnes' is perhaps the most elaborately and continuously patterned of these poems, many passages from the 'Grecian Urn' are remarkable for their sound, and we might instance the spell-binding pattern of the initial three lines, in ee.*t, i, l, r, è, v, sh ây, d, n, s, dh*, with its already mentioned progression in ee.*s, l*, of which the italicized word may have been selected partly for the pattern:

> Thou still unravish'd bride of quietness,
>   Thou foster-child of silence and slow time,
> *Sylvan* historian, who canst thus express . . .

In stanza II. 4, tight patterns in *it, nəw/əwn* knit together on the third *t*-component and link with a series in e.*p*: 'Pipe to the spirit ditties of no tone': a jingle but a typical Keatsian trick. In lines 7–8 of this stanza the repeated *əwl* enclosing the triple post-accentual '-ver' and the *k-s* sequence-pair and *in(in)ni* switch or chiasmic bracket ('winning near') seem to aid the verbal picture of eternally frozen motion by producing a cyclic effect:

> Bold Lover, never, never canst thou kiss,
> Though winning near the goal—yet, do not grieve.

It should now be clear that the Keatsian incantation is composed of an enormous number of intertwining sub-patterns, an almost continuous web of sound-strands, here more richly flowering, there more soberly, but in these poems almost never thinning quite away. On this magic carpet the reader/listener is perpetually airborne, though at times he may find himself nearer the ground than at others. One group of sub-patterns hands him over, thread by thread, to others, and often some of the first group stealthily reappear further on.

---

1 Keats, *Poetical Works*, ed. Forman, p. 233.

Of course, mere complexity *within* a pattern is not restricted to Keats or even to the Romantics. Indeed, Pope's 'heart'/'heat' sequence (bracket) earlier cited is merely an abstraction from the larger vowel-shunting sub-pattern *fii' | —h-t| |-t'â'f-'ât — |hiit*, which, with its lengthened 2.1, together with a tight chiasmus in ee.*l, S* and a loose expanding one in ee.*n, f*, suggests the emotions uncoiling, unfreezing ('Now feels my heart its long forgotten heat'). What is especially Augustan here is the precision and the tendency to syntactical parallelism. It is possible to isolate Keatsian lines of this sort, but their patterning is more gentle, more luxurious, more magical, less related to the argument. Thus, anticipating the sound of '*legion'd* faeries' on the coverlet in XIX, 'St. Agnes', xv. 9 reads: 'And Madeline asleep in lap of legends old.' The original version of this line was 'Sweet Madeline asleep among those legends old',[1] a far inferior pattern altogether, which, moreover, splits the line into two parts respectively dominated by the two assonant couples in ee.*iy, əw*, instead of helping to bind it together as do the chiasmically placed ee.*è, i* in the final version. Altogether there are some seven ee.*è, n, d, S, l, i, p*. The most obvious sub-pattern, (a), is the circumsyllabic sequence-pair in *l-p* mentioned before (cf. 'heart'/'heat'). Add ee.*è, d* (including the *d*-sound of /dʒh/) and we have (b), a complicated progression. A notable sequence-bracket (c) is next perceptible, *l-n-Sl—| |-nl—| |—l'-'n'S-l*, appropriately gracing the imagery with its soothing expansion in 3 and the overtaking of the accent by 3(4) compared with 1(4). More purely decorative is a tight progression (or interchange-bracket?) (d), *lin| |—li(y)|in| |l-*.

The close of the penultimate stanza of the 'Ode to a Nightingale', VII. 5-10, represents, perhaps, the crown of the Keatsian incantation. To attempt to map out this hallowed precinct may seem sacrilege; but it has indeed been thoroughly discussed from many points of view, and cannot lose from a new analysis.

> Perhaps the self-same song that found a path
> Through the sad heart of Ruth, when, sick for home,
> She stood in tears amid the alien corn;
> The same that oft-times hath
> Charm'd magic casements, opening on the foam
> Of perilous seas in faery lands forlorn.

1 Ridley, *Keats's Craftsmanship*, pp. 130-1.

These lines were originally set down with the versions 'Perhaps the self-same voice . . .', 'Charm'd the wide casements . . .', and 'Of keelless seas . . .' (the last perhaps first altered, according to Ridley's argument, to 'ruthless seas').[1] 'Voice' was at once altered to 'song' (presumably to avoid the word-repetition from line 3 of the stanza); this change gives us a crude series (a) in e.*s* (continued in the next line) in place of the original chiasmic bracket *s* — *F* | | *s* — | | *F*-*s*: a doubtful gain. But it also gives a more sonorous vowel and a booming -*ng*. The casements line would originally have had a -*d* series, but the amended version gives (b) an interchange-bracket *DJ*-*m* | | | *D* | | | *m*-*DJ* and a hesitating or doubled /k/ at 'casements'. Moreover, the stressed vowels of the line now afford greater variety, the first three *â è əy* contrasting with the couple (c) in *əw*.[2]

'Keelless seas', which would indeed have alliterated with the /k/ of 'casements', would produce a crude assonance hardly desirable here. 'Ruthless', as Ridley remarks, would echo 'Ruth' unduly; indeed, in carrying over the rhyme-like patterning of (g) below into line 10 it would not only perpetrate a meaningless and disagreeable pun, but would have disturbed therewith the sound-pattern of (d), (l), which is so essential to the last line. Keats's good angel seems to have restrained him on this occasion so that he might achieve perfection. What is interesting here is that in 'perilous' the -*l*-*s* of his first and second thoughts is essentially preserved: obviously Keats felt the sequence-pair in ee.*l*, *S* with 'lands' to be desirable. But, even better than this, 'Of perilous' now forms (d) a more or less tight sequence-pair in ee.*F*, *e*, *r*, *i*, *l*, *S* with 'faery lands', which becomes a bracket with 'seas in' (*SiySin*) for its centre. (The sub-alliteration of /p/ with /f/ is also perhaps relevant here, and 'opening', 'foam', 'Of perilous' make (e) a tightening chiasmus significantly picked out by the couple (c) in e.*əw* which surrounds the first member.) With 'ruthless' ee.*F*, *e* would have escaped, and ee.*l*, *i* have suffered interchange.

Returning, for the moment, to line 5, we find (f) more of ee.*p*, *f* in a loose chiasmus. Then comes (g) the interchange-progression *âth*/*thruw*/ | | . . . *â'* — *ruwth* ('path Through', 'heart

---

1 Ibid., pp. 229–30.
2 In a written communication, Miss M. M. Macdermott has drawn attention to the importance of vowel-modulation here.

DAVID I. MASSON

of Ruth') in which the hollow, remote, and brooding syllable /ruw/[1] is passed by the insinuating blade of the interdental *th*, suggesting the perception of the bird's song stealing through the echoing vestibule of her ear and the echoing loneliness of her mood into the brooding girl's consciousness. The small vertical tongue-tip movements in the loosening chiasmic bracket (h) in ee.*S*, *D* ('stood in tears') faintly suggest Ruth's small upright figure, and contrast with the vowel-like nasals and soft *l* of 'alien corn', more appropriate to the gentle horizontal expanse of the unfamiliar fields.[2]

Meanwhile 'self-same', 'sick for home', 'stood in tears amid', 'same', 'oft-times', carry (i) a loosening-and-tightening switch-progression, 1234/5, in ee.*S*, *m*, and (*j*) a complicated pattern embracing these with ee.*F*, *D*, which bursts into flower in line 9 and continues, its independent significance subsiding, as a contributory factor in the wonderful last line: *DJ-m/ /D/ /m-DJ . . . / / /Sm/ / /-nDS . . . F-m/ /-F . . . S/ /S-/ /S-nF . . ./ /-nDSF . . .* (group III as a chiasmic bracket contaminated by e.*n*, set within a sequence-pair contaminated by e.*m*; II as a motif-repetition from (i): '*Charm'd magic casements . . . foam Of perilous seas in faery lands f*[orlorn]'). The sub-alliterative affricates *ch*, *g*, *ts* here form a series, (k), with a whispering effect of mystery.

Another sub-pattern in the last line which is of great importance is (l) *F . . . l-S/S-S-n/ /F . . . l-n's/ /F-l-n*. Of this the most significant feature, (m), is the gradually tightening sequence *F . . . l . . . n/ /F . . . l-n/ /F-l-n*, with a stress-shunt in member 3. This produces an effect, not foreign to Augustan 'rhetorical' patterning, of a supra-logical argument, here clinched at the end of the line. But unlike Augustan patterns, and like most Keatsian patterns, it is separated from the syntax, and even from the 'rhetoric of the emotions'. It has attained, in fact, the transcendental quality of great music. Even at the most humdrum valuation, the patterns of this last line would seem to serve

1 For /ru/, etc., as dark and brooding, compare Rilke's *Le magicien*, line 4: 'Le trouble sourd d'un gros remous fécond', though a uvular *r* may have been intended; and the partly lexical associations in such words as 'brood' itself, 'croon', 'rumour', 'ruse'; 'gloom', 'doom', 'moody'. For the association of *u*-sounds with gloom, mystery, brooding emotions, cf. Maurice Grammont, *Traité de phonétique*, 3rd ed. (Paris, 1946), p. 407; and M. M. Macdermott, *Vowel Sounds in Poetry*, pp. 89 (foot), 92 ('Deep-band' vowels).

2 Cf. Sir Richard A. S. Paget, *Human Speech* (London, 1930), pp. 146–8.

178

as a magical incantation which, though it may carry certain connotations, works chiefly to subdue the critical-analytical faculties in the reader or listener, and to free his imagination.

Very much the same picture is obtained from a consideration of 'The Eve of St. Agnes', XIX. 5–9, perhaps the most intensely charged musical passage of that poem, though not equal to the lines just analysed. Here there are some fifteen to twenty sub-patterns. Those in 'legion'd faeries', 'coverlet and', 'pale enchantment', 'held', 'sleepy-eyed', for example, make a perfect spell of '*pale enchantment*' themselves, with a strong similarity to the abracadabras of magic. Sub-patterns in ee.*v*, *ə*, in ee.*n*, *S*, and in ee.*S*, *m*, *n*, *d*, suggest muttering and whispering, connecting the images of lovers' clandestine trysts, danger, and magic. The Daemon king is closely linked to these incantations, although the exact relevance and nature of Merlin's transactions with his demon has not been satisfactorily settled.[1] It may be that here the sound did partly override the sense, and this is also possible for the 'pale enchantment' patterning, where Ridley finds a discrepancy with supposed sources.[2]

> And win perhaps that night a peerless bride
> While legion'd faeries pac'd the coverlet,
> And pale enchantment held her sleepy-eyed.
> Never on such a night have lovers met,
> Since Merlin paid his Demon all the monstrous debt.

The original versions produce greatly inferior patterning.[3] An

---

1 Ridley, *Keats's Craftsmanship*, pp. 135–6; Werner W. Beyer, *Keats and the Daemon King* (New York, 1947), pp. 168–70.

2 Ridley, *Keats's Craftsmanship*, pp. 135–6.

3 'While legion'd faeries round her pillow flew' (at once altered to fit the rhyme), and 'O when on such a night. . . . Since Merlin paid the demons . . .'; spellings here normalized. 'O when' contains a vowel and a semivowel which would have had no echoes in this passage, whereas 'Never' gives (a) a striking subpattern *'ne— | | on—t(sh) | | -n-t | | . . . 'et | | | . . . 'on't— | | ''et* ('Never *on* such a night . . . met . . . mo*n*strous debt') together with the tight muttering progression (b) ('Never . . . have lovers'; cf. 'lover, never' in 'Grecian Urn' II. 7 quoted before). The alteration 'his Demon' for 'the demons' avoids the repetition of 'the', tones down the over-rich echo of *monS*, and instead introduces (c) a tight syncopated sequence-pair in *SD* ('his Demon . . . monstrous') which ties up the two ends of the principal incantation (d): in view of their places in the pattern we may consider /*db*/ here an allotype of e.D, and the unaccented *o* one of e.*o*, so that 'his Demon . . . the monstrous debt' makes the stress-shunting sequence-and-interchange *S*D-*mon | | —*D-*monS | | | —S*D.

unusual form of pattern is the vowel-modulation of the last two lines.[1]

Although his patterns bear a general resemblance to those of others, each musical poet employs them as personally as he does other devices, conscious or instinctive. In the phonetic patterns of such an Augustan as Pope, we are aware of the touch of an expert hand putting our thoughts through their paces. With the Romantics, sound-patterns express depth rather than clarity, excitement rather than control. Even in Wordsworth, when simplicity will allow him, an inward vision is matched by an unconscious aptness of gesture.[2] In Shelley we feel that the poet is mouthing at us, trying to bully us into sharing his emotions. In Keats, a suaver orchestration than Shelley's meets a richer vision than Wordsworth's, and a purer, deeper harmony is the result. However unconscious his patterning may have been, Keats's delight in sound is evident. It led him into specific lapses, as well as into a too unrelieved lushness of pattern. But it also brought him to the crowning achievement, in which the half-autonomous patterns cast an extraordinary spell on the scene, like the unspeakable otherness of a landscape transformed by fear, like the dark meaning of a dream, or the untranslatable message of true music.

1 $'e$ | ϑ o | | $'a$ | ϑ $\hat{a}y$ ϑ | $'a$ | | ϑ | $'e$ | | | i $'\vartheta\vartheta$ | i $'\vartheta$ | $|y$ i $'iy$ | | | ϑ $\hat{o}$ ϑ | |
$'o$ e | $'e$: group I is nearly symmetrical, while II and III each move from 'grave' to 'acute' stressed vowels; I 1 reversed = III 2 $\simeq$ I 3; I 2·2 $\simeq$ III 1; $\hat{a}$: $a \simeq \hat{o}$: o; in II the stressed vowels gradually rise toward the unstressed, /i/ and /ə/ having functions exchanged until /iy/ (heralded by /əy/) gives the signal.
2 *Resolution and Independence*, xii. 1–4.

Index